Praise for *Endless Referrals* by Bob Burg

"Any entrepreneur or salesperson who doesn't own this book is losing money because of it. Read what Burg has written, internalize it, and then take it to the bank with more money than you'll ever be able to spend. His system works!"
> —Wilson L. Harrell, former publisher of
> *Inc.* magazine and contributing editor of
> *Success* magazine.

"Bob Burg's book is a masterpiece! A must for anyone in sales and for anyone wanting to expand their financial and relationship resources."
> —Anne Boe, author of
> *Is Your Net-Working?*

"Reading *Endless Referrals* was worth the price of a Harvard MBA. What a great way to have new business beating a path to your door! Free advertising, free pre-sold prospects, free business! A true breakthrough in real world prospecting."
> —Tom "Big Al" Schreiter, author of
> *Big Al Tells All*

"Bob takes the art of sales and the art of relating to people and combines them in an incredibly effective roadmap to success and great profits. Buy this book and watch your personal and professional network, and your bank account, grow and grow."
> —Pam Lontos, author of
> *Don't Tell Me It's Impossible*
> *Until After I've Already Done It*

"The title of the book says it all. In a clearly written, well organized, easy-to-follow format, Bob Burg shows how anyone can become a master at the art of business networking. Most important, his strategies and techniques are in step with the present and future world of successful selling. Follow Burg's advice and you'll get what the book promises—a steady and growing number of endless referrals."
> —Michael LeBoeuf, author of
> *How to Win Customers and Keep Them for Life*
> and *The Perfect Business*

"A quick and powerful read packed full of value. This is great! These are the time-tested, simple things that really work! All of our sales leaders *will* own the book."　—Richard B. Brooke, President and CEO, Oxyfresh USA, Inc.

"Bob Burg has just taken away all the excuses for not finding clients by showing you step-by-step how to find 'diamonds' in your 'acres.'"
> —Danny Cox, author of *Leadership When the*
> *Heat's On*

Endless
Referrals

Endless Referrals

Network Your Everyday Contacts Into Sales

Bob Burg

Burg Communications, Inc.
Jupiter, Florida

New and Updated Edition

McGraw-Hill

New York   San Francisco   Washington, D.C.   Auckland   Bogotá
Caracas   Lisbon   London   Madrid   Mexico City   Milan
Montreal   New Delhi   San Juan   Singapore
Sydney   Tokyo   Toronto

Library of Congress Cataloging-in-Publication Data

Burg, Bob.
    Endless referrals : network your everyday contacts into sales /
Bob Burg.—New and updated ed.
        p.   cm.
    Includes bibliographical references and index.
    ISBN 0-07-008997-3
    1. Selling.   2. Business—Communication systems.   3. Social
networks.   4. Business referrals.   I. Title.
HF5438.25.B86   1998
658.85—dc20   98-33518
                                                            CIP

McGraw-Hill

A Division of The McGraw·Hill Companies

    4 5 6 7 8 9 0   DOC/DOC   0 4 3 2 1 0

ISBN 0-07-008997-3

*The sponsoring editor for this book was Betsy Brown, the editing supervisor was
Carol Levine, and the production supervisor was Tina Cameron. It was set in
Palatino by McGraw-Hill's Professional Book Group composition unit.*

Printed and bound by R. R. Donnelley & Sons Company.

Gender Usage
The author feels very strongly regarding the utilization of gender equal-
ity in his writing. The pronouns *his* and *her*, *he* and *she*, etc., have been
used interchangeably and randomly throughout the text.

This book is printed on recycled, acid-free paper containing
a minimum of 50% recycled, de-inked fiber.

Contents

Contents

xiii

Preface

From the on-the-street salesperson to the doctor, from the entrepreneur to the accountant, endless referrals are important. From the home-based business owner to the insurance agent, and from the network marketer to the software consultant, endless referrals are the cornerstone of business. Without a business based on endless referrals from present customers and clients to everyday contacts, the fate of anyone's business is a nerve-wracking mystery, dependent upon current economic conditions and buying moods.

But a business based on endless referrals brings peace of mind. Endless referrals is going to sleep at night knowing that the chances are good that you'll have new business waiting for you the next day, and the next, and the next for as long as you desire.

Prospecting is, and always will be, a key to building a business based on endless referrals, but these days, the rules of the game are changing. No longer do standard prospecting techniques work. The average consumer is more knowledgeable, less trusting, and wants to have a "know you, like you, trust you" relationship with his or her salesperson. Nowadays, in order to build that business based on endless referrals, we do it another way. We network!

But, in actuality, that is a confusing word, as misunderstood today as ever. Does it mean handing out business cards? Or aggressively shaking hands with everyone who comes within 3 feet of us? Do we tell people we are networking? Where can we do it? Exactly what is networking?

In essence, networking is the mutual give and take that results in a winning situation for everyone involved in the transaction.

While the term networking wasn't prominent until the 1980s, it has always existed in some form—as the old boys' network, or the grapevine. Recently, however, networking has become more of an art and science. I realized this as I listened to humorist Roger Masquelier at a National Speakers Association convention. Roger was telling a story about networking at a meeting. "Of course," added Roger, "in the old days, we just called it talking." This brought laughter from the audience, and thousands of heads nodding in agreement.

What I realized at that point was that most people actually do believe that networking is merely "talking," as well as indiscriminately handing out business cards. *It isn't.* As misunderstood as networking is, there is a real need for individuals and companies in our modern business scenario to use it effectively.

Why? Because in today's tough business climate, where competition is so incredibly fierce and many markets are already saturated, people are realizing that it's vital to be able to cultivate new business without spending a lot of money doing it.

I like to define *networking* as cultivating mutually beneficial, give-and-take, win-win relationships. For the purpose of this book, the end result may be to develop a large and diverse group of people who will gladly and continually refer a lot of business to us, while we do the same for them.

Throughout this book you will have the opportunity to meet and learn from people who have successfully developed businesses based on referrals by using the techniques described. Do each use all the techniques mentioned? Not at all. Certain people find that some ideas are more applicable than others to their particular profession or method of operation.

This book, therefore, is based not on theoretical pap but on time-tested, proven ideas that have worked for many of us. As you read through, you may at times begin to say to yourself, "That technique wouldn't work for me," or "I could never see myself doing that." If this is the case, you have two choices, one is to not even try it, but the other, more profitable choice is to mold the technique to your particular business style and type of work.

If you follow the techniques with a ready, willing, able, and most of all, open mind, you will soon find yourself cultivating a network of endless referrals.

Bob Burg

Note from the Author

Since 1994 when *Endless Referrals* was first released, I've had a chance to meet many of you in person at various sales rallies and speaking engagements. This has been very enjoyable for me, and your kind words are always appreciated. I've also listened to your questions and noticed that many of them involve a desire for information on specific topics that since 1994 have become even more a part of the free enterprise system and the sales and marketing process.

For this revised edition of *Endless Referrals*, aside from updating information in the general text, a chapter has been added for each of the topics in which you expressed interest: Home-based businesses, network marketing, mail order (aka direct marketing), and marketing through the Internet—or *Inter-net-working*, as we refer to it. These four topics have one thing in common; they all pertain to people who are either in business for themselves, or would like to be. As America goes full circle (at the turn of the twentieth century a significant percentage of the population owned their own business, many right out of their home), I hope you can use the information in these chapters as part of a foundation to reach your personal goals and achieve your dream of financial freedom.

Bob Burg

Acknowledgments

There are so many people I need to thank that it would take a separate book just to list them. Instead, let me thank several groups of people. One is the National Speakers Association, which has over 3500 of the nicest, most supportive, sharing, and caring people in the world.

Also, my fellow speakers, authors, and salespeople who were so willing to lend their ideas and success stories to this book for the benefit of my readers. Jeff Slutsky, you're a prince.

And those who gave me moral and written support when it was needed (which was always). Dean Shapiro, thank you. Your expert writing skills rescued my readers from many of my overused expressions and amateurish syntax. Lloyd Jones, a wonderful agent and entrepreneur and a true salesperson, and Betsy Brown at McGraw-Hill, your knowledge of the publishing business, encouragement, and professionalism were a guiding light. And you were incredibly great to work with, as well.

I must thank my office staff, who help make my speaking habit possible by keeping me on the road constantly. (Come to think of it, that's probably where they like me best!) Thank you for your loyalty, love, and support.

Of course, I thank my clients, without whom I wouldn't have an audience and the pleasure of involvement in a wonderful, rewarding career such as this.

And you, the reader, for your participation, feedback, and help in making this book a best-seller.

To each and every one of you, I wish you the best of success . . .
AND GREAT NETWORKING!

Bob Burg

Endless
Referrals

1

Networking: What It Is, and What It Does for You!

The late Og Mandino was an extremely successful man. A renowned speaker and storyteller, he is probably best known as author of the classic best-seller, *The Greatest Salesman in the World.* This book alone has sold well over 30 million copies. Yes, that's 30 *million* copies! And that was just one book. His others also continue to sell extremely well.

In July 1992, Og was the keynote speaker at the annual National Speakers Association convention. For about 45 minutes he talked about the fact that nobody who is truly successful ever does it alone. He talked about his wife, his family, his associates and friends—all the people who had helped him through the rough times and over the hurdles.

But What Does That Have to Do with Networking?

Let's go back to the definition of networking that I gave in the preface. Networking is the cultivating of mutually beneficial, give-and-take, win-win relationships.

Now let's take a look at how Webster's dictionary defines the term *network:* 1. Any arrangement of fabric or parallel wires, threads, etc., crossed at regular intervals by others fastened to them so as to leave open space; netting; mesh. 2. A thing resembling this in some way.

Now, let's leave out the words and thoughts in both definitions that don't apply to us and the purpose of this book and keep in those that do. Oh, and let's substitute the word *people* in the dictionary definition for the words *fabric, parallel wires,* and *threads.* This is what we get:

> *Networking:* An arrangement of people crossed at regular intervals by other people, all of whom are cultivating mutually beneficial, give-and-take, win-win relationships with each other.

The Basic Setup

Let's look at the first part of what we have.

```
 •        •        •        •        •        •        •

 •        •        •        •        •        •        •

 •        •        •        •        •        •        •

 •        •        •      YOU        •        •        •

 •        •        •        •        •        •        •

 •        •        •        •        •        •        •

 •        •        •        •        •        •        •
```

Just as we are all at the center of our own particular universe, we are also at the center of our network. We realize, of course, that all the other people are at the center of *their* network, and that is as it should be.

Each of the people in this network serve as a source of support (referrals, help, information, etc.) for everyone else in that network. Those who know how to use the tremendous strength of a network realize this very important fact:

> We are not dependent *on* each other; nor are we independent *of* each other; we are all interdependent *with* each other.

The true strength really comes through when we realize that all the people in our network are also part of other people's networks that we ourselves don't personally know. And that, indirectly, makes each of those people part of our network too.

Sphere of Influence

Are you familiar with the term *sphere of influence?* Sphere of influence is simply the people you know—people who are somehow, some way a part of your life, directly or even very indirectly.

Your sphere of influence includes everyone from immediate family members to distant relatives—close friends to casual acquaintances, the person who delivers the mail, the plumber, the tailor, the person who cuts your hair—practically anybody who in some way touches your life and whose life you touch.

Have you ever heard of Joe Girard? Based out of a Chevrolet dealership in Detroit, Michigan, he was one of the world's most successful car salespeople. Officially, he was actually the most successful car salesperson in the world for 14 years. That's how long he was listed in the *Guiness Book of World Records* for selling the most cars in the world in a year's time.

In his book, *How to Sell Anything to Anybody,* Girard explains what he calls Girard's Law of 250. Basically, the law states that each of us has a personal sphere of influence of about 250 people. According to Girard, 250 people will attend our wedding and funeral.

Even if his number for a wedding or a funeral seems somewhat high, the 250 figure still works out. For instance, right now, take a pencil and paper and write down everybody you know. Everybody! Add them and you'll see the number will be around 250.

Therefore, figure that every time you meet someone new, that person, even that *average* person, also has about 250 people in his or her sphere of influence. You know that once that person becomes part of your network, another 250 people indirectly become part of your network as well. Cultivate a network of enough new people, and your personal sphere of influence will soar to incredible heights.

This Network Will Increase Our Sales

These days, buyers are different. They are educated, trained, and skeptical. They are backed by consumer protection laws, as it should be. The adage *caveat emptor,* "let the buyer beware," is no longer apropos. Probably the biggest change of all is that buyers are much more relationship-oriented. People want to buy from people they know, like, and trust.

That's where our network comes into play, but in a different way than you might imagine. You may be thinking, "All those people in our network already know us, like us, and trust us. They are our buyers."

No! They are merely the tip of the iceberg. They are a given, and all things being equal, they will buy from us. But if we stop there, we are walking away from a lot of potential business.

Remember, those people are at the center of their own individual networks. They themselves can connect you to at least 250 people. Keep in mind, those 250 have their own 250. Knowing that, and knowing how to work the situation, will result in a ton of new business.

The Golden Rule

All things being equal, people will do business with, *and refer business to,* those people they know, like, and trust.

This is absolutely the bronze, silver, golden, and even platinum rule of networking. The intent and theme of this entire book is to show you how to get people to know, like, and trust you. Let's take this one more step forward. We also want these people to *want* to see you succeed and *want* to help you find new business. You might say we want these people to be your personal walking ambassadors. That goal isn't particularly difficult to accomplish.

Things Aren't Always Equal

No matter how well people know us, like us, and trust us as a person, we have to be able to come through for them when they give us their business or referrals. If we can't or don't, we'll be in danger of losing not only their direct business but that of their 250-person sphere of influence as well.

For instance, there is a dry cleaning company in my town. The owners and employees are lovely people who I believe *try* to do a good job. However, it just doesn't seem to work. Personally, I can honestly say I know them, like them, and trust them. Trust them, that is, to do practically anything in the world for me—except clean my suits.

Now, the fact that they happen to be dry cleaners doesn't work out particularly well for them. They nearly ruined three of my best suits. They seemed to have trouble following instructions as well. I would tell them that I wanted very light starch on my shirts, but when I'd arrive to pick up my clothes, my shirts would practically be standing at attention waiting for me. It just didn't work out.

After a while, despite my positive personal feelings about these people, I felt I could no longer justify either doing business with them directly or giving them my referrals. If they were anywhere close to their competition, they would, to this day, continue to get my direct business as well as my referral business. But they are not, so they don't. Again, all things being equal, people will do business with, and refer business to, those people they know, like, and trust.

It Isn't Just What or Who You Know

Sure, we've all heard the old axiom, "It isn't what you know, it's who you know!" That saying was usually related to us by a crusty old, macho businessman type, while he knowingly put his arm around us, proud of himself for sharing his eternal wisdom.

Of course, what you know is also important. Let's face it—we must know what we're doing and talking about. We must be able to provide proper guidance to our prospects, customers, and clients. Also, if we can't provide excellent, or at least adequate, service after the sale, we can rest assured we won't be doing business with that person ever again.

We will also lose out on the business of those in their 250-person sphere of influence. Why? Because nothing gets around faster than negative comments. You can also bet those comments will somehow make their way back to the person who used their influence with that person to get you the referral in the first place. That original person will then, of course, have to be removed from your "who you know" list.

Let's face facts, though. In today's world of sales and business, often, in order to get the opportunity to do business with someone in the first place, who you know has become vitally important. But that's not all there is to it.

> It isn't just what you know, and it isn't just who you know. It's actually who you know, who knows you, and what you do for a living.

That is, when that person, or someone that person knows, needs your products, goods, or services. And...

> providing that first person knows you, likes you, and trusts you.

As previously mentioned, our goal is to get as many new people as we possibly can to feel as though they know you, like you, and trust you; to feel that they *want* to see you succeed and actually *want* to help you find new business. Remember, I said that goal isn't particularly difficult to accomplish. It isn't. We do that by networking.

What Networking Isn't

Since we've been discussing the basics of what networking is, let's talk a bit about what it isn't. You see, networking really is the buzz word of the late 1980s and early 1990s. Everyone seems to use the word, and yet many people don't really know what it is and isn't. Generally, the term *networking* is thought to be when a person hands his or her business card to everyone in the world that he or she meets or comes into contact with. The often aggressive shoving of said business card in said contact's face is many times followed by, "Give me a call. I'll cut you a deal," or "If you ever need to buy a whichamahoozee, I'm the one to call."

That is not networking. That is hard-selling, which is the antithesis of networking. We'll talk more about that later. For now I want you to forget about business cards. Well, don't forget about them altogether—they do serve a purpose, albeit a very minor one. In fact, as far as I'm concerned, business cards have three main benefits.

1. The first "benefit" is very tangible, though not to be taken too seriously: you can win a free lunch at a local restaurant by dropping your business card into a fish bowl. Have you ever done that? Won a free lunch? Paid for your business cards, right? Maybe there is such a thing as a free lunch after all.

You can also win a door prize at an association meeting by, again, dropping your business card into a fish bowl. Or you could even win a free book or cassette tape program at a seminar via the same means.

2. This second benefit is a more legitimate one depending upon your profession, although it absolutely is not networking: you can include your business card with your bill payments or with a tip after your meal.

Let's face it, we all have our bills that have to go out each and every month—electric bill, cable TV, water, telephone, mortgage payment, and more. Doesn't it make sense that someone is at the other end receiving the bill payment, opening up the envelope?

Depending upon the type of product or service you represent, if it can potentially fit anybody's needs and you will probably never get to meet that person anyway, you might as well include your business card with your bill payment. You never know what may happen. That person, or someone in their 250-person sphere of influence, may need to buy what you have to sell.

Are you familiar with a man by the name of Tom Hopkins? Tom Hopkins is an internationally known speaker and author of the book, *How to Master the Art of Selling*. Tom got his start as a real estate sales person, and he used to do that very same thing: include his business cards with his bill payments.

One day Tom got a call from a woman who said, "Mr. Hopkins, you don't know me, but my husband and I want to buy a bigger home and would like to talk to you about it." After agreeing that he'd be delighted to do just that, he asked her how she got his name. She replied, "I handle your account at the Gas Company, and I've got about two dozen of your cards in the top drawer of my desk." Apparently, she didn't know who else to call.

Well, I'm sure that the fee Mr. Hopkins earned by helping that woman and her husband acquire a new home more than paid for his business cards for the rest of his life. Now that's probably not going to happen too often. But if it happens even once in your selling career, that's great—you made out on it. The fact is, business cards are so inexpensive that you might as well include them any time you have the chance, again, because you have nothing to lose.

Another thought along the same line: you can also leave your business card with your tip at the end of the meal at a restaurant. You never know. Your waiter or waitress, or someone in his or her 250-person sphere of influence, may need to buy what you have to sell. But when you do that, you need to make sure you leave a big enough tip; otherwise you will be remembered, but it will be for something else.

3. Finally, you can use your business card to get the other person's business card. As far as I'm concerned, this is the one truly legitimate benefit of business cards. But we'll discuss that in greater detail in the next chapter.

Although I make light of business cards, and totally believe they are not worth much more than the paper stock on which they are printed, when used correctly, they do have some genuine value. Obviously, successful salespeople such as Tom Hopkins, Joe Girard, and many others who believe in them are living proof of their use an an effective business tool.

What I'm trying to point out, and even emphasize, is that business cards by themselves are not about to make you, me, or anyone else successful. They are simply an extension of ourselves and what we are doing right.

Now that we've looked at the benefits of business cards and learned how relatively unimportant they are to effective and profitable networking, let's move on.

What we'll discover throughout this book is that networking involves giving to others and helping them succeed in their lives and careers. When accomplished in a pragmatic and organized fashion, we find that we get back tenfold what we put out, both personally and professionally.

Key Points

- Networking is the cultivating of mutually beneficial, give-and-take, win-win relationships.

- We are not dependent *on* each other; nor are we independent *of* each other; we are all interdependent *with* each other.

- Each of us has a personal sphere of influence of about 250 people. And so does every new person we meet.

- All things being equal, people will do business with, *and refer business to*, those people they know, like, and trust.

- It isn't just what you know, and it isn't just who you know. It's actually who you know, who knows you, and *what you do for a living*...providing that first person knows you, likes you, and trusts you.

- Business cards are not a big deal. We need them mainly to get the other person's card.

2

Questions Are the Successful Networker's Most Valuable Ammunition

The famous sales trainer J. Douglas Edwards was among the first, if not *the* first, to utter the phrase, "Questions are the answers." What exactly did he mean by that?

Simply this: In sales, the person who asks the questions controls the conversation. One may ask, "But wouldn't the person doing the talking lead the conversation?"

It would seem that way, wouldn't it? However, when we ask the right questions, we lead the other person exactly in the direction we want them to take. That's why great salespeople aren't pushy. Great salespeople *never* push. They lead!

In fact, Mr. Edwards had another statement that I think is right on the mark.

The only reason for making a statement is to set up another question.

Of course, he was speaking in the context of a sales presentation. Ask questions—the right questions—that will ultimately lead a person to the right decision: buying that salesperson's product or services.

It's Just As Valuable in the
Networking Process

The same theory also applies to networking. Recall the basic fact we learned in Chapter 1. Coming on strong—handing your business card to someone and asking for their business or referrals right off the bat— is ineffective.

What we need to do is make an impression at the first meeting that will simply elicit the "know you, like you, trust you" feelings that are necessary for a mutually beneficial, win-win relationship. We do this by asking questions—the right questions, which we'll discuss in a moment.

When and Where Can We
Network?

Networking opportunities occur almost every day, practically any-where and any time. We might expect to network at business func-tions, at chamber of commerce functions, on the golf course, in associ-ation meetings, or in organized networking or lead exchange groups.

That's just the beginning, however. Opportunities to meet new net-working contacts and prospects also occur in places and at times we may not realize. Or we may think the situation is not appropriate for networking.

What are some examples? A PTA meeting, the racquetball court, night school class, shopping mall, airplane, casual introduction by a third party—the list goes on and on. How many times have you found yourself in one of these places and you were certain there were some potential business contacts waiting to be discovered? But you also felt that networking would definitely be frowned upon, that it would be considered…well, *tacky* by some…maybe even yourself? Please keep this in mind:

> If you are networking correctly, the other person will never know that you are networking.

The first thing you do is simply introduce yourself to a person you want to meet. Of course, you don't do this in an aggressive, intimidat-ing, turn-off fashion. You don't walk over with your arm stretched out and business card extended. That's important to keep in mind when meeting this person for the first time.

You tell him your name and offer a firm but nonaggressive handshake. He will respond reflexively by telling you his name. Then ask what he does for a living. He'll tell you and ask you the same question. You tell him briefly, but go right back to showing interest in *his* business.

Now ask him for *his* business card. He'll give it to you. *If* he asks for your business card, give it to him. Realize, however, that your card will be thrown out at the person's earliest convenience. More correctly, either it will be thrown out directly, or it will travel through a never-ending dimension of time and space, lost forever in The Rolodex Zone, never to be seen or heard from again. But, as we learned earlier, the main reason for having your business card is not to give it to someone else but *to get the other person's card.*

The next step is very important.

> After the introduction, invest 99.9 percent of the conversation asking that person questions about himself and his business. Do not talk about you and your business.

Why? Because at this point, contacts don't care about you or your business. Let's face facts: your business and my business are probably two of the things in this world that person cares least about. That's just the way it is. He wants to talk about himself and his business. Let him! This is known as being you-oriented. Most people, of course, are I-oriented.

Will this get you off to a good start with your networking prospect? Let me answer that question by asking you a question: Have you ever been in a conversation with someone who let you do practically *all* the talking? If so, did you say to yourself afterward, "Wow! What a fascinating conversationalist!" Sure, we've all done that. Isn't it true that the people we find most interesting are the people who seem most interested in us? You bet!

Warning!

There's a sneaky kind of danger that you need to be aware of at this particular point. Let's pretend the person just asked what you do for a living. When you answer, it just happens to be something that person really needs.

For instance, imagine that you are a stockbroker. You responded not by saying, "I'm a stockbroker," or even "I'm a financial planner," but instead by giving a short benefit statement such as "I help people create and manage wealth."

Now the person looks at you and says, "What a coincidence. My spouse and I were just talking about the fact that we are very weak in that area and need to do something about it. After all, we're working hard, but we have no financial future, nothing put away for the later years. We know we definitely need to talk to a person such as yourself right away."

Let's face it. At this point, everything inside you wants to go *Yesssss!!!!!!*

That, unfortunately, would not be the correct response. As tempting as it might be to try to set up an appointment with that person and his spouse right on the spot, realize that they are just not ready yet. The "know you, like you, trust you" stage has not yet been established. Bombarding that person right now will do just the opposite of what you want to accomplish. Instead, just go right back to asking questions about him and his business.

> The type of questions we need to ask are called open-ended, feel-good questions.

Let's look at both. Most of us who've either read books on sales or taken any kind of sales training are already familiar with open-ended questions. These are simply questions that cannot be answered with a yes or a no, but require a longer response. I first learned about open-ended questions when I was a television news anchor for an ABC affiliate in Oklahoma. Management decided that we should have more live interviews, lasting about 3 minutes, during our newscasts. Now, 3 minutes doesn't seem like a particularly long time to most people. On live television, however, 3 minutes can be an eternity! Especially when it came to some of my guests.

Understandably, they weren't necessarily used to being interviewed on television. Or they might have been brilliant people, but not especially charismatic. For instance, during the oil crisis of the early 1980s, I was interviewing Mr. Johnson from the local bank:

> ME: So, Mr. Johnson, how do you feel the current oil problems will affect the local banks as well as the local residents?
>
> MR. JOHNSON: Uh…it's gonna be tough.
>
> ME: Okay, it's gonna be tough. Can you elaborate on that point?
>
> MR. JOHNSON: It's going to be *really* tough.

I was thinking, "This would be a fantastic time to take a commercial break!" But then I heard the director through the earphones screaming, "Stretch! Stretch! You still have 2 minutes, 30 seconds left!" That was tough! But it taught me that if I was going to survive these 3-minute live interviews, I needed to learn how to ask questions that would get and keep my guests talking.

What I did—and my suggestion to you is to do likewise—was to watch some of the top network television interviewers, people such as Ted Koppel, Larry King, and Barbara Walters. Whether you personally enjoy watching these outstanding professionals, the fact is, these people know how to ask questions that get people talking.

Barbara Walters, of course, asks questions that get people *crying*. That's not good for our purposes. We want to accomplish just the opposite. We want to ask questions that make people feel good about being in a conversation with us. We want to ask questions that make our new networking prospects feel good about us as people, even though we've just met and they hardly know us.

Ten Networking Questions That Work Every Time

I have 10 questions in my personal arsenal. They are absolutely *not* designed to be probing or sales-oriented in any way. You'll notice that they are all friendly and fun to answer and will tell you something about the way that person thinks. You'll never need or have the time to ask all 10 during any one conversation. Still, you should internalize them. Know them well enough that you are able to ask the ones you deem appropriate for the particular conversation and time frame.

Here are the 10 questions.

1. *How did you get your start in the widget business?*
   People like to be the Movie of the Week in someone else's mind. "I worked my way through college, then started in the mail room, then blah, blah, blah, and finally began the fascinating career of selling widgets." Let them share their story with you while you actively listen.

2. *What do you enjoy most about your profession?*
   Again, it's a question that elicits a good, positive feeling. And it should get you the positive response you're seeking. By this time you've got him on a roll.

3. *What separates you and your company from the competition?*
   I call this the *permission-to-brag question*. All our lives we're taught not to brag about ourselves and our accomplishments, yet you've just given this person carte blanche to let it all hang out.

4. *What advice would you give someone just starting in the widget business?*
   This is my *mentor question*. Don't we all like to feel like a men-

tor—to feel that our answer matters. Give your new networking prospect a chance to feel like a mentor by asking this question.

5. *What one thing would you do with your business if you knew you could not fail?*
   This is a paraphrase of a question from noted theologian and author Dr. Robert Schuller, who asks, "What one thing would you do with your *life* if you knew you could not fail?" We all have a dream, don't we? What is this person's dream? The question gives her a chance to fantasize. She'll appreciate the fact that you cared enough to ask. And you'll notice that people always take a few moments to really ponder before they answer.

6. *What significant changes have you seen take place in your profession through the years?*
   Asking people who are a little bit more mature in years can be perfect because they love answering this question. They've gone through the computer age, the takeover of fax machines, the transition from a time when service really seemed to matter.

7. *What do you see as the coming trends in the widget business?*
   I call this the *speculator question.* Aren't people who are asked to speculate usually important, hot-shot types on television? You are therefore giving them a chance to speculate and share their knowledge with you. You're making them feel good about themselves.

8. *Describe the strangest or funniest incident you've experienced in your business.*
   Give people the opportunity to share their war stories. That's something practically everyone likes to do, isn't it? Don't we all have stories we like to share from when we began in business? Something very embarrassing happened that certainly wasn't funny then but is now. The problem is, most people don't get the chance to share these stories. You, however, are actually volunteering to be that person's audience.

9. *What ways have you found to be the most effective for promoting your business?*
   Again, you are accentuating the positive in this person's mind, while finding out something about the way he thinks. However, if you happen to be in the advertising field, absolutely *do not* ask this question. Why? Because right now, it would be a prob-

ing question, and it would be perceived as such by your networking prospect. Eventually you will get to ask that question, but not now.

10. *What one sentence would you like people to use in describing the way you do business?*
    Almost always, the person will stop and think really hard before answering this question. What a compliment you've paid him. You've asked a question that, quite possibly, the people who are closest to him have never thought enough to ask.

It's *How* You Ask

You may be wondering if a person will feel as though you are being nosey asking these questions during a first meeting. The answer is no.

Remember, you won't get to ask more than just a few of these questions during your initial conversation anyway. But more importantly, these are questions people enjoy answering. If you ask them the way I have them worded, you won't come off like Mike Wallace conducting an interrogation for *60 Minutes*. We wouldn't want that. These questions are simply meant to feel good and establish an initial rapport.

There are also extender questions, which can be utilized effectively when the person's answer needs lengthening. For instance, the words, "Really? Tell me more." The person will usually be only too happy to accommodate you.

Then there is the echo technique, taught to me by my friend and fellow speaker, Jeff Slutsky, author of *How to Get Clients*. According to Jeff, you only need to repeat back the last few words of a networking prospect's sentence in order to keep him or her talking. For instance:

NP (NETWORKING PROSPECT): ...and so we decided to expand."

YOU: "Decided to expand?"

NP: "Yes, we thought the increase in our revenue would justify the cost."

YOU: "Justify the cost?"

NP: "Yes, you see, if the amount of..."

As Jeff warns, however, we must every so often adjust the phrasing of our echo, or eventually the person is going to look at us and say, "What are you anyway—an echo?"

The One Key Question That Separates the Pros from the Amateurs

This next question is key in the process of getting this person to feel as though he knows you, likes you, and trusts you. It must be asked smoothly and sincerely, and only after some initial rapport has been established. The question is this:

Learn this Q ✱

"How can I know if someone I'm talking to is a good prospect for you?"

✱

Let's discuss why this question is so powerful. First of all, just by asking the question you have separated yourself from the rest of the pack. It is the first indication that you are someone special. You are probably the only person he has ever met who asked him this question during the first conversation.

During my live seminars where I often address audiences numbering in the thousands, I'll ask for a show of hands from those who have ever been asked that question or even one similar by somebody they have just met. Seldom do more than a few hands go up. Often, none!

You have also just informed that person that you are concerned with his welfare and wish to contribute to his success. Most people would already be trying to sell their own product or service, but not you. You are wondering out loud how you can help the other guy.

You can be sure that your prospect will have an answer. I was recently talking to a person named Gary, who sells copying machines, and asked him the question. He suggested that the next time I walk by a copying machine in an office, I take a look at its accompanying wastepaper basket. "If that basket is overflowing with tons of crumpled-up pieces of paper," he said, "that's a good sign the copying machine is not working well. That's a good lead for me."

Don't we all have ways of knowing when someone may be a good prospect that the general public does not know? People you meet from now on will be glad to share their knowledge in that area with you. And don't you think they'll appreciate your sincere interest? You bet they will!

Again, that question will be the first indication that you are somebody special and different—a person worthy of doing business with, either directly or by way of referrals. My advice is to learn that question word for word until it becomes part of you and you could ask that question, as the saying goes, "in your sleep."

That question will serve you profitably throughout your life. Loring "Snag" Holmes, an insurance sales professional, found that out right

after he attended one of my seminars. About a week after the program,
he was introduced to a prospect through a mutual friend.

According to Snag, "When he found out I sell insurance, he immediately became defensive—not the first time I've experienced that response. Before learning these techniques I would've tried to keep selling this person on an appointment. Instead, what I did was focus on him and his business. He seemed to loosen up a little. It turned out that he sold office products. After I asked, 'How can I know if someone I'm talking to is a good prospect for you?' his attitude turned 180 degrees. I should've been asking these questions for the last 30 years."

Alison Oliver, an account executive for a billboard company, was nervous about her brief luncheon appointment with a corporate buyer. He had been tough on the phone, and she was not looking forward to a battle over soup and salad.

"We met for 1 hour and 15 minutes," Alison said, "even though it was obvious he had planned on a much shorter meeting. All I did was talk about his favorite subject—him! Within a week I made the sale, and he personally called my boss to commend me on my selling skills."

These are two incidents that resulted in almost immediate sales, and that isn't even the purpose of this questioning technique. All we are looking to do is establish a positive relationship, which will result in direct business and a lot of referral business *down the road.*

However, these techniques are powerful. Often, they will result in immediate sales. Then we need to maintain the relationship and still work that person's 250-person sphere of influence.

Here's a funny story that truly confirms the power of you-oriented questioning. A good friend of mine in the National Speakers Association, Sydney Biddle Barrows, gained both acclaim and notoriety after her book *Mayflower Madam* hit the best-seller list. It was the true story about the rise and fall of the escort service Sydney had owned. The most successful in New York City.

Understandably, because of the nature of her business, Sydney was not anxious for her friends to know what she did for a living. When people asked her, she would simply ask them something about themselves. According to Sydney, keeping her little secret from her friends was one of the easiest things for her to do.

Countless times, via you-oriented questioning, I've been able to establish excellent contacts on airplane trips. On one occasion in particular, I kept a person talking about himself for the last hour and 45 minutes of the flight. Yes, that took some concentration on my part.

As we landed I said, "If I can ever refer business your way, I definitely will." He replied, "Me too," and I could tell he meant it. Then with an embarrassed smile, he asked, "By the way, what do you do?" Amazing! Just by my focusing on him, he was totally sold on me without even knowing anything about me.

Another time I was sitting next to a syndicated columnist on a flight from Chicago to San Francisco. I asked all about her and her career as a journalist. The result? A feature story on me and my program that ran in all the papers that syndicate her column. This process works!

Back to Your Prospect

So your conversation with your new networking prospect has concluded, and you hardly mentioned yourself and what you do for a living. That's okay, as long as you have *their* card. Later on, we'll look at how to successfully and profitably follow up with this person.

Key Points

- Networking opportunities occur constantly, anywhere and any time.
- If you are networking correctly, the other person will never know that you are networking.
- After the introduction, invest 99.9 percent of the conversation asking that person questions about himself and his business. Do not talk about yourself and your business.
- Even if what you do interests the other person right away, turn the conversation back to that person and his business.
- Ask several of the 10 open-ended, feel-good questions to find out more about your networking prospect. Remember, these questions are not intended to be probing in nature, but simply to establish a rapport.
- The one key question is, "How can I know if someone I'm talking to is a good prospect for you?"

3
How to Work
Any Crowd

Mention the term *networking* to many business owners or salespeople, and images of their local chamber of commerce will immediately spring to mind. Why? Because across North America and throughout the world chambers of commerce have instituted monthly events known as Business before Hours, Business after Hours, Networking Functions, or Card Exchanges.

Regardless of what they're called, the concept is that chamber of commerce members attend these get-togethers with plenty of business cards in tow ready to exchange them with each other. If all goes according to plan, when one of the members eventually needs a particular product or service, he or she will simply have to check their business card file and *voila!* They will know who to go to.

The purpose of this exercise, according to chamber of commerce executives, is, and I quote, "Chamber members doing business with other chamber members." In other words, creating a self-sufficient business environment within the membership.

A Good Thought, But...

It's a great concept! There's only one minor problem—it doesn't work. Why not? Because no matter how loyal people may be to their chamber of commerce, they will most likely only do business with someone for the reason mentioned in Chapter 1. *All things being equal, people will do business with, and refer business to, those people they know, like, and trust.*

Pressing the flesh and handing out an endless number of business cards will not convince people to feel any of these things about you. And most people simply don't know how to work a chamber of commerce *audience* in such a way as to elicit those feelings. In this scenario, every time you *don't* get somebody's direct business, you also *don't* get the business of her 250-person sphere of influence.

Let us now look at the proven techniques that will allow you to take advantage of a wonderful situation: having tons of good prospects right in front of you for about 2 straight hours.

First, Let's View the Situation

Picture in your mind's eye the typical chamber of commerce card exchange scenario. Let's make believe this one is an after-hours event, usually running from 5 to 7 p.m. The majority of attendees sit at the bar or hang around the hors d'oeuvres table. They have a few drinks, something to eat, talk with each other, flirt with members of the opposite sex, and get absolutely nothing done in the way of business. It's basically a party, and maybe even a darn good party at that, but it isn't networking.

Many people however, rationalize that they are indeed networking. They believe they're doing business because they are at this event after normal business hours. About the most productive thing anybody there is doing is every once in a while meeting somebody they don't know and exchanging business cards. Now, no disrespect meant, but *big deal!*

Oh, occasionally by sheer luck, some business will take place. One person might just happen to need what another is selling, or vice versa. But the chances of that happening are small, and the odds for success are certainly not being played to their full advantage.

The First Thing to Do Is Join

Let me ask you this. If you currently belong to your local chamber of commerce, do you attend these card exchanges? If your answer is yes, have you gotten a ton of business from them? No? Would you like to get a ton of business from them? You can!

The first thing I suggest you do is—if you're not already a member of your local chamber of commerce—join today. For two reasons. One is to do your part in supporting your local business community. The other, and even more importantly, is to have an opportunity to use these techniques during those card exchanges as a real networking and selling tool.

So how do we make these usually social functions become networking and *work for us?* You have to know why you are there—you're not just after these people's business, but that of their 250-person spheres of influence as well. Here are three steps to help you accomplish that goal.

1. *Adjust your attitude.* When I say adjust your attitude, I mean understand that the only reason you are at that particular function is to *work.* That doesn't mean it can't be fun. Networking *is* fun. Establishing mutually beneficial relationships with people is fun. Making more money is fun. But we are there at that card exchange, networking function, or whatever we want to term the occasion, to work.

2. *Work the crowd.* To do this be the "sincere politician"; that is, be sincere, but with an air of confidence about you. Be open, but don't come off like a sharp hustler. Be nice. Have a smile on your face. Very simple, right? Okay. That's a start.

3. *Introduce yourself to someone new.* If possible, introduce yourself to someone who is a center-of-influence type person. These are the people who have a very large and important sphere of influence themselves. Typically, they have been in the community for a long time. People are familiar with them. People know them, like them, and trust them. These centers of influence may or may not be particularly successful in business, but they know a lot of other people whom you want to know.

But How Do We Find Them?

My friend, fellow speaker, and author Rick Hill has a great rule of thumb for locating the function's centers of influence. He notes that people are usually broken up into groups of four, five, or six. According to Rick, each group usually has a dominant person—that one man or woman who seems to control the conversation.

He's right. Next time you're at a chamber of commerce function or social gathering, notice how easy it is to find that one person in every group. When someone in the group makes a point, all heads turn to that person for her response. When our dominant person speaks, everyone hangs on her every word. The group laughs when she laughs. They usually agree with whatever this dominant person says. Remember, that person, while not necessarily financially successful, probably knows a lot of people. Make a point of meeting that person one-on-one.

How do we do that, though, if they are always around other people who are hanging on their every word? Basically, keep your eyes on the few centers of influence as you're walking the perimeter of the room. Eventually, one of them is going to leave his or her present group.

It's the Manner in Which You Introduce Yourself That's Important

Just wait for your opportunity and then walk up and introduce yourself to that person. Perfectly acceptable behavior! Again, that's what you're there for, and so is that person.

If you're sort of embarrassed about introducing yourself cold to somebody, that is understandable. Everyone has those feelings at times, including myself. But realize that if you simply approach that person politely and nonaggressively (without a business card in the person's face and ready to pounce), 99 times out of 100 that person will be quite receptive.

Again, such people know that everybody, including themselves, is there for the purpose of networking, regardless of whether most people know how to go about it successfully. The center of influence is just as anxious to make another contact in you as you are in them.

Now the Process Begins

After you have exchanged names, ask your center-of-influence person what line of business she is in. She'll tell you and ask you the same. That's a start. Respond *briefly* with your benefit statement, then quickly move on to the next step. Remember...

> After the introduction, invest 99.9 percent of the conversation asking that person questions about herself and *her* business. Do not talk about you and your business.

After reading the last chapter, you know why. Your networking prospects don't yet care about you and your business. They want to talk about themselves and their business. Let them. Now is the time to ask several of the 10 questions we discussed in Chapter 2. If you don't remember what they are, go back and review them before you attend your next business function. And *memorize* them: they are the tools you'll need here.

The Question That
Separates the Pros from
the Amateurs

Remember the most important question in Chapter 2? Now's the time to ask it.

> "How can I know if someone I'm talking to is a good prospect for you?"

We discussed previously why this question is so important. I guarantee you will be the *only* one there asking that question (unless somebody else at that function has already taken my course or read this book). In any case, that person will be more than happy to tell you what to look for in a prospective customer. They will be impressed with you and your concern for them. Believe me, this technique works!

At this point you might be asking yourself, "If everybody knows these techniques, doesn't that take away my advantage?" Here's my answer. These techniques are intended to result in a mutually beneficial, win-win situation for everyone involved in the process. That being the case, doesn't it figure that the more people who know these techniques, the better for everyone involved?

The main thing is to learn this important networking principle, internalize it, and apply it consistently. Those who do will likely attain great success. But the fact is, most people won't. I sincerely hope you are one of the small percentage who will.

Now's the time to *ask for your prospect's business card.* Again, if she asks for yours, give it to her, but realize that the key is to get *her* card. We'll see why in great detail in the next chapter.

Remember Her Name

Later on, *pop back by and call your networking prospect by name.* Let's say it's half an hour later. You're standing at the hors d'oeuvres table by a recently met center of influence. You very pleasantly say, "Hi, Ms. Gregory. Are you enjoying yourself?"

That's really going to impress her, especially because by this time she has more than likely forgotten your name. Well, I guarantee you that at that point she will take notice of your name.

Remembering peoples' names and faces is a very valuable skill, and one that virtually anyone can learn.

Matchmaker, Matchmaker, Make Me a Match

If you have the opportunity, *introduce people you have met to others.* Preferably, people who can be of mutual benefit to one another. You should be able to make several good contacts at these meetings. So introduce these people to each other.

I call this "creative matchmaking." Position *yourself* as a center of influence—the one who knows the movers and shakers. People will respond to that, and you'll soon become what you project.

Give each person a nice introduction and explain what the other does. Suggest ways they can look for leads for each other. Remember the critically important step we talked about earlier: asking that person how you can know if a person you're talking to can be a good prospect for them?

Tell Jerry how to know what would be a good lead for Mary, and vice versa. Wow! Will they be impressed! They're going to be reminded that you cared enough about them to really listen and remember. It will show sincere interest on your part, and that will make those people more interested in helping you.

All this time you're just beginning to give them a hint of the fact that you are an ace, someone to do business with or refer to others.

Decide in Advance Who Your Networking Prospects Are

Incidentally, another way you can ensure meeting people with whom you can have mutually beneficial networking relationships is to introduce yourself to people involved in professions complementary to yours. For instance, a mortgage broker should try and meet Realtors® who can refer plenty of business their way. Why? Because Realtors are always working with people who need to borrow money.

How will you know that a person is a Realtor before introducing yourself? Be creative. You can check your chamber of commerce directory beforehand and find out who does what. Ask others who might know who the most influential Realtors happen to be.

Keep Your Eyes and Ears Open

Another method is name tags. You may have spotted a real estate company name on someone's name tag as you passed by each other.

Or you might have overheard a part of a conversation indicating that the person is a Realtor. You'll find a way to know if you want to know badly enough.

If you create computer software programs, then meeting a person who sells computer hardware would certainly be a positive step in the right networking direction, wouldn't it? A sign shop owner should try to meet those who either buy signs or, more importantly, are in a position to talk to many other people who buy signs. In any case, regardless of how you meet your best contacts, our next step will be to cultivate them successfully.

Now the business function has ended. Hopefully, you've met about five or six good contacts. Even one or two would not be bad—that's all you need. One or two good contacts are much better than just handing out a bunch of business cards to people with whom you will never end up doing business. That's what everyone else was doing. You've taken a different, more personal approach. The scenario is now set for the follow-up.

Every so often people ask me how they can overcome their shyness or lack of confidence to meet new people and proceed through the entire process we've just covered. The answer is in five words: *Build on your small successes.* There is nothing unusual about having fear in this area. If you feel out of your comfort zone, if you are shy and feel uncomfortable about starting a conversation with someone new, begin by commiting yourself to go to this event and simply say hello in passing to a few people. Success!

Next event, commit to saying hello, shaking hands with a few people, and exchanging names with a smile. Success! The next time set yourself to say hello, exchange names with a few people, and ask what line of work they are in. If you're up to it, ask one or two of the open-ended, feel-good questions. Success! And, as you begin to feel more and more comfortable (and you will!), you'll stay in the conversation longer, and before you know it, the process will become completely natural. You'll become a master at working a crowd.

In the next chapter, we'll look at some methods of profitable follow-up. Simple in their application, they are designed to ensure that when the time comes that your prospect needs your products, goods, or services (or knows someone else who does), you will be the only one who could possibly be in that person's mind.

Key Points

- Chamber of commerce functions (as well as other business and social events) are excellent sources of networking if used correctly.

Otherwise they are practically worthless.

■ There are seven proven techniques that will ensure your success at business functions:

1. Adjust your attitude. Realize that the purpose of attending this function is to work and build your network.
2. Work the crowd. Be pleasant and approachable.
3. Introduce yourself to someone new. If possible, have that person be a center-of-influence person. (You can also predetermine with whom you wish to network based on complementary professions.)
4. After the introduction, invest 99.9 percent of the conversation asking that person questions about herself and her business. Do not talk about yourself and your business.
5. Ask for *your networking prospect's* business card.
6. Later on, pop back by and call that person by name.
7. Introduce people you have met to others.

4

Profitable
Follow-Up
Techniques

Thus far, we've done well in finding and meeting our networking prospects. Maybe we've done this by way of chance meetings or non-business occasions, or possibly during an organized chamber of commerce function. We've made a great, positive impression on those we've met. Now comes the follow-up. By systematically and consistently implementing the following techniques we will separate ourselves, the successful networkers, from the "wanna-bes."

I know. You're thinking to yourself that follow-up is a royal pain. It can be, but only if you do a lot of unnecessary, time-consuming tasks that don't get results. What I want to do is show you some techniques that, once internalized as good habits, will not seem like a hardship. But they will help you build a powerful network, resulting in a lot of referral business.

Hit Them Right Away

First off, *send a personalized thank-you note.* Sure, we've all been taught that. Basic Sales Training 101, wasn't it? However, very few people actually do this, not realizing they are missing out on an important step. People who send notes get remembered for two reasons.

1. They stand out from the competition, since they are one of the few.

2. The recipient will actually see who it is sending them that note.

More on that in a moment.

In most communities you can mail a letter before midnight and it will arrive at its intended location the very next day—assuming, of course, that the destination is local. A letter that shows up at the person's desk or home the day after you meet is a nice touch.

This note should be a nonpushy, simple, brief note, written in blue ink (research indicates blue ink is more effective both in business and personally). It should say something like, "Hi Dave (or Mary, or even Mr. or Ms., depending upon the particular situation), Thank you. It was a pleasure meeting you. If I can ever refer business your way, I certainly will."

The Impression That's Being Made

Let's look at what you've done. First of all, you have again shown that you have a lot of class and that you are conscientious. You've shown that you are a person worthy of doing business with directly or having business referred to.

What you didn't do was come on strong and try to do a hard sell. You simply thanked him or her just for the meeting (we all like to be thanked, don't we?). You also let that person know once again that you have *their* best interests in mind, with the promise to make an effort to send business their way.

Sure, you could add something about keeping you in mind if they, or someone they know, ever needs your products or services. I'm going to strongly suggest, however, that you don't do that. They understand why you sent them the note and are already impressed with you. Sometimes the more we understate our case, the more dramatic an impact we'll make. Besides, you're going to give them plenty of opportunities to be thinking of you in the very near future.

Let me share with you what I do, regarding the type of stationery for the note you send. I send mine on an individually designed post-card that measures 8 by 3½ inches. In the top right-hand corner is my company name and logo. Beneath that is my picture. Just beneath the picture is my name. Below that is my company address and telephone number. All of this is on the right-hand side of the postcard, leaving plenty of room for writing the note.

Picture This

The picture is very important. You want them to *know* who sent that note, and without your picture they might not. People today meet

BURG COMMUNICATIONS, INC.

BOB BURG

P.O. BOX 7002
JUPITER, FL 33468-7002
561-575-2114 • 1-800-726-3667
FAX: 561-575-2304

Author: *ENDLESS REFERRALS: Network Your Everyday Contacts Into Sales (McGraw-Hill)*
WINNING WITHOUT INTIMIDATION: How To Master the Art of Positive Persuasion (Samark)

Actual size is 8 × 3-1/2 inches. Notice there is lots of space in which to write your note.

many other people during the course of a day. As impressed as they were with you during the meeting, as the saying goes, "out of sight, out of mind." What we're doing is giving them a quick reminder right off the bat.

Although this is only the first step toward having them see your face whenever they, or someone they know, need your products or services, it is still an important one. For maximum effectiveness you must put your picture on an individually designed postcard.

Ask your local printer to typeset and print these for you. The expense is minimal; the payback is well worth it. I highly recommend that you get this type of postcard.

First Class All the Way

Now, back to the sending of this note. Although it can be sent as a postcard, I suggest instead enclosing it in a regular number 10 envelope. Address the envelope by hand (again, in blue ink) as opposed to typing it. Do not put a mailing label on it, or on anything else you ever send to this person. I'm not a big believer in using mailing labels because I want the person receiving the information to *know* I really care. Hand-stamp the envelope (as opposed to using a postage meter). An even nicer touch is to use a large, commemorative stamp.

In other words, personalize it. Make it special in your networking prospect's mind's eye. You want this envelope to be opened and the message actually read. If it looks like junk mail, it could be thrown out before ever having been opened. A hand-addressed, hand-stamped envelope will grab people's attention more effectively than one with an impersonal mailing label and postage meter.

Since we've done it the right way, let's take a look at our networking prospect's probable response. He sees the envelope on his desk the next morning. Because it appears to be a personal letter, he opens it. Chances are he still won't, at this point, even associate you with the company name on the envelope. Remember, out of sight...! Now, as your networking prospect pulls out your postcard note and sees your picture, he remembers the good feelings associated with you. You are the one who asked all those questions. You made him feel important. You asked how you could help him, and even introduced him to others.

However, your prospect now thinks, here comes the solicitation. "If I can ever sell you, or someone you know, a whichamahoozee, let me know." But you didn't do that, right? Far from it!

All you did was say thank you for the meeting and let him know you'll try to refer business to him. He will certainly appreciate you for thinking that highly of him, and will remember the effort.

Make the Time

Some people might be thinking, "I'm too busy. I don't have time to write a thank-you note to every new networking prospect I meet." My answer to them is, "Yes, you do!"

The pros, the champions, the ones who are determined to succeed (and you're one of them), do the little things right, consistently. That includes writing and sending the notes.

I say that because through the years I've noticed that successful people share similar traits. One is that they are avid note-writers. They write thank-you notes all the time. It's a known fact that George Bush did this from early on in his career; he networked his way up to the position of chief executive of the United States of America.

There are those who will put the cart before the horse and say it's because these people are successful that now they have the time to write those notes. But we all *know* that's not true. They were doing the little things right, such as writing notes, *before* they were successful. Now it's simply something called "habit."

It's the same in practically every profession. Show me an avid note-writer and 9 times out of 10 I'll show you a success. It's ironic that one trait, such as writing notes, seems to separate those who are successful from those who are not.

From Negotiating to Horse Races

One person who's been a big influence on me is Dr. Jim Hennig. He is an authority on the art of win-win negotiating. Dr. Hennig points out that in negotiating, "It's often the little differences that make the big differences." He goes on: "Doing the little things right can often be the difference between the successful and the unsuccessful negotiation."

That's so true, isn't it? It's true of just about everything else in life. After all, don't they say, "Baseball is a game of...inches." In boxing a split decision is often the difference between the champion and the person who's name we forget 2 weeks later. Maybe even the next day. An average of just a few strokes makes the difference between the top PGA or LPGA money winners and those that barely survive the tour.

My brother Rich is a big horse-racing buff. Recently he gave me an excellent analogy of how little things mean a lot. Typically, in a $200,000 purse, the horse that finishes first brings in $120,000 for its owner. The second horse, who may have lost by just a nose in a photo finish, brings in $40,000 for its owner. The third horse, who lost by just a neck, brings in about $12,000. And the fifth horse, who lost by just a length, one-fifth of a second, brings in the *whopping* sum of $3,000 for its owner!

In that case, couldn't we say that one-fifth of a second was what made the difference of $117,000 between the owners of the first horse and the fifth horse? As Dr. Hennig says, little differences make the big differences.

Back to our thank-you notes. Those of us who are committed to realizing the benefits of effective networking write them even when we don't want to. Let me share with you a shortcut that will make the process a bit easier.

During some downtime, simply take 25 or 30 of your personalized postcards. Leave room at the top for the salutation, and write, "Thank you. It was a pleasure meeting you. If I can ever refer business your way, I certainly will." And sign your name.

I think you know what I'm getting at. Put an elastic band around the postcards, and place them neatly in a shoe box inside the trunk of your car, along with an equal number of already hand-stamped envelopes.

From now on, whenever you meet new networking prospects, simply go to your car, write their name at the top of the note, hand-write their name and address on the envelope (that's why you took their business card), and drop it in the nearest mailbox. Sure, it's still a little bit of extra work, but as speaker and best-selling author Zig Ziglar says, "You don't pay the price for success, you enjoy the benefits of success."

Keep in mind that sending the note is simply a way of establishing yourself and your credibility with this person. It usually will not get immediate results. However, that's not to say, never.

As a speaker and member of the National Speakers Association, I know that other speakers, because of the diversity of topics, are often a tremendous source of referral business. On one particular occasion I was in the audience while a fellow speaker I had not yet met gave a wonderful presentation. We talked briefly afterward and I sent him a note. He, also being an active networker, responded with a note of his own. He also gave me a referral, which turned into a booking.

Naturally, I immediately wrote him a note to thank him for the referral and to assure him that the meeting planner to whom he referred me would receive the highest professional courtesy and so forth.

He then wrote me back a very nice note thanking me for the thank-you note for the referral. In his note he wrote, "It's obvious, Bob, that you are a true professional, and I'm happy to give you referrals."

Remember, at that point he had never actually seen or heard me speak. Since then we've become friends, and I've had the opportunity to refer him to many meeting planners and vice versa. A true win-win.

Another example of the power of sending these postcard type notes was related to me by a man named Tom, who began applying this suggestion immediately after attending one of my seminars. He met a gentleman named David at a business-after-hours event, and after going through the steps to establish the initial know you, like you, and trust you feelings, Tom followed up immediately with his note. Several days later he received a letter back, which he was nice enough to forward to me. The following includes most of that letter:

> Hi Tom, Thanks for dropping me that nice note! I really appreciate it. Enjoyed talking with you at Tuesday night's event. Of course our discussion was the most enjoyable of the night for me, but I am sure it was because you allowed me to talk mostly about myself. I've enclosed some literature about my company. I hope this helps when referring anyone to me. I appreciate your help, more than anything, I hope we can somehow stay in touch. Sincerely, David.

Would you say Tom has got himself a great contact? When reading though the letter another time, it's easy to see that Tom asked all the right questions and did an excellent job of establishing rapport. I know of others who, immediately after sending their postcard type note, were invited to meetings set up by the person to whom they sent the note in order to meet that person's contacts.

Again, the purpose of these postcard type notes is not the type of instant gratification you just read about. It usually doesn't happen that quickly, nor is the process designed to. It will set the stage, however, for future follow-up on your part. And every so often, a quick payoff for your consistent effort will happen.

So don't forget, a simple note or two or three can do wonders when it comes to networking. Don't you enjoy receiving thank-you notes? I do. And I remember those who send them.

Keep Them in Your Thoughts

Be sure to send any articles, newspaper or magazine clippings, or other pieces of information which relate to your networking prospects or their business. If you hear of something that may be helpful to them, send it on your personalized postcard.

For example, a networking prospect sells temporary services to businesses. You hear a rumor that a large company is about to open in a certain building. That would make an excellent and much appreciated informational note, wouldn't it? You could simply call the person, but I would drop a note as well. Dropping that note is so effective and will work to your advantage. A sample might be, "Mary, a quick note to let you know Amalgamated International is about to open in XYZ building. Thought it would be a good prospective lead. Good luck." Then sign your name. Now can't you see how the person on the receiving end of that note would appreciate your unselfish gesture?

Sending newspaper or magazine articles affecting our networking prospects is a very valuable idea. I know, it's another point we all learned in Basic Sales 101, but how many people actually do it consistently?

One challenge people might create is to limit their horizons. You might be thinking, "Well how often does someone in my network actually get his name or picture in the newspaper? Maybe the special Monday business section if they got promoted or something, but how often does that happen?"

Here's a suggestion: as you look through the newspaper, *scour* it to see what bits and pieces of news or information somehow, in some way, affect those in your network. If something you read has anything to do with them, their profession, personal interests, hobbies, whatever, send it along with a short note.

Let me sight a firsthand example. When I was in local sales, I did my networking locally, of course. One prospect in particular was definitely a center-of-influence person whose business and referrals I very much wanted. He was also a direct prospect, as he owned and ran a local franchise business.

One morning in the newspaper, I saw a rather uncomplimentary article about the headquarters of that franchise. This can be a rather touchy situation because we don't want to send our people bad news. Nonetheless, I cut the article out of the paper and wrote a note on my postcard, saying, "Although I don't agree with the article, I thought it would still be of interest." I enclosed the article and note in an envelope and sent it.

He called the very next day to thank me for my consideration. He hadn't seen the article and was glad I cared enough to send it. In fact, he planned to write a rebuttal letter to the editor as a result, which he did. Let me ask you, did I get his business that day? No. But I did 2 months later when he was ready.

In other words, when he needed the products or services that I handled, I was the only one who came naturally to his mind. The founder of the National Speakers Association, the late Cavett Robert, said it best: "People don't care how much you know until they know how much you care—about them and their problems."

After knowing how much I cared, he was more than willing to find out how much I knew. Over time, I also received numerous referrals from him, and totally believe I would to this day if I were still in that or any other type of local business.

Small Investment—Big Payback

Next, *send your networking prospects a notepad every month or so to keep you on their mind.* This notepad should contain your company name, logo, and your picture, and as on the postcard, your name should be directly beneath the picture.

Your address and telephone number should also be included. Make sure to keep all the information about you on the top quarter of the page. That way they will have plenty of room to write their notes. Otherwise, of course, they'll throw it out.

Practically everyone uses scratch pads or notepads, and when people constantly see your picture, you become familiar to them. Your networking prospects are going to have your face right in front of them a lot of the time. Your visibility and credibility will increase in their mind.

You see, what you really want is for your networking prospects to think of you and *only* you whenever anything is brought up concerning your business. If you're a Realtor, you want them thinking of you whenever they think of buying or selling a home. And more importantly, whenever they hear anybody else talk about buying or selling a home. In fact, whenever they think "home," you want them to think of you. If you're an insurance agent, you want them to think of you whenever "insurance" comes up in a conversation. If you're a copy machine salesperson, you want them to think of you whenever "copy machine" comes up, and so on.

One time, my director of marketing called a prospect on the other side of the country, because she knew it was planning time for their annual convention. The moment my name was mentioned, the meeting planner said, "Oh yes, I have his notepad right here on my desk. How's he doing?" Please keep in mind, at that time I had never personally spoken to that meeting planner. Nevertheless, she felt she knew me, by virtue of seeing my picture every single working day.

The result was that we got the booking. I'm positive the decision to have me present a program at their convention was *not* based solely on the notepad. But I *am* certain that it opened the door, kept me in the ball game, and kept the benefits of my program on that person's mind.

The Opposite Is Also True

Ethel is a Realtor and a member of a large office. She has lived in her community all of her life and is well liked and respected. One day she ran into a woman with whom she had been friends for years. The

woman said excitedly, "Ethel, you're going to be very happy to know I just listed my home for sale with one of the salespeople in your office."

Ethel, for reasons easy to understand, was not exactly delighted by that news. She nicely, but disappointedly, asked, "But we've known each other for years. Why didn't you list it with me?" The woman, now realizing the situation replied, "Ethel, I'm so sorry. I just didn't think of you at the time."

What that shows is that people generally don't care about our success as much as we do. That isn't surprising. People are concerned with their own success. If we are not somehow in front of them at the very time of a buying decision (whether they are buying directly, or in a position to refer business), there's a chance they may not think of us until it's too late.

Another case in point concerns a person in my town who tried to sell me a cellular phone for two years. Every so often I'd get a call from him, and he'd ask me if I was ready to buy. I'd always decline. I mean, I really didn't feel I needed one and wasn't in any particular hurry.

As far as one day possibly doing business with him, that wasn't a problem. He certainly fit into the "knowing, liking, and trusting" category. I always figured when I was ready to invest in a cellular phone, he'd get a call.

But something happened to change that. My parents live just 5 miles from me, and every couple of weeks they travel 2 hours to Miami to visit their two grandchildren. There's one stretch on the Florida turnpike that is fairly deserted. I was always concerned about their car breaking down in the middle of nowhere, with them not being able to contact anyone for help.

We have a rule in our family. Whenever any of us takes a trip of any substance, whether by car or plane, we always call to say we arrived safely. On this particular occasion, however, they didn't call until well after the time they should have. When my dad finally called, he told me what had happened. Their car had broken down in that very stretch I mentioned earlier.

Fortunately, a tow truck happened to be in the area and everything turned out fine. (Thank goodness that kind of luck is typical with my dad.) Nonetheless, the incident was enough to motivate me or, more correctly, panic me into purchasing a cellular phone for them!

I immediately reached for the Yellow Pages and began looking for car phone companies to call. Later that day, a salesperson returned my call. We immediately set up an appointment. We met, I bought a car phone, and gave it to my parents.

The question I ask you now is, what happened to the local cellular phone guy I knew? I'll tell you what happened. I don't know!

Actually, I hadn't even thought about him. I was so emotionally wrapped up in the situation with my parents that I didn't even consider calling him. I ended up purchasing the phone from another salesperson, a relative stranger.

However, what if every other month or so I had received a notepad from this guy with his name and picture on it. Wouldn't he, especially in time of panic, when I wasn't thinking logically, have been the only person I would have thought of? Absolutely. I would have reached for his notepad just as easily as I did for the Yellow Pages!

We've got to keep ourselves in front of our networking prospects constantly. Of course, we must accomplish this in a very nonpushy, nonthreatening, almost subliminal manner. The goal is to be the only one they think of when it comes time for them, or anyone in their sphere of influence, to need or want our products, goods, or services.

Newsletters, pens, magnets, and other promotional items are fine. They can never hurt. The problem is that either their shelf life isn't long, as in the case of the newsletter, or they don't have your picture on them and can't always be seen by your networking prospect anyway. A pen will run out of ink and be thrown away and there goes your name and phone number. The scratch pad will be kept and used.

This Sums It Up

In a nutshell, here's why the scratch pad, always on their desk or near their telephone, with your picture on it, is so important. You want them, when they *hear* your name, to know your face and what you do for a living. You want them to *see* your picture and make the connection between your name and what you do for a living. And when they, or someone they know, want or need what you have to offer, you want them to immediately *think* of your name and know your face.

Thanks for the Referral

When you receive a referral (and after implementing these techniques you'll receive plenty), be sure and follow up every time, immediately, with a handwritten, personalized note of thanks. I suggest using the personalized-postcard format we discussed earlier. Again, enclose it in a number 10 envelope for that extra touch.

The note should read something along these lines: "Dear Mary, thank you so much for your nice referral of Bob Jones. You can be assured that anyone you refer to me will be treated with the utmost caring and professionalism."

Now isn't that effective? Short, sweet, professional, and to the point. It says it all. Not to mention that it will surely reaffirm the referrer's feeling that you were the right person for that referral.

Of course, depending upon the situation you can alter the wording of the note or even the type of thank you. I've sent flowers to people who gave me really big referrals. It's certainly worth the investment, as well as a nice way of saying thank you to someone you genuinely like and to whom you feel grateful.

However you thank them, do it in such a way that separates you from the rest. Constantly show that person why *you* should be the only person in your particular line of work receiving the referrals of his or her 250-person sphere of influence.

Key Points

- Follow up on networking prospects in these ways:
    1. *Send a personalized thank-you note* on a 8-by-$3^1/_2$ inch personalized postcard which includes your picture. The note should be written in blue ink, enclosed in a number 10 envelope, and hand-stamped. Make the time to consistently write and send these notes.
    2. *Send any articles, newspaper or magazine clippings, or other pieces of information which relate to your networking prospects or their business.* If you hear something which may be helpful to them, send it on your postcard.
    3. *Send your networking prospects a notepad regularly to keep you on their mind.* Include your company name, logo, picture, and contact information.
    4. Send thank-you notes after receiving referrals.

5

Training
the People Who
Network for You

Thus far we've learned a method for effectively meeting people and winning them over in a very nonaggressive, nonthreatening way—everything from the initial introduction to your networking prospects through genuinely caring follow-up.

You may have even already matched some good people with other good people and had a hand in the success of those you've chosen to include in your network. It's probably safe to say that these people feel good about you. They know you, like you, and trust you. They want to see you succeed, and they want to help you find new business.

However, there is still a challenge: although these people might *want* to help you find new business, they might not know how. Even though you may be in a profession in which your prospects seem obvious, and people might be totally familiar with what you do, it doesn't matter. For them to know how to network for you may be more difficult than you realize.

Help Them Help You

What you've got to do is make it easy for them. Train the people who want to network for you. Sometimes, things we take for granted are confusing to someone else. Have you ever had a good acquaintance or a close friend whose means of making a living was not known to you?

A friend of mine named Tom is vice president of an engineering firm. When asked what he does for a living, he replies, "I'm an engineer." What does that tell me? What does that tell anyone? Nothing. I'd like to refer business to him when and if the opportunity arises, and I've asked him numerous times to explain, in layperson's terms, just what it is he does and who his prospects are. I still don't understand. He hasn't developed a simplified method of explaining it.

Another friend is a computer consultant. A computer consultant? What is that? It could mean anything, couldn't it? It reminds me of the movie *Father of the Bride*, starring Steve Martin. His soon-to-be son-in-law described himself as an international computer consultant; then he quickly added that he realized it sounded as though he were unemployed everytime he said that.

Even the more tangible types of professions can also be trouble for those who are not versed in that particular field. So let's use a technique usually involved in a one-on-one sales presentation to get our point across.

Features Versus Benefits

What's the difference between a feature and a benefit? A feature is what something *is*, whereas a benefit is what something *does*, or can be something that solves a problem. The difference between features and benefits is often stressed in sales training classes for use during a sales presentation. That's because it is important for sales professionals to realize that people buy a product or service not for its features but for the benefits they will realize by taking ownership.

Keep in mind that benefits often encompass opposite ends of the spectrum. In other words, the benefits include the fulfillment of a desire and/or the solution to a problem.

When I was in direct sales we used to use the analogy of the elderly woman from the cold Northeast. She visited an appliance store in the middle of a freezing winter in order to purchase a heater. The salesperson began rattling off all of the heater's wonderful features, and he was undoubtedly a glib presenter.

He expertly informed the woman what type of material the heater was made of, the way it was crafted, and even the BTU output. He described the engineering and research that went into it, the bells and whistles. He even told her about where it was made and how long the manufacturer had been in business. After patiently listening to this salesperson's eloquent description of the impressive list of features, the woman asked meekly, "But will it keep an old lady warm at night?" *That's* the difference between features and benefits.

A friend of mine and fellow speaker, Frank Maguire, is one of the founders of Federal Express. According to Frank, "We decided early on that we were not in the `delivery' business...but in the business of `peace of mind.' Our clients' biggest fear was late delivery."

Late delivery could ruin their business or, at the very least, ruin a good account. It was their biggest perceived problem, or pain. Frank knew his clients needed to feel assured that, regardless of the situation, their package would "absolutely, positively" be there when it was supposed to be (overnight!).

Life insurance is a feature. Protection and security are the benefits one derives from owning a life insurance policy. For a life insurance sales professional to say, "I sell life insurance" is to merely point out a feature. On the other hand, "I show people how to plan for a sound financial future while protecting themselves and their loved ones for the present, through insurance" is the benefit to the prospective client. In this case, it both satisfies a want (a sound financial future) and solves a problem (protecting the insured's loved ones).

"I sell real estate" is a feature. "I help people successfully market their home and purchase their perfect dream home" is the benefit one will derive by working with that salesperson.

"I am a dentist" is a feature. "I provide healthy teeth and smiles, with no pain" (as opposed to, "I stick metal objects into people's teeth") is the benefit to the prospective patient. And the referrer will easily understand that.

Remember, as we network we have to realize that it isn't only the person to whom we are speaking whose business we are after: more important is his or her 250-person sphere of influence. Stating the benefits of what we do provides our networking prospect with a much clearer picture of who would be a good prospect for us.

Actually Tell Them *How* to Know

There's another step to this as well. Remember the one key question you asked this person during your first conversation: "How can I know if someone I'm talking to is a good prospect for you?" Well, after your win-win rapport is established with that person, you can also let him or her know, in plain and simple language, how to recognize if someone would be a good prospect for you.

For instance, there was the earlier example I cited of Gary, the copying machine salesperson. He made reference to the fact that when walking by a copying machine you might notice a lot of crumpled-up pieces of paper overflowing from a wastepaper basket. According to Gary, that's an indication that particular copying machine has not been working well lately. Its owner might need a new one, and you could be giving an excellent lead.

You can also give others the same type of coaching. If you are a printer, you might suggest that a person just starting a new business may be a good prospect for you. If you are a solar energy equipment salesperson, then suggesting that your fellow networkers keep their eyes and ears open for people complaining about high energy costs would also serve you well. Even though *you* know what it is you need, the chances are, the other person doesn't. Help them to help you.

Keep in mind that no matter how good a rapport is established during your initial conversation with networking prospects, it's only after you have earned their loyalty that you can legitimately expect your benefit statement and prospecting tip to carry any weight with them. That's okay. We're assuming that at present, they are quite grateful to have you in *their* network, and are only too happy to be your walking ambassador.

Your Personal Benefit Statement

We've covered possible benefit statements for several professions. Later in this chapter, I'll list a few more suggestions. Unfortunately, there is not enough room to write out a different benefit statement for every single profession, but you will at least get a sampling of how it's done.

So you need to come up with your own. Let me give you some guidelines first. Your benefit statement should be a short, succinct, descriptive sentence no more than 7 seconds in length. It should describe what you do and how it will benefit the person using your services.

What I suggest is that you develop this benefit statement and practice it on people you know. A family member or close friend is ideal, as well as a trusted associate with whom you work. Get their critique and ask them to be totally honest. Don't worry about perfection. Don't worry about getting your feelings hurt. Your first try isn't etched in stone. You'll keep improving on it as time goes on.

In my case, when I first began teaching networking techniques, my benefit statement was, "I show people how to network for profit." It was a decent benefit statement because it had a desired benefit to the person attending my seminar, namely, profit.

It was decent, but not spectacular. I kept working on it and asked myself the benefit my prospects would get out of my program. Benefits that were tangible, that they could relate to, and that would tell them *how* they were going to achieve all that profit.

Well, I knew my prospects fit into two main categories. The first category was direct salespeople depending on referrals in order to accelerate their business. The second was professionals such as chiropractors, dentists, lawyers, and accountants—people whose business greatly depended on referrals, but who definitely do *not* consider themselves to be salespeople (even though they are). And they had to be very discreet in seeking out referrals from those who were not already patients or clients.

Notice that both groups wanted, needed, and had to have *referrals*. So that word had to be included in my benefit statement, and it had to be plural. They needed continuous, *endless* referrals. Hmm? That's it! My new benefit statement became, "I show people how to cultivate a network of endless referrals."

That benefit statement has become my trademark, and it helped me position myself as an authority in the networking field. And I know it's an effective benefit statement because of the positive comments I receive from those in the mail-order advertising profession.

These people are masters at writing headlines that grab our attention. They *have* to be. After all, they have just split seconds to get us interested enough to keep reading the message. Their "benefits-laden" headlines are often the difference between the successful and unsuccessful advertising campaign. When a prospective mail-order buyer sees that headline, it must immediately present enough of a benefit to get that prospect to continue reading the ad.

Let's Put It Together

Often, a benefit statement will begin along the lines of, "I show people how to..." or "I help people to...." Usually, it isn't a good idea to begin a sentence with the word "I," but in this case we almost have to. If you come up with another beginning that works as well for you, by all means, use it.

What's vital is that you show where you help some*body* do some*thing*, or you do some*thing* for some*body*. That something can be to help them achieve a positive goal or avoid or conquer a particular pain.

One of the best benefit statements I ever heard was from a young man during a seminar in Minneapolis. I was suggesting benefit statements for people in the audience involved in different professions. Somebody then asked me to suggest a benefit statement for stockbrokers, or financial planners. After I gave a few of my standard suggestions, a gentleman named Gregory Zandlo of North East Asset Management raised his hand. He had a benefit statement he'd been using which he thought was also worth mentioning. It was, "We help people create and manage wealth."

Wow! That says it all, doesn't it? How much more effective could a benefit statement possibly be? It's short, sweet, and to the point. It can also fit into any conversation without sounding pushy. And it points out a desire (creating wealth) while solving a problem (managing that wealth).

So follow that lead. Take a moment right now to come up with a benefit statement in the fewest possible words. Do it now. Please do not worry about perfection—just take the first step and put something in writing. Use a separate sheet of paper.

How did you do? It doesn't matter; you are on your way! Keep thinking about it and working on it. Ask those in your network to lend you their ear and provide feedback. Mold this statement. Reshape it. Then memorize it. Internalize your benefit statement so that you know it without first having to think. Then experiment with it and check out responses.

Rick Hill, whom I mentioned earlier, uses what he calls the raised-eyebrow test. According to Rick, "When you tell someone your benefit statement and they start looking around the room for someone else to talk to, you probably need to continue working on it. If, however, they raise their eyebrows with interest and say, `Hmm, tell me more,' you're probably on the right track."

That's as good a description as you'll ever find. And Rick, whose program focuses on prospecting, has an excellent benefit statement himself. When asked what he does, he responds, "I teach companies large and small how to develop a never-ending chain...of new business." Great! And notice the pause after "never-ending chain." "That," says Rick, "is to help that person *literally* picture the never-ending chain."

Let's List a Few More Benefit Statements

The following are just a few benefit statements used by those in particular businesses. A few are repeated from earlier, but I feel it's worth recapping them again.

Chiropractor: I help people heal themselves naturally, without drugs.

Accountant: I give companies large and small timely and accurate financial information while legally minimizing their business and personal tax liability.

Realtor: I help people successfully market their home and buy their perfect dream home.

Financial planner: We help people create and manage wealth.

Advertising agency: We show you how to dramatically increase your company's revenues through strategic positioning in the marketplace.

Life insurance agent: I help people prepare for a sound financial future while protecting themselves and their loved ones for the present.

Graphic artist: I show you how to present your perfect image to those with whom you want to do business.

Solar energy salesperson: We help people save energy and save money all at once through solar heating.

Transactional attorney: Our firm helps people successfully arrange transactions while helping them avoid costly mistakes.

Litigating attorney: Our firm helps people resolve disputes in various forms and avoid costly consequences.

Tell Them How to Know If Somebody *They* Are Talking to Would Be a Good Prospect for *You*

You should take this step *only* when you are sure the other person is ready. If you have already won this person over, they will *want* to network for you. You can come right out and mention to this person that you could use her help.

Because she is grateful for the business you've referred to her, she may actually say to you, "What can I do for you now that you've been such a help to me? You've thrown business at me, you've thought of me. Now what can I do to know if somebody I'm talking to would be a good prospect for you?" This is when we let them know the answer.

If you are a chiropractor, you might respond, "Anyone with neck pain or back pain is a good prospect for me." An accountant might say, "If you know of someone needing help managing the financial end of the business, that person would be a good prospect for me." A banker could suggest that, "A family that mentions adding on to their home would be an excellent prospect for me."

This transaction of information can occur in either a formal or informal session. Since a win-win relationship has been established, there should not be any resentment on the other person's part whatsoever.

One idea is to invite a center-of-influence person you've won over to lunch. Assure her that you look forward to continuing to help her find new business. At the same time, show and teach her how to network for you as well.

How to Ask for Referrals
(So That You Get Them)

Years ago, shortly after I had joined the local sales force of a company, the sales manager held a meeting one morning focusing on how to increase referrals. The question he asked was, "How do you get referrals?" One of the young salespeople who had just come over from another company was supposed to be a real dynamo. He immediately threw up his hands and said, all-knowingly, "You *ask* for them!"

To my amazement, the sales manager said, "That's right." I remember thinking to myself, "How naive!" Actually, they were both half right. You do have to ask. Where they missed the boat, however, is the fact that you have to ask better than that.

Here's why. Have you ever asked someone, either after a sale, or at any other time when you really felt good about this person wanting to help you: "Kay, do you know anybody else who could benefit from my products or services?"

I'll bet Kay began to stare off into space. She was thinking about it—and thinking about it in earnest, really concentrating. Finally, she said, "Well, I can't think of anybody right now, but when I do, I'll definitely let you know." You then probably never heard from her again regarding a referral. And it wasn't Kay's fault.

When we ask people if they "know anyone who..." we are giving them much too large a frame of reference. A blurry collage of 250 faces (their sphere of influence) will run through their mind, but no individual will be singled out. They may feel frustrated, as though they let you down. After everything you've done for them, they feel badly that they can't come through for you as well. It might even make that person feel resentful toward you.

A definite solution to this challenge is to isolate—funnel their world down to just a few people. We've got to give them a frame of reference that they can work with.

Have You Heard the One
about the...

Let me explain it this way. Has anybody ever asked you if you knew any good jokes? Now, you probably know plenty of good jokes, but can you actually think of one when someone asks you? I can't. Here's another example. One night I called my local golden oldies radio station and requested the song "Only in America" by Jay and the Americans. The announcer told me they no longer carry that song on their play list. "But" he asked, "do you happen to know any other oldies you'd like to hear?" I can tell you right now that I know hundreds of oldies I'd like to hear, but could I think of even one at that moment? No way!

It's virtually the same situation when we ask people if they know "anybody" who could benefit from our products or services. Most likely they know plenty of people who could, or who might. Try to get them to think of even one person at that time using that methodology, however, and it's probably not going to happen.

Instead, give them a frame of reference. Let's take the following example. You are talking to Joe, a center of influence in your community. Joe really likes you. You've sent him business, provided him with some background information for one of his projects, and, who knows, maybe you even fixed him up with a blind date that worked out. You are well aware, through asking the right questions during previous conversations, that Joe is a golfing enthusiast and member of his local Rotary Club. Let's see how we can make this situation work.

> YOU: Joe, you were telling me you're an avid golfer.
>
> JOE: Yes, I am. Been playing for over 20 years. If I ever get to retire, I'll probably play every day. Right now, though, it's only on weekends. And I mean, *every* weekend.
>
> YOU: Hmm. Is there a specific foursome you play with most of the time?
>
> JOE: Well, yeah, there's Joe Martin, Ken Stevens, and Nancy Goldblatt.
>
> YOU: Joe, as far as you know, would any of them happen to need...

And then you get into the benefits of what you do. Now, none of the three Joe mentioned might be a good prospect at this particular time, but at least you are increasing his odds of being able to help you. You gave him three people he could *see.* And maybe one or more of them *might* need your product or services. If he tells you, "I'll ask them next time we go out," it may result in some business for you down the line.

Now let's move along to the next frame of reference.

> YOU: How long have you been involved with your local Rotary Club?
>
> JOE: About 6 years now. Great bunch of people.
>
> YOU: Joe, are there one or two people in your club that you tend to sit next to every meeting? (Notice you didn't ask, "Does *anyone* in your club need...")
>
> JOE: Really just one person—Mike O'Brien. Been friends with him and his family for years.
>
> YOU: Has Mike ever mentioned needing a...?

Do you see where we are going with this? The process continues until your networking associate has come up with a few names. Oftentimes, what will happen is this: when one name comes to mind, it will naturally trigger off the names and faces of many others who would also be excellent referrals.

You might be wondering if this will seem pushy. The answer is no, not if this person has genuine good feelings about you and wants to see you succeed. You can also arrive at your meeting with a few names of your own for your friend to call. Nothing at all wrong with doing that.

Keep this in mind: when using this method of asking for referrals, we are, in essence, limiting the number of potential people they might know, but increasing the number of referrals we'll actually receive. Very effective.

One thing I always do is to tell the referrer, "I promise I'll call." And when I call that person, I say, "Hi, Ms. Johnson. This is Bob Burg calling. I *promised* Tom Stevens I'd call you." Sort of positions us a little better in that person's mind right off the bat, doesn't it?

In sales we always want to make it easy for a potential buyer to buy from us. When seeking referrals, we want to make it as easy as possible for a potential referrer to refer to us. Know the frame-of-reference questions you are going to ask *before* you ask them. If *you* feel comfortable with the process, they will too.

Key Points

- We need to train people to know how to network for us.

- Know the difference between features and benefits. A feature is what something *is,* whereas a benefit is what something *does,* or something that solves a problem.

- Develop a benefit statement for the product or service you provide.

- Tell people how to know if someone *they* are talking to is a good prospect for you.

- In order to ask for referrals so that you get them, you must isolate people in the referrer's mind so they can "see" them.

- Isolate people in their mind by giving them a frame of reference.

6

Six Essential Rules of Networking Etiquette

Just like any game, relationship, or business, networking has its rules, procedures, and etiquette. Knowing what to do and following the road map to success is great. Knowing what *not* to do can often be just as beneficial. There really aren't many rules when it comes to networking; however, the few that exist need to be adhered to. If not, there is great risk of destroying the wonderful environment we have created through effective networking.

Don't Ask for Immediate Repayment

When you give something to, or do something for, someone, *do not ask for (or expect) an immediate repayment*. Or a repayment within any time frame at all. We've seen throughout this book how important it is to be a giver. We know that the more we give the more we will receive.

Is there anything more maddening than someone doing something for you, with the unspoken (and sometimes actually spoken) implication, "Now what are you going to do for me?" That isn't networking—it is trading. It is no more than keeping a running tally of who owes what to whom.

Asking for repayment, or letting people know that you feel they *owe* you, will only elicit resentment. Imagine giving someone a lead, a direct referral, or some advice; or maybe you helped their son or daughter get an after-school job at the local hamburger joint. If you then turn around and overtly make that person feel indebted to you, the win-win relationship has been sabotaged. It will only serve as a warning sign to that person that you don't do "something for nothing!"

An incident from my direct sales days immediately comes to mind. I was trying to help a prospect find a product he needed and was having trouble. Suddenly, a man I knew rather indirectly gave me some unsolicited advice on how I could find what I was looking for. Yes, his advice was unsolicited—but extremely helpful.

Later that day he called and asked if his advice was of any help. I told him it certainly was, and that I appreciated his assistance very much. He then politely informed me that, should a sale ensue, he expected a referral fee for his help. I told him that if his advice did lead to a sale, I would honor that, and I said nothing more about it.

The Actual Result, Though, Was Bad Feelings

Needless to say, I very much resented what he did. I decided right then and there I would never ask for or accept his advice again, and I wasn't really anxious to do anything that would benefit him.

Had he not mentioned the referral fee, I would have felt obligated—and even wanted—to return the favor down the road. And knowing how I feel about give and take, you can be certain that what he did for me would have come back to him many, many times over.

Let me clarify something. When I advise you not to make people feel they owe you, I need to qualify that statement. Of course, we want people to feel they owe us, but we want them to *want* to owe us.

When we do something for someone, to help him reach his goals or just to show we care, we elicit good feelings. We foster a mutually beneficial, win-win relationship. That person feels good about us, and either consciously or subconsciously will work hard to give back in kind (if not more).

When we make someone feel threatened or inferior, as though he *owes* us, we cause anger and resentment. In that case, the person may *say* he wants to help us, when in reality, he may want to sabotage our success.

There are times that payback is mentioned by a person as a segue, or bridge, into asking us for help. As wrong as this is, we need to be aware that the person may not feel comfortable asking us for something. In fact, it is more a defense mechanism than anything else.

A fellow speaker was kind enough to send me some information he thought I might find useful. I immediately called to thank him. During our conversation, he discovered that some information I had could be of help to him. Instead of simply asking me to send it, he said, "Listen, since I gave you the other information, would you send this to me?"

Had I not understood his discomfort in making that request, I might have felt resentful. Someone else might actually have been offended and thought, "Oh, so that's why he did that for me." This is the reason we need to be careful in that aspect of networking.

Do something for somebody without the goal being a payback, and you'll usually be paid back anyway. Again and again and again.

Find a Mentor

When seeking a mentor, approach modestly, unassumingly, respectfully, and with the intention of giving more than receiving. A mentor is a person, usually already successful, who wants to take us under his or her wing and help us become a success in our own right. A mentor is the teacher; we are the student.

It's like a good friendship in the way it develops over time. When seeking a mentor, approach modestly, unassumingly, respectfully, and with caution. I've actually heard people just starting in business announce out loud for the world to hear, "I am looking for a mentor." They're probably not going to find one with that approach.

But if you approach your objective correctly, you *can* find people out there who are looking to share their knowledge with an eager young beginner or an eager older professional. You might start by taking them to lunch. (Be sure and pick up the check.) Ask them questions and pick their brains, but do it with sincere respect and appreciation. Make them feel good about the knowledge or skills they possess. But mainly, find out what you can do to help *them,* and then do it!

In many ways, it's similar to what we discussed earlier about cultivating a center-of-influence person to supply you with endless referrals. The same rules apply. You wouldn't walk up to that person and say, "Hi, will you be my unlimited referral source and help me to succeed beyond my wildest dreams?" Of course not. You wouldn't do that in trying to acquire a mentor, either. You've got to establish the relationship gradually, based on mutual give and take, and always try to do more for that person than he or she is doing for you.

Most Mentors *Want* to Be Mentors

Here's the good news: successful people *enjoy* being mentors. They even seek out students. Why? Because it makes an already-made person feel good to share just how he got there, and even to be able to give that student a boost. Mentors want to be remembered fondly by those who follow their advice and go on to be successful themselves.

Ego probably has something to do with it as well. As an established professional speaker, my advice on how to make it in the field of professional speaking is constantly being sought by speakers just starting their careers. And I love to help them. It boosts my ego and allows me to share and teach, which I love to do. And when they become successful and famous, it gives me great pride to know I had a hand in their success.

When I was just beginning in the speaking profession, I was lucky enough to have found the National Speakers Association. Just by joining, I had access to thousands of other professionals. What I found in this benevolent organization was a great bunch of people ready, willing, and able to share their knowledge. You, too, may find it advantageous to join an organization made up of others in your field. It's a good place to find your mentor or mentors. It worked for me.

There isn't any *one* person I would call my mentor, but I can easily think of *several* whom I called constantly with questions. It was amazing the number of questions they answered and the amount of information they shared. Of course, I did the right things as well. I sent a thank-you note after each and every conversation.

Not only that. Whenever I spoke with a prospective client and didn't get the booking, I always made sure to plug one of my mentors. And they knew it. Even though they weren't helping me with the expectation of getting something in return, you can bet that when they saw it happening, it made them feel even better about taking their valuable time in order to help me.

I can genuinely say that much of my quick success as a professional speaker is due to these wonderful people who mentored me, without qualification or reserve. I'm glad I could give something back to them, and I continue to do it now.

One of the nicest compliments I received was after addressing the National Speakers Association at our 1992 national convention in Orlando, Florida. During my speech I hit hard on the importance of finding a mentor and establishing give-and-take relationships. Afterward, numerous members of the audience came up and told me that people who were sitting near, or next to them, had commented out loud, "Burg practices what he preaches. He's referred plenty of business to me."

Keep an Eye on the Clock

When networking, especially if we are asking someone for advice or information, it's extremely important that we respect their time. If I'm calling that person on the phone, the first thing I will always ask is, "Do you have a real quick minute to (answer a question) (give me some advice) (refer me to someone in the widget industry), or is this a lousy time?" If it is a "lousy time," find out when might be a better time. Remember, we want them to feel good about being a part of our network. Wasting their time and not being sensitive to their needs will obviously not help us to accomplish that goal.

Respecting others' time is especially important when contacting someone who doesn't know us personally. Let's take an example. We are considering a direct-mail campaign for our product or service and we realize that before jumping right in, it would be wise to hear some thoughts from someone who's already been there. So we ask someone in our network to connect us with a person he knows in the mail-order industry and he gives us a name.

Imagine how this person would feel if, immediately after our introduction, we started machine-gunning him with question after question after question. How would he feel about our imposing on his time (and expertise) without showing any sensitivity as to his needs? Among those needs is the time he requires to conduct his own business. Every minute he spends answering our questions is a minute away from getting his own job done.

A friend of mine in Philadelphia is a schoolteacher by trade who has amassed a small fortune buying and selling real estate. She went to a lot of seminars, read a lot of books, and suffered numerous setbacks before becoming successful in this venture. People who hear about Sandi will often call her and say that a friend suggested they call and talk to her about investing in real estate.

Enough Is Enough

Knowing Sandi as I do, that is fine. She's a giver and likes to help. Unfortunately, she tells me, most people take advantage of that quality. They will keep her on the telephone for a long time, trying to extract as much information as possible. And, they'll call back time and time again. Eventually, Sandi has to tell them that if they want a *seminar* from her, they'll have to pay.

Imagine people doing that to her—or anyone. How obnoxious! And the truth is, it needn't be that way. Most people love to help and are glad to share what they know. In fact, they want to, if only for ego's sake alone. However, we need to be totally respectful of their time and let them know how much we appreciate it. A little consideration goes a long way.

Follow Through on Promises

One of the more deadly sins of networking is not following through on what we promise to do. Have you ever been exchanging ideas or leads with a fellow networker who has said, "I'll send you that information right away"? After a couple of days, though, the information doesn't arrive. You don't really want to call and remind him because that would appear pushy.

A week later, you still haven't received the information, or even a call from that person. On a scale of 1 to 10, how does that make you feel about that person? How do you rate them for dependability? How much do you trust their word? Also on a scale of 1 to 10, how effective a networker do you feel that person probably is?

Now let's look at a different scenario. Suppose you sell printing, and during a conversation with a fellow networker who's in the business of leasing office space, you learn that a new company will be moving into one of their larger spaces very soon. You recognize the type of business and know they'd be a huge purchaser of printing services. The person with whom you are networking mentions that he'll get you some information on the company and who's who within the organization.

Two days later you receive an envelope with the letterhead of this leasing agent. Upon opening the envelope and pulling out its contents, you notice that the information includes the following: the date the company will be moving in, their purchaser's name and telephone number, and other valuable data that will surely give you the definitive edge over your competition.

Now go back to that 10-point scale and answer those very same questions regarding *this* person. After giving them a score of 10 all around, ask yourself this: Isn't he or she the kind of person you will absolutely go out of your way to help? I know I would, because networkers like that are hard to come by. Also, the more of those types you know and associate with, the more successful *you* are going to be. I guarantee *they* are, and we become like the people with whom we associate.

Be Extra Careful Not to Annoy a Referred Prospect

Let me paint you a picture of a very ticklish situation. One of your fellow networkers calls you and excitedly says, "I've got someone for you to contact. Our regional manager's name is Carol Davis, and she would be the person with the authority to purchase more of your widgets than you ever thought you could sell to any one company. Just mention my name and she'll take your call."

You like that! In fact, it makes your day—you think. So you eagerly and confidently pick up that ordinarily intimidating instrument known as the telephone and begin dialing. As the secretary begins the screening process, you nonchalantly say, "Just tell her that Dave Smith suggested I call."

Dave Who?

When the secretary questions you as to who Dave Smith would happen to be, you feel a slight pull in your stomach. Something doesn't seem right. Nonetheless, you do not retreat. You say, "Dave is with the Centerville branch of your company." Unimpressed, she puts you on hold and you now find yourself listening to the Musak rendition of "Danke Schoen" over the telephone system. Finally, after about 4 minutes, you are greeted by a somewhat irritated voice. The conversation goes as follows:

CAROL DAVIS: This is Carol Davis.

YOU: Hi, Ms. Davis. This is Joe Taylor calling from Widgets Unlimited.

CD: (silence)

YOU: Uh, Dave Smith referred me to you.

CD: (silence)

YOU: Uh, Dave said you would be the person to speak to regarding the purchasing of widgets for your company.

CD: We don't need any right now. Just send me some information and we'll call you when we're interested.

Obviously, this was not a good referral. At this point I might ask one or two qualifying questions, but if there's any resistance in her voice, I will politely end the conversation.

Although it may be tempting to tell this person to take a long walk off a short pier, it isn't the right thing to do. Such a comment merely serves to lower you to that person's level. Also, there's a good chance your return rudeness would get back to Dave, who had given you the referral in the first place.

"So what?" you may be wondering. "It was a terrible, unqualified referral which did me no good at all!" True, but at least he was thinking of you, and, with a little coaching on your part, his future referrals could be all-stars.

Coach Him on How to Help

This goes back to a technique I discussed earlier in the book, and that is training those who network for us. As far as I'm concerned, anyone who refers us once certainly thinks enough of us to give referrals again in the future. If, however, he gets a nasty call from Carol Davis's office or a letter asking him to keep his nose out of corporate headquarters' business, he won't ask you about how rude Carol was. No, he'll assume *you* came on too strong, and he may not risk the prospect of another introduction.

Here's a way to tactfully handle this situation. First, call Dave and thank him very much for thinking of you. Let him know that friends such as him make your job so much easier. Assure him you look forward to referring even more business to him, as well. Then tell him that, as a friend, you feel you should relate to him the circumstances of your contact with Ms. Davis. Let him know that you're telling him this simply for his knowledge, in the event that he may be thinking of referring someone else to Ms. Davis.

In a very matter-of-fact, unemotional manner, review with him your unpleasant conversation with Ms. Davis. Be careful, though. You don't want to embarrass him. Remember, he felt like a big-shot when he gave you the referral ("Just tell her that Dave Smith suggested I call"), so it's imperative you *don't* make him regret that.

Let him know that a similar situation has happened to you, so you can understand and still appreciate his thinking of you. Then just explain that, in future situations, it would probably be helpful to make sure either that the prospect is expecting you to call or that his relationship with the prospect is solid.

Again, it isn't *what* you say but *how* you say it. Using the above as a guideline and spoken with tact (tact—the language of strength), you'll defuse any resentment and turn that lemon into lemonade in the future.

Say (and Write) Thank You

By this time, that should go without saying but it bears repeating anyway. Regardless of whether the lead turns into a huge sale or a bomb like the one in the example above, let that person know how much his thoughts are appreciated.

Another good reason for doing this is to let the referrer know something happened. Once I had to turn down an engagement to speak because I was already booked for that day. Always networking, however, I gave the prospect the name of another speaker who deals with a similar topic. After a week, I realized I had not heard from the other speaker. It wasn't the thank you itself I was after, but the desire to know whether a connection had ever been made. I found out from the *prospect* that it had. Between you and me, I'd have liked the thank you as well. We all like to feel appreciated.

Thanking your referrer is one of those automatics. It never gets tiresome to receive a thank-you note. I have people who consistently refer business to me, and they've made it a point to tell me they *always* appreciate my thank-you notes. I'm convinced it's a major factor in why they continue to refer business my way.

Key Points

In order to maintain and build our network, we must adhere to certain rules of networking etiquette.

- When you give something to or do something for someone, do not ask for (or expect) an immediate repayment.
- When seeking a mentor, approach modestly, unassumingly, respectfully, and with the intention of giving more than receiving.
- Keep an eye on the clock.
- Follow through on promises.
- Be extra careful not to annoy a referred prospect.
- Say (and write) thank you.

7
Prospecting for Fun and Profit

The very first question one might ask when beginning to read this chapter is, "Isn't this entire book about *prospecting?* After all, when we network, aren't we prospecting for business?" Yes—and no. When we network, we are prospecting. When we prospect, however, we aren't necessarily networking.

Let me qualify this statement by explaining that networking and prospecting are like first cousins—same family, but different. In this chapter, we're going to look at prospecting from this angle: Prospecting is getting to the point that the networking relationships begin. Networking, in turn, becomes a vehicle for long-term, lasting results.

Here's a rule to live by:

Never stop prospecting!
    Yes, even when we reach the point that all, or almost all, of our business comes from referrals, we continue to prospect within our network.

Let's look at prospecting here as the intangible we've always heard about and most of us have experienced in sales: the endless telephone calls, knocking on doors, and hearing the words, "I'm not interested."

It Doesn't Have to Be
That Way

There are ways to prospect that are fun, exciting, and profitable. Sure, you'll prospect by telephone and see people face-to-face. The difference will be in the results, your methods of attaining those results, and your attitude along the way.

You must realize first that sales and prospecting have always been, and always will be, a numbers game. If you make enough calls and see enough people, you will make your share of sales...even if you do things wrong. Of course, the key is to do things right. That way, you'll make more sales in much less time, calling on many fewer people.

A neat formula in practically any type of prospecting takes into account the relationship between calls and contacts, contacts and appointments, and appointments and sales.

For instance, let's say that for every 100 numbers you call (or people/ businesses you call on in person), you actually get to speak or make contact with 40 decision makers. Out of those 40 contacts, you will close 10 appointments. And out of those 10 appointments, you'll make 4 sales.

Letting the numbers and percentages work for us, we realize that every time we call and don't make contact, make a contact but don't get an appointment, or make an appointment but don't close the sale, we're one step closer to success!

That sounds strange, doesn't it? Here's what I mean. You know the chances are 4 in 10 that when you call or visit, you'll contact the right person. If you miss your first one, fine! You've just increased your odds on the next call. If you miss the next, congratulate yourself— you're yet another step closer to your first contact.

Obviously, it isn't quite that simple. The numbers work over a long period of time. Nonetheless, the more calls in which you don't hit your goal (contacting the right person), the greater your odds that the next one will be it.

How to Put a Dollar Value
on Small Failures

Let's take those same 100 calls and the same ratios. Let's say in this scenario that each closed sale makes you $300 in commission. If it's going to take 100 total calls to make four sales ($1200), then can't we break that down into $12 per call? That's right! Every time you pick up the phone or visit a business or knock on a door, you net $12. If you can't make the initial contact, that's $12. If you make the initial contact but can't close the appointment and can't close the sale, that's $12. When someone says, "I'm not interested!!!!" simply say (to yourself), "That's $12, please."

How to Prospect Yourself into a Raise

You can raise your salary one of two ways: by making more calls or by turning a higher percentage of initial calls into contacts, contacts into appointments, and appointments into sales. That's what we'll discuss for the remainder of this chapter. We'll look at effective ways of prospecting, individually and both by telephone and by visiting in person.

Turn Your Telephone into $$$

It's understandable that the telephone can be an intimidating object. After all, people can be rude, which means prospects can be rude. We realize that when we make prospecting calls, we are probably taking people away from something they are already doing to increase their own business. Since they don't yet know the benefits of our products or services, they may not like that. Their resentment might come across to us in a most obvious way.

If you are like me, you are naturally sensitive to rejection. Hey, I like to be liked! It isn't fun when people say they're not interested, or hang up the phone, or fib to quickly rid themselves of our pesky presence. But realizing that this is the worst-case scenario and that their rejection isn't personal (after all, they've never met us), we can now turn these calls into the beginnings of making money.

Let me point out something right now about using the telephone. Depending upon your particular business, you might be using the telephone simply to get in-person appointments. That is the usual case. In direct sales we had a saying that you never tried to sell your product on the telephone. The only thing you tried to close on the telephone was the in-person appointment!

There are businesses, however, where the telephone is used both to prospect *and* to close the sale. As a professional speaker, my business definitely fits that description. After all, if my marketing staff or I had to visit meeting planners and decision makers all over the country in order to close a booking, we'd spend much more time in travel and money in travel-related expenses than we could ever recoup by actually speaking and marketing our books and tapes.

Other businesses fall into that category as well, so I'll discuss this aspect of teleprospecting before talking about phone techniques for simply closing the appointment.

As I've shared at live seminars the techniques my staff and I use to prospect and sell by telephone, I've heard from many people selling numerous other products and services that these techniques work for them as well. So as you read how we do it, simply imagine how you can bend and twist the techniques to your own unique situation.

"Know You, Like You, Trust You" Is Even More Important Now

Probably the most difficult aspect of teleprospecting is that you are not right in front of the person during your presentation. There is less control in this situation because you can't read their facial expression and body language and you don't know if they are giving the conversation their undivided attention or working on something else while you're speaking to them.

And it is certainly easier for someone to get rid of us on the telephone than it is in person. After all, what's to keep that person from saying, "Listen, something just came up and I have to go. I'll call you if I'm ever in need of your product." Sure she will—in your dreams.

So, needless to say, establishing a relationship with this person based on good feelings is essential right from the start. And this process begins with the secretary, especially if that person has assumed, or been asked to assume, the role of screener or gatekeeper.

Find the Person Who Can Say Yes

The first thing we need to do is make sure we are asking for the right person, the decision maker. We can do a wonderful job of getting past the secretary, make a great impression on the person to whom we are presenting, and close the sale beautifully. If, however, the person we've just sold on our product or service does not have the authority to say yes, we've wasted our time (as well as hers).

In many instances, it is obvious who the decision maker is. In that situation, you already have a step up. But let's take a look at various ways to qualify a prospect before we go too far into the presentation.

First might be the receptionist. Sometimes receptionists don't know who the actual decision makers are, but usually they do, or at least they can refer you to someone who knows. When calling a corporation or association to book a speech, I will say to the receptionist, "Good morning, my name is Bob Burg. Who's the person in charge of hiring outside professional speakers for your annual convention?" In your case, the proper question might be, "Good morning, this is Jane McGregor. Who's the person in charge of purchasing widgets?" Or handling advertising? Or purchasing office products? Same thing, right?

That question will send me in the right direction. I'll then ask to be transferred to the decision maker's office, realizing I'll probably get his or her secretary. *Warning:* If the person answering the phone is the secretary or wants to know why you are calling, find a reason to politely get off the telephone (after, of course, finding out the information you wanted). When speaking with the person who'll decide whether or not to screen us or put us through, we need to already have that information and appear to be "in the know."

Getting Past the Gatekeeper

Let's pretend that the decision maker is Mary Jones and her secretary is Julie Smith. Julie answers the phone.

> JULIE: Good morning, Mary Jones's office. May I help you?
>
> ME: (informal and friendly, as though I belong) Good morning, this is Bob Burg. May I speak with Mary, please?
>
> JS: And where are you calling from, Mr. Burg?

She wants to know the name of our company, doesn't she? That way, she can decide if what we do will be of interest to Mary or if she should discourage us. What I'll do at this point is answer with the name of my city, and then segue right into a reflexive closing question, "What's your name?"

> JS: And where are you calling from, Mr. Burg?
>
> ME: Jupiter, Florida—I'm sorry, what's your name?
>
> JS: Julie Smith.
>
> ME: Oh, thank you, Julie.

Notice there was no pause between "Jupiter, Florida" and "I'm sorry, what's your name?" I didn't want to give her an opportunity to say, "No, I mean what company are you with?" Instead I went right into my reflexive closing question, "What's your name?"

A *reflexive closing question* is simply a question that produces an automatic response. When asked, "What is your name?" most people respond reflexively. Hopefully, she will put us through at that point. Does that technique work every time? No! It works some of the time.

If, instead, she says, "No, I mean, what company are you with?" or "What's your call in reference to?" you need to have a short statement which says just enough to raise her interest and position your call as worthwhile enough to be put through, but not enough to say what it is you actually do.

I might say, "This regards your upcoming convention. Mary would be in charge of profit-making programs, wouldn't she?" If you sell computer systems you might say, "I can show her how to dramatically increase her department's profitability for little cost. Julie, I'll explain to her just how to do that."

Does this technique work every time? No! It works some of the time. Let's say that in this case it didn't work and Julie wouldn't put you through. Or possibly, Mary isn't in. Make sure you've written down Julie's name, because you will use her name as a positioning tool for credibility on your next call, which is a few days later. After all, you don't want to go through the same song and dance again.

JS: Good morning, Mary Jones's office. May I help you?

ME: (very friendly) Hi, Julie?

JS: Yes.

ME: (very friendly) Julie, hi! This is Bob Burg, how are you?

JS: (wondering who the heck Bob Burg is) Uh, f-fine, and you?

ME: Great. Hey, is Mary in?

Keep in mind that Julie talks to many people every single working day. She can't possibly recall every person and conversation. Also remember that, although it may be Julie's job to screen calls, it isn't her job to keep people from getting through who *should* be put through. In this scenario, I sound as though I belong. As though I've been there before. Does this technique work every time? No! It works some of the time.

There are many ways to get past the gatekeeper. I come across more and more of them every day in various books and sales newsletters and at seminars I attend. Not every idea will work for you, or for me, but some will. Let me share just a couple of techniques that have consistently worked for me.

Try These—They Work!

The first technique is use of priority mail, available from your local post office. For $3.00 (at the time of this book) you can send a letter to the decision maker in a huge, attention-getting, red, white, and blue cardboard envelope. Usually, because of the perceived value of this package (it *must* be important if it was sent priority mail), it will, in fact, get in front of the boss.

Inside this huge, multicolored, cardboard envelope is your letter enclosed in a regular number 10 envelope. It should be brief, businesslike, and to the point. It should let the person know who you are and should also contain a short benefit statement and a request to be put through next time you call. Here's a generic example:

> Dear Mr. Thomas,
>
> Would you like to know more about a sure-fire way to cut down on your sales staff's wasted, nonproductive time? Gadger Gidgets. These profit builders, designed specifically for your particular industry, will show you how to increase production and profitability by up to 34 percent, and at a very affordable price.
>
> When I've called, you've been very busy. I'm sure that's the norm for you. May I make a request? I'll call Thursday, October 17, at 2:10 p.m. If you are in, I'd appreciate your taking my call. I promise to be brief and help you determine quickly if our system may fit your needs.
>
> If you are not in and would like to speak with me, could you have your secretary schedule a time for me to call back at your convenience.
>
> > Sincerely yours,
> > *Steve Larkin*

One quick point: notice that the time I gave was 2:10 p.m. Whenever scheduling any appointment you should suggest an odd time, as opposed to 2:00, 2:15, 2:30, or 2:45. This gives the impression of your time being clearly slotted, accounted for, and important. The same goes for percentages: 34 percent is actually much more credible than 35 percent. Why? Because it's much more specific, and it suggests documentation.

By the way, you should only say that if it is a fact. And if the exact percentage result was 35 percent, you're *still* better off going with 34 percent. But if increased production and productivity are not at least 34 percent, absolutely don't state that.

Back to your letter. If Mr. Thomas is impressed by the possible benefits mentioned in your letter, he'll take your call. If not, it is up to you to decide whether to blow that one off or try another tack. Here's a technique that I learned from Harvey Mackay's book *Swim with the Sharks without Being Eaten Alive*. In it, Mackay tells how to get to the person he calls the "tough prospect," the one who won't take your calls. Mackay's technique (which I am loosely paraphrasing in this explanation) can also be used as a way of getting past the screen. This has earned positive results for my staff and myself on numerous occasions. Here's how.

Simply put a money value on the time you'll take to speak with the decision maker. The following example is a conversation I had with a secretary who had consistently denied me access to the boss for over 3 weeks. After reading Mr. Mackay's book, I decided to go for it.

ME: May I speak with Mr. Prospect, please?

SECRETARY: No, he's busy.

ME: May I make a telephone appointment to speak with him?

SECRETARY: No, he's too busy even for that. Just send whatever it is you have in writing! (charming individual)

ME: I'll tell you what. Please put me on hold and ask Mr. Prospect if I can take just 200 seconds of his time. Tell him that if I go even 1 second over, I'll donate $500 to his favorite charity.

SECRETARY: (bewildered) Hold on a moment.

COMPANY MESSAGE OVER EASY LISTENING BACKGROUND MUSIC: "You'll find this to be one company that really loves people." (The message was actually pretty close to that.)

SECRETARY: He'll take your call at 9 tomorrow morning…and his charity is the Heart Fund.

TELEPHONE: Click!

Nonetheless, at least I got to speak to the decision maker. As an off-shoot to this story, I have found that this technique works quite often, and most secretaries are happy to go along with it. Also, in many cases, the decision maker will come right to the phone, probably curious as to what kind of person would make that kind of statement. Again, does it work all of the time? No, but I can guarantee it will *never* work if you don't try it.

Before going on to our conversation with the decision maker, I ask you to keep this in mind: always be pleasant to the secretaries, and realize that they are just doing their job. Maybe a bit overzealously, yet we're not going to win them over by being testy or argumentative. We have to make these "key" people our friends. We do that by being courteous, using their names, finding mutual points of interest, and establishing a rapport.

Now You've Got the Decision Maker

Okay, so I've been put through to Mary Jones. She is the decision maker who could hire me to do a networking speech or seminar. You'll have to take this example and modify it to accomplish what you want to accomplish with *your* product or service.

> MARY JONES: Hi, this is Mary Jones. How can I help you?
>
> ME: Good morning, Ms. Jones (not "Mary" yet), this is Bob Burg. I understand you're the person in charge of hiring outside professional speakers for your annual convention. Is that correct?
>
> MJ: Yes, it is. What can I do for you?
>
> ME: Well I...by the way, do you have a real quick minute?

There are those from the "old school of sales" who will probably groan as they read the words, "do you have a real quick minute?" I can almost hear them say, "Burg, why on earth would you ask a person that question? You're just giving them an excuse to say they're busy and get rid of you!"

Here's what I've found in my 10 years of teleprospecting experiences. People generally will answer that question in one of three ways:

Number 1: "No!" Actually, that answer will probably be more along the lines of, "No I don't have a minute. I don't have any time at all. I'm between meetings, trying to make a deadline, and I especially don't have time to talk to anyone who wants to sell me anything."

As far as I'm concerned, that answer is fine. They are letting us know in no uncertain terms that this would not be a good time. We won't have their full, or even partial, attention. Trying to share the benefits of our product or service with them now would only bring about resentment from their end, destroying any chance of establishing a relationship with them. Our job at this time is to politely get off the phone. We'll try again later.

Number 2: "Yes." I know that sounds good. If, however, that "yes" is followed by, "I've got all the time in the world. I'm not doing anything anyway. What can I do for you?" then be warned: that person is probably not the decision maker.

I say this only somewhat tongue-in-cheek. There are people out there in nonpower positions who like to play king for a day. They will lead you on forever, yessing you to death. Then, when it's time to take action, they have no authority. I speak from experience. It's happened to me!

Number 3: "Yes, real quick." Typically, the response might be more like, "I have a *real* quick minute, but that's it. I'm very busy." As negative as that may sound, that is exactly the response you want.

At this point, we'll give them a quick benefit statement. This benefit statement will, of course, explain the benefits of what they can expect by doing business with us, without telling them enough to make an instant decision to say no. When they respond positively, we will then be in a position to take control of the conversation. And you know that we don't take control by telling, but by asking questions. Remember, no one is going to hang up the phone on you while *they* are talking.

> ME: Well I...by the way, do you have a real quick minute?
>
> MJ: Real quick, I'm very busy. What can I do for you?
>
> ME: I do a program entitled "How to Cultivate a Network of Endless Referrals." Does that sound like a program that may be of value at your next convention?

Usually, the prospects I call will answer yes. That's because before I target a particular market, I qualify the "need it" and "want it" aspect of that market. [There are three parts to what is known as the marketing bridge we all need to cross when working with prospects: (1) Do they need it? (2) Do they want it? (3) Can they afford it?] Whether or not they can afford my fee will often need to be determined later.

If you are in a business where you can prequalify the wants and needs of your market, great. If not, you'll have to make a few more calls in order to qualify the same number of prospects.

Obviously, you'll want to come up with a benefit statement that works as well for you as mine does for me. If the prospect does show interest, it might be appropriate (depending upon the situation, you may need to wait) to further qualify her position by asking, "Mary, along with you, who else will be in on the decision-making process?" That, of course, is much more tactful than saying, "Are you really the decision maker, or are you just pulling my leg?"

Again, tongue-in-cheek, but understand the difference. The first way of asking shows respect and gives our prospect an *out* without causing her embarrassment. And it lets you know that there are other people to whom you may have to make your presentation. If you come right out and ask if your prospect is actually the decision maker, she might have to say yes in order to save face. By the time she finally admits she is not, 3 months have gone by. Again, that will only waste your time and your prospect's time.

Where the Selling Process Actually Begins

From this point on it is now a matter of making a good presentation by asking questions to determine wants and needs, being able to answer objections, and closing the sale. After qualifying and question asking, you should have a good idea of what you need to do for the next tele-meeting. If you need to send information to your prospect before speaking with her again, take the proper steps to ensure she will receive your material and actually review it before your next call.

Jeff Slutsky recommends describing to prospects in detail the type of package and envelope they will receive, including size, color, and insignias or logos. Then you must get a commitment from them that they'll review your information. After determining with your prospect the exact day and time you will have your follow-up conversation, I suggest words along the lines of, "Mr. Dennison, many people, after reviewing the information, have questions on two key points, the whichamacallit and the whichamahoozie. I'll look forward to discussing those points with you."

That day, send a note on your personalized postcard as discussed earlier in the book. If you have your picture on it, prospects will feel more like they know you and will be more comfortable in doing business with you. And, if nothing else, it will remind them that you were serious about getting back in touch and expecting them to have reviewed your material.

Since the focus of this book is not sales presentation skills or how to close the sale, I suggest you turn to other sources on these subjects and learn the proper techniques that will best suit you and your prospects, customers, and clients.

There are many excellent books on the market today regarding these skills, and some to keep away from. Two books I strongly urge you to purchase and devour are *Secrets of Closing the Sale* by Zig Ziglar and *How to Master the Art of Selling* by Tom Hopkins. Both books are packed with real-world knowledge, and they dispel the myth of the "born salesperson."

Contrary to popular belief, people are not born salespeople, nor are they born closers. Selling and closing are both developed, learned skills. An art and a science. Both authors are excellent at each, and I personally give them a lot of credit and thanks for helping me become the salesperson I have become. Their books are listed in the resource section at the conclusion of this book.

Selling the Appointment
by Telephone

Ironically enough, even though most people use the telephone simply
to set appointments, this section of the chapter will be brief. Here's
why: the toughest part is still just getting to the decision maker.
You've already learned how to do that!

Now it's simply a matter of closing the appointment. If you are
involved with a product that must be demonstrated or explained in
person, do *not* get sucked into giving your presentation over the telephone. It won't work, especially for high-ticket items. When I was selling solar energy systems, which averaged around $10,000 per unit, I
was constantly asked on the phone how much it cost. Can you imagine
answering "$10,000" without first their knowing the benefits of what
the system would do for them and how much they would actually
save? Depending upon the individual family, water usage, and home,
and available tax credits, these solar energy systems were of enormous
value. But do you think a salesperson ever got the chance to come over
and explain that once they divulged the price? No way!

If this is the case with your product or service, you need to have a
learned, memorized response for every question or objection you will
receive on the way to setting that appointment. Price won't be the only
one. If you are worried that your presentation will sound "canned,"
have no fear.

If you practice beforehand to the point that the information is internalized, your responses will sound completely natural. Think of stage,
television, and movie actors and actresses. They would never imagine
just getting up there and winging it.

Again, when first speaking with decision makers, you must hit them
with a benefit statement (even if it's in the form of a question) that will
pique their interest without giving away too much information. Then,
after a brief presentation or several qualifying questions, go into closing for the appointment. If I were selling a solar energy system, the
conversation might go as follows:

ME: Hi, Ms. Prospect, this is Bob Burg. Do you have a real quick
minute?

PROSPECT: It depends. What do you need?

ME: I'm with Sunstrong Solar Energy Company. May I ask you just a
very few questions regarding the rising of your monthly hot water
bills? (If rising hot water bills are a concern for that prospect, the
answer will probably be yes.)

After a few more questions enhancing the prospect's interest, it is time to set the in-home appointment. It might, however, not go without a couple of questions or objections from them.

> PROSPECT: Before we waste each other's time, how much does your system cost?
>
> ME: Good question, and very important. It really depends on several things. Every home and family is different, and has its own individual needs. The nice thing is that it's my job to see that *your* needs will be met.

Now go into closing for the appointment. It has been taught for years that the best way to do this is to give the prospect a choice of two yeses, as opposed to a yes or a no. In other words, if we ask, "Would Tuesday evening at 8 be good for you?" the prospect might say no. Now we have to guess on another convenient date and time. "How about Wednesday at 7?" to which the prospect responds, "Naw, that's no good either. I'll tell you what, let me think about it for a while, and if I'm interested I'll get back to you." At that point you've probably lost your prospect.

Instead, we give them a choice of two yeses.

> ME: Would tomorrow evening at 7:15 be good, or would Wednesday evening at 7:45 be more convenient for you?
>
> PROSPECT: Tomorrow's no good. I guess we can do it Wednesday.

This technique is called the "alternate of choice." It's very effective, yet we need to be careful when using it for two reasons. First, people are more educated to sales techniques, and this one has been around for a while. Second, if you phrase the alternate of choice the same way too many times it *sounds* salesy and manipulative.

Instead, let it flow with genuine concern regarding the convenience of your prospect. If he or she fires another question or objection at you, simply respond and go back into another alternate-of-choice question in order to set the appointment.

Listening Is the Key

Whether using the telephone as a complete sales tool or simply to get appointments, the key to success is having a game plan, following it religiously, and listening to your prospect. Fellow speaker Jim Meisenheimer, who specializes in personalized sales training programs, recommends the following 10 tips for telephone success:

1. *Prepare in advance.* Prepare your questions and responses in

advance. Know your product or service well, and your mind will be free to listen to the customer and focus on his or her needs.

2. *Limit your own talking.* You can't talk and listen at the same time. Jim makes an excellent point. We have a saying at my company: "If *we* are doing the talking, nothing is being sold."

3. *Focus.* Concentrate on your conversation and the customer's needs. This means temporarily shutting out your personal problems and worries. Difficult at times but possible, and definitely necessary.

4. *Put yourself into your prospect's shoes.* Understand their needs and concerns by thinking like them. Take their point of view in order to help them solve their problems.

5. *Ask questions.* We know the importance of asking questions during a presentation. Asking questions will also help clear up any points or prospect concerns you are not sure you completely understand. Paraphrasing the prospect's concerns back to them in the form of a question, followed by, "Do I understand you correctly?" or, "Is that what you're saying?" will keep you on the right track.

6. *Don't interrupt.* Nothing will turn a prospect off quicker than interrupting them. The same goes for finishing their sentences for them. Don't assume you know what they are going to say (even if you have to bite your lip to keep from doing it). Jim also suggests that just because the person pauses, he or she is not necessarily through talking.

7. *Listen for the whole idea or complete picture.* Words alone are not necessarily conveying what your prospect fears or desires.

8. *Respond (as opposed to react) to the ideas—not to the person.* Don't allow yourself to become irritated or insulted. Objections and questions are not personal. Also, don't let a prospect's mannerisms, such as an accent, distract you.

9. *Listen between the lines.* Often, what is *not* said by the prospect is just as important as what is said. Listen for overtones, doubts, concerns.

10. *Use interjections.* Show the customer you are listening by occasionally saying, "Uh-huh," "I understand what you're saying," "I see what you mean," or other fillers. Don't overdo it, though.

Several Quick, Final Tips for the Telephone

Use a mirror to check your attitude. Every telemarketing authority I know will always suggest hanging a mirror on the wall in front of you so you can see yourself as you converse. Why? Because your mood and attitude absolutely *will* come across to your prospect. If the reflection in the mirror is up and smiling, that's how you'll come across on the telephone. The opposite is also true.

Be careful with the hold button. If you must put a person on hold, do so for as short a time as possible—15 to 30 seconds, no more. If you leave prospects on any longer, you'll notice a change in *their* attitude, and it won't be for the better. To better understand why, notice what happens when you are the one stuck on hold for any length of time. It's frustrating, and definitely not fun.

In fact, try this experiment. Glance at your watch and notice the second hand. Then sit there doing nothing for about 2 minutes, and then glance back at your watch. As long as the time seems, it probably won't even come close to 2 minutes.

Hang up last. One definite fact of life is that none of us likes the cold sound of the "click" in our ear. When you hear that awful sound, don't you sometimes feel as though the person was in a hurry to get rid of you and go on to the next person? That's how your prospect might feel as well. Let her hang up first.

Finding Prospects from Conventional and Unconventional Sources

The key to effective prospecting is to work smarter, not harder—to get yourself in front of qualified people with the least amount of time and effort. There are just a few methods for accomplishing that goal.

Physically Position Yourself in front of the Right People

Speaker and author Rick Hill says, "If you're going to go fishing, go where the fish are." Makes sense, doesn't it? The same could be said about prospecting for gold, meeting members of the opposite sex, and prospecting for new business.

Back when Rick was setting records as a radio advertising sales representative, he used to leave his office at 2 p.m. every Friday. When his sales manager would ask where he was going, Rick would give him the name of a local watering hole. When the manager questioned him as to why he was doing this before the workday ended, Rick would reply, "How are my sales this month?" At that, the manager would stop his questioning.

Actually, Rick was going to the local club where advertising agency representatives hung out on Friday afternoons. Rick couldn't have put his prospects in front of him any better if he had sprung for an elaborate party.

Ask yourself where your prospects hang out. Are there certain clubs, organizations, and associations you could join that would give you continuous access to these people? If so, invest some time and money and join. The dividends will more than justify the expense.

Find the Orphans

When you begin with a new company, or even if you have been there for some time, realize that every time a salesperson leaves the company, he or she leaves behind a number of customers and clients that are no longer being serviced. They are your orphans.

If your product is one that can be purchased again or upgraded—a car, a computer system, or a copying machine—contact that customer and establish a relationship. One copying machine salesperson was referred to as "Mr. Upgrade." That's because as soon as he joined the company, he began calling orphans and talking to them about upgrading their present system. From what I understand, he did extremely well.

When I joined the solar energy company, I used orphans as sources of referrals, since their systems should last for life (no resales) and upgrades are seldom. I'd introduce myself and ask how happy they were with their system. Since the product was great, I could count on many ecstatic answers. I'd then ask for referrals of those they knew who might also be able to benefit from a similar system. Did it work all of the time? No, but it worked a lot of the time. Use your imagination and always wonder how you can assist someone in meeting *their* needs. Zig Ziglar says, "You can get everything in life you want if you just help enough other people get what they want."

What's the Itch Cycle?

I first learned about this great idea from Tom Hopkins. Statistics will show that, depending upon the product, there is an average time expectancy between purchases. In other words, a time length before one itches to buy again. For instance, the average home owner will move every 5 years. The average new car buyer will buy every 2 to 3 years.

Go back to the orphans again. How long has it been since they last purchased? What is the average itch cycle for that product? Have they purchased more than once? If so, what was their time frame, or itch cycle, between purchases?

Look in Local Newspapers

It was mentioned earlier in the book that we should always scour the newspaper for information of interest to those in our network. That way, we let them know we care and that they are on our mind—a very effective networking technique.

The newspaper can also be used as an excellent prospecting tool. For instance, if you are a life or health insurance sales professional and read about someone receiving a big promotion, don't you think his or her insurance needs to be increased? What about people who have a new baby? Check out those birth announcements! Find out where they live and send them a congratulatory note. Maybe they have an insurance person already—but then again, maybe they don't. Or possibly their insurance agent doesn't pay attention to those things and you do. A nice congratulations note and follow-up phone call could work wonders, couldn't it?

If you are in real estate, you know where to find the "For Sale By Owners" list in the classified section. Get up a little earlier than your competition and make your calls. Find out the owners' address and get yourself over there. Be nice, nonpushy, and caring about their needs. Once you've established a rapport, begin doing the things you've learned in this book about networking and cultivating relationships.

Go Door-to-Door, Business-to-Business

Although this method is the most time-consuming, it is very effective for this reason: whenever you make your contact with the decision maker, you are in the very best position to establish the rapport necessary to close the sale.

Again, depending upon your particular business, your sales might be of the one-call, two-call, or several or more calls variety. Regardless, getting in front of your prospects cuts out every other step in between. You can read their body language, gather your facts, and answer objections without their having a quick escape. The more people you see face-to-face, the more sales you will make and the more lives you will enhance.

A Lesson on How *Not* to Prospect Door-to-Door

Davis Fisher is a training consultant for SDA Corporation in Rolling Meadows, Illinois. At a recent speaking engagement I had in Chicago, he shared the following story with me.

Our offices are located in a 10-story building, not too far from O'Hare International Airport. For some reason we are in a perfect location for salespeople who make cold calls. A few years ago there was a unique moment in the day when I was in the office alone. It was around noontime. The receptionist had stepped down the hall and our coworkers were either at lunch, on errands, or out of town.

A knock on the door. "Come in," I said, and in walked a young salesman. He said to me, "Do you have a minute?" and I said, "Sure." And with that he pulled up a chair, sat down at my desk, opened his briefcase, pulled out some brochures, moved a couple things on my desk, and spread the brochures out.

For the next $13^1/_2$ minutes we went through his brochures. He told me all about what he was selling—computers for the small office. I sat there looking at his brochures, nodding my head, saying "Uh-uh," "Ooooh," "That's a big one," "Wow," "Color on that one's neat."

At the end of the $13^1/_2$ minutes, he picked up his brochures, put them back in his briefcase, set it down next to him, looked around, and said, "Nice office you have here." I said, "Thank you." He looked over my shoulder through a big picture window looking out on the spaghetti bowl intersection of a major expressway and toll road. He said, "Wow, you really have a view of the toll road from here." I said, "Yeh, we do." He looked at me and asked, "What do you folks do here?" I replied, "We teach people how to sell." "No kidding," he replied. "How am I doing?" And I said, "Not very well."

Why not? Because in his 15-minute sales call, this salesperson spent $13^1/_2$ minutes telling me how much he knew about what he was selling. He never asked me any questions. Had he asked, he would have discovered that we had bought a computer for our office 6 months earlier and had no immediate need.

At that point he might have asked questions such as, "No kidding, what kind did you get? How did you happen to go with them? What's been your experience over the last 6 months? Who was involved in making that decision? If you were going to make that decision today, what would be different about it? I realize that you are tied into a contract now with those people, Mr. Fisher, but let me leave a brochure describing several of our products, including one here that I think may give you some assistance based on some of the problems you have had.

"Feel free to give me a call over the next three months in the event I may help you out. In fact, if I haven't heard from you, may I call you? Do you have a brochure describing what you do? I always like to know what some of my prospective clients do. Possibly I can refer some business your way. May I have one of your cards? Thanks...I'm curious: do you know of anyone in the area who might be in a similar position to the one you were in 6 months ago, so I might talk to them and see if I may be of some assistance? Thanks. Bye."

And then leave—saving himself $13\frac{1}{2}$ minutes on a 15-minute sales call so that he could use that valuable time down the hall or across the street where he might encounter someone who, indeed, could become a qualified prospect based on appropriate probing and listening! Good selling is not telling!

Davis makes an excellent point. The worst thing a salesperson can do is simply walk in, introduce himself, sit down without being invited to do so, and start "machine-gunning" through a presentation. If faced with the decision maker, we must first discover (or create) a need, a want, and a financial capability.

With just a bit of questioning, the salesperson in the above example would have discovered earlier that there was no need. With some creative questioning, however, he also could have discovered the prospect's itch cycle, and maybe even picked up a few referrals along the way. As professionals, we don't want to waste our prospects' time. We don't want to waste our time, as well.

Some Thoughts on Effective Prospecting

A friend of mine, Sonia Cooper, is a salesperson and prospector par excellence. Her motto is, "Put the needs of your customers/prospects/referral sources first...and your paycheck will follow." A few years back Sonia was an account representative for a title insurance company. One day she noticed a real estate agent from the neighboring county stuffing the mailboxes in a real estate office in the county where she worked.

Sonia felt that as a commercial real estate broker he had better things to do than travel office to office (which Sonia did as part of her job), so she offered to pass out his fliers for him since she'd be there anyway. To which title account representative do you think that commercial broker referred his title orders from resulting sales? The answer should be obvious.

A true believer in self-promotion and "keeping your name and telephone number in front of prospects," she constantly looks for new and creative ways to accomplish this goal. Once, when she was on a cruise ship, she noticed that each day the crew would pass out word games for the passengers to solve. Each day was a different theme.

She had the social hostess put together a packet of all 12 games and the answers—not knowing exactly how she would use them. Upon returning to work, she came up with the idea of passing out the word quiz to all of her individual prospective agents. Each month, on appropriately colored paper, she would distribute her and her firm's name along with a different word quiz. Answers to the previous month's quiz were on the back.

According to Sonia, this was a huge hit. In a very subliminal way, they saw her name and phone number all month long. They were especially effective during normally slow times. Instead of just sitting around doing nothing and waiting for the phone to ring, her prospects were actively having fun with her word quizzes. Some of the offices actually had internal contests as to which agent could come up with the most correct answers. According to Sonia, "This was one of the most inexpensive and successful prospecting promotions I ever implemented."

Sonia is now an account executive with BellSouth Communications, Inc. in West Palm Beach, Florida. Upon joining the company, she got off to another impressive start, racking up huge sales numbers. Sonia knocks on a lot of business doors and is often faced with having to get past the gatekeeper. She has six techniques she uses with great success:

1. *Treat them like they own the company.* Not only because one day they might, but they are probably the person their boss looks to for protection from the outside world. If you can make them feel good about themselves, they'll help you do the same, by ensuring you get to see the decision maker.

2. *Know them by their first name.* Show them that they are important to you by using their name.

3. *Tell them that you need their "help."* The fact is, most people want to help, and to feel that you know they have the power to help.

4. *Include them in the promotional materials you pass out.* Keep them in the loop. Make them a part of the sales process.

5. *Put yourself in their shoes.* How would you like to be treated in the same position? Respect them as people, unlike other salespeople who treat them like nonentities whose sole purpose in life is to keep the salesperson from achieving his or her goal of seeing the decision maker.

6. *Be of service to them.* Ask them if there isn't any way you can help them—maybe drop something off at the post office for them on your way there?

And of course, make them your ally. Smile, be sincere, and appreciate the importance of the job they have to do.

Pat Hance, broker-owner of Pat Hance Real Estate Company in

Plantation, Florida, feels it's very important, when prospecting, to continually have your name out to the public. She believes that everyone she meets, anywhere, is either a prospect or an excellent source of referrals.

Pat is also an expert at prospecting other Realtors. She attends every real estate convention she possibly can, handing out a flyer with her photo on it, containing the words, "Pat Hance wants your referrals!" in huge print. She says consistency is important, keeping the same message year after year after year, making only minor changes to show additional designations and honors she's received.

In Pat's own words, "This little flyer has been given to every attendee at every real estate convention since 1969. Do they remember me? You bet! I've received comments when the new updated photo replaces the less recent one (e.g.: I see you're no longer using your high school photo).

"I've received referrals from agents I've never met—agents who received this flyer somehow, somewhere. It's not important that they remember how or where, just that they remember Pat Hance!"

After discovering that a New York ERA real estate office had blown up her picture to poster size and tacked it up on the bulletin board, she arranged a neat cross-promotion with that office's broker. When he visited Florida on vacation, he took a video recorder to Pat's office and taped her saying, "Come on to Florida. Send your buyers! Send your sellers! We want to work for you in sunny, south Florida." This resulted in numerous sales and referrals for Pat.

Pat considers herself the biggest "flesh presser" of them all, meeting people in all walks of life, from the supermarket to her church. Yet, wherever and whenever she does this, she focuses on the other person's needs, not her own. She knows that eventually, with the way she is positioned and known in her community, that person will remember her when the time is right for business or referrals. One introduction and handshake, through the twists of fate, resulted in referral fees on approximately 35 transactions over the course of several years.

Yes, whether prospecting by telephone or in person, the basic rules apply. Follow the road map, be creative at times, and most of all, always have the other person's wants and needs in the forefront of your mind.

Key Points

- Never stop prospecting.
- Prospecting is a numbers game. The more things we do right, how-

ever, the more sales we will get in less time and after calling on fewer people.

- There is a definite relationship between calls and contacts, contacts and appointments, and appointments and sales. Learn yours and use it to your advantage.

- When using the telephone as a prospecting tool, establishing a relationship with that prospect becomes even more important.

- Knowing how to talk to (and get past) the gatekeeper is vital to teleprospecting success.

- Ask the prospect, "Do you have a real quick minute?"

- Qualify to ensure you are speaking with the decision maker!

- Use your short benefit statement to pique prospects' interest so they'll want to hear more.

- If using the telephone simply to set in-person appointments, be sure to limit your conversation to just that. Give too much information and you may disqualify yourself right then and there.

- Utilize the following tips from Jim Meisenheimer:
  1. Prepare in advance.
  2. Limit your own talking.
  3. Focus. Concentrate on your conversation and the customer's needs.
  4. Put yourself into your prospects' shoes. Understand their needs and concerns by thinking like them. Take their point of view in order to help them solve their problems.
  5. Ask questions.
  6. Don't interrupt.
  7. Listen for the whole idea or complete picture. Words alone are not necessarily conveying what your prospect fears or desires.
  8. Respond (as opposed to react) to the ideas—not to the person. Don't allow yourself to become irritated or insulted.
  9. Listen between the lines. Often, what is not said by the prospect is just as important as what is, or the way it is said.
  10. Use interjections.

- A few final tips for using the telephone effectively:
  1. Use a mirror to check your attitude.
  2. Be careful with the hold button. If you must put a person on hold, do so for as short a time as possible.
  3. Hang up last. No one likes the sound of the "click" in their ear.

- Prospects can be found from both conventional and unconventional sources.

1. Physically position yourself in front of the right people.
2. Find the orphans. They are company customers and clients that a departing salesperson left behind when leaving the company. You may adopt them.
3. What's the itch cycle? Depending upon the product, there is an average time expectancy between purchases. In other words, a time length before one itches to buy again.
4. Look in local newspapers. Always scour your local newspaper for prospects.
5. Go door-to-door, business-to-business.

- Follow Sonia Cooper's motto: "Put the needs of your customers/prospects/referral sources first...and your paycheck will follow."

- Follow Sonia Cooper's six tips for winning over the gatekeepers.
    1. Treat them like they own the company. They are both the bodyguard and direct link to their boss.
    2. Know them by their first name.
    3. Tell them that you need their "help."
    4. Include them in the promotional materials you pass out. Keep them in the loop.
    5. Put yourself in their shoes. How would you like to be treated in the same position?
    6. Be of service to them. Ask them if there isn't any way you can help them.

- Listen to Pat Hance's sage advice: "Continually keep your name in front of the public."

- Follow the road map, be creative at times, and most of all, always have the other person's wants and needs in the forefront of your mind.

8

Begin Your Own Profitable Networking Group

Here is a concept that will make you a lot of money over the long run: begin, run, and maintain your own organized networking club. You'll have to work at it. You'll have to cultivate it. The results, however, will truly pay off many times over. This is an extremely valuable way to network your way to endless referrals.

This is where you involve a diverse group of people who are either business owners or salespeople representing a certain business. You may be familiar with the concept and may possibly even have participated in a similar organization yourself. Unfortunately, however, quite often these groups are run incorrectly and do not live up to their full potential.

My mentor in this particular area is a woman from Sudbury, Massachusetts, named Tanny Mann. Tanny founded and runs a group called Sales Networks, Inc.—SNI for short. In fact, she now runs several of these groups and has attained tremendous success with them.

Tanny's organization was the first of this type in which I was involved. An excellent networker, she was a true inspiration when I began my own group after I moved to Florida several years later. I began selling for a local company and, having just relocated, had no sphere of influence to speak of to help me get started.

Tanny organized her group. She taught people how to network within the group, and she genuinely cared for the success of her members.

This went a long way toward Tanny's own success. I'd like to share with you the setup and running of an organization such as Tanny's.

This chapter is based on a combination of what Tanny taught me, techniques I have learned from others, and those I've cultivated myself. The group I ran resulted in a lot of business for a lot of people, including myself. If you'll follow this advice, the group you begin, or even the group with which you are now involved, will prove to be just as successful and rewarding for you.

One Is the Magic Number

There's a limit of one person for a particular type, or category, of business: one printer, one chiropractor, one florist, one Realtor, one sign maker, one insurance person, one banker, and so on until you run out of categories. The total membership in this group can grow to be as high as you'd like, but should include just one person for each type of business so there is no competition within the group.

The intention of this networking club is to (1) develop and maintain a give-and-take relationship with as many other businesspeople as possible, (2) to train each of these people to know how to prospect for you, and (3) to know how to match you up with their 250-person sphere of influence. The intent is qualified leads, leads, leads, and more leads.

We already know how important it is in networking to give to others. It is *vitally* important to do this within your new networking club—in this case, especially, to be able to refer business to others.

Let's even give a special definition of networking as it relates specifically to this type of group. How about this: "the developing of a large and diverse group of people to and from whom you effectively and pragmatically give and get worthwhile leads." That's a mouthful, isn't it? It is also the way this group benefits everyone.

Knowing how to sell your products, goods, or services after acquiring these worthwhile leads is, of course, another very important subject. There are many excellent books on these subjects, and I hope you have either begun, or plan to begin, your own resource library. What we're talking about here, however, is simply how to get these leads and what types of leads to give.

The Different Types of Leads

In a group situation such as this, there are basically three types of leads: (1) general group leads, (2) individual leads of the "feel free to use my name" type, and (3) individual leads of the "please *don't* use my name" type.

General Group Leads

These are leads given by one member which could possibly benefit several members of the group. For example, an office building is going up along Highway 1 in Tequesta. This lead could be useful to the copier salesperson, Realtor, the insurance salesperson, the cleaning person, the sign person, and many others.

Individual Leads—Feel Free to Use My Name

These are leads given by one member to another. The lead may be a person who could use that particular service. In this case, the lead giver is friendly enough with the prospect that using the lead giver's name would be a help.

It should be made clear whether or not the prospect expects a call from the person to whom the lead was given. If that is the case, make sure you call or the lead giver will be made to look bad. That, in turn, will not result in additional leads from that person. Also, it should be made clear whether the lead is simply a lead or a presold.

A presold is where the lead giver has already established your credibility with the prospect to the nth degree and all you need to do, basically, is show up.

Individual Leads—Don't Use My Name

These are also leads given by one member to another. However, they are given with the stipulation that the lead giver's name not be mentioned to the prospect. Why not? For whatever reason, it would not be appreciated by either the prospect, or the lead giver, or both.

Possibly, that person is still a prospect for the lead giver and the lead giver might feel the prospect will resent the idea that his or her name is being given out to others.

Or the prospect could be a person who doesn't like the lead giver. That still isn't to say that person is not a good prospect. The lead giver might say, "Joe Sprazinski, I know he needs a new fax machine. Unfortunately, he and I didn't exactly hit it off, so I wouldn't use my name." Okay, so find another reason to get in there and see Mr. Sprazinski.

Important point: when lead givers don't want their name revealed to the prospect, their wishes *must be respected.* Otherwise, you'll never get a lead from that person again—or from anyone else in the group who hears that you went ahead and used the lead giver's name despite a request not to.

A Definite Agenda

Now let's turn to the procedure for these meetings. Lasting about an hour, it is a very structured type of setup and it needs to be followed to the T. If not, it will turn into just another group of people getting together and socializing, *thinking* they are networking but not accomplishing much. As the leader of the group, ensuring that the procedure is adhered to is your responsibility.

Meetings have two distinct segments: the *prenetworking* and the *formal networking* phases. Encourage members to arrive early in order to business-socialize during the prenetworking period. This helps along the "know you, like you, trust you" feelings necessary for effective networking. And it should be informal. Get as many group members as possible to know you on a personal basis.

During the formal networking phase, after calling the meeting to order, ask each person to briefly address the group, stating his or her name, company, type of product or service with which they are involved, and types of leads desired.

Here's a hint which worked very well for me when I ran my group. For your turn, develop a sort of vignette, a profile, or short commercial. You'll use that every single time, and the message will become implanted in your group members' minds and memories. Even though you might imagine it to be boring for people to hear, don't let that concern you.

You are there to do business, and as group members become more and more familiar with your word-for-word commercial, what you do will become a part of them. That is what all successful networkers strive to achieve.

Can You Relate to This?

Aren't there commercials from years ago which you can identify and still remember? "I can't believe I ate the *whole* thing" from Alka Seltzer. Two insurance commercials that come to mind are, "You're in good hands with Allstate" and "Get a piece of the Rock" (Prudential). How about this fast-food commercial: "You deserve a break today. So get up and get away." To where? Of course, McDonald's. And you know what, that particular McDonald's campaign hasn't been around for years! But you remember it, anyway, don't you?

Therefore, play your commercial over and over again, once a week, at every group meeting. Before long, what you do will be ingrained into your fellow networkers' brains. Here's an example of a short, effective commercial. If I were in real estate, I might say, "My name is Bob Burg, Realtor associate with Ocean Realty. I successfully market homes for people who wish to sell, and help those who want to buy the perfect dream home. If you hear a person mention selling a home or buying a home, that person would be a good lead for me."

That's all you need to say that week, next week, and every week in the future. As mentioned earlier, what you want to avoid is talking technical. If you're a Realtor, you wouldn't want to say, "When I list a home, first I do this, then that, then hold an open house, then this," etc. The accountant in the group would absolutely *not* talk about how to prepare a form 11-20 U.S. corporation tax return. The copy machine salesperson would not describe the bells and whistles in his product. That's not important.

You might think, "Well, the others in the group should know as much as possible about my products or service so they can help sell them." That's not so! You can sell your products or services much better than they can. You simply want them to get you the *leads*.

Here's a perfect example. There was a woman in my group who sold paper products. All kinds of paper products. Every week she would give her brief vignette, or commercial, and conclude by saying, "And remember, when you think of toilet paper, think of me."

Everyone laughed every time she said it. But I'll tell you what: when you met somebody in business who might need paper products, any type of paper products (not just toilet paper), you thought of this woman. How effective! She is a very successful salesperson. In fact, last time I spoke with her I discovered she had been promoted to sales manager of the entire company.

Your commercial should total no more than 15 or 20 seconds. Following that, thank those who gave you leads at the previous meeting or during the week. Recognition is very important, and they will appreciate the fact that you recognize them publicly. After thanking those from whom you received leads, you now give out your leads to the group and individuals.

Out Loud!!!

Please realize how important it is to state your leads publicly and enthusiastically. Do not wait until afterward and give out your leads privately. There were people in my group who feared being thought of as conceited or braggadocio for giving their leads out loud.

Why? That's just what you want to do, isn't it? If the people in the group know you're giving out leads, even to others, then they know you have the potential to get leads for them. That, of course, will make them work harder to find leads for you and will result in a "delightful cycle of success" for everyone.

As you recruit members for your group, you need to sell them on the fact that they will not necessarily receive many leads right away. Success in this group is similar to planting the seeds in an enormous garden. It takes care, commitment, diligence, and most of all, patience. Eventually, all will reap plenty.

Teach them these exact techniques. Assure them that *if* they are willing to stick with it, they will receive the rewards they desire: lots and lots of qualified leads and the foundation of a terrific network.

They must *not* miss these meetings, except in an emergency. They must schedule the meeting as a business appointment each and every week. There were people in my group who quit after two sessions because they "didn't get business from the group."

Well, they hadn't given anyone a chance to get to know them, like them, or trust them. Even then, the timing might not have been quite right. Joining a networking group won't necessarily result in instant gratification. Some people will not be willing to accept that fact and will, therefore, quit.

But another member named Tom, who sold a fairly high-ticket item, patiently cultivated the group for over a year. He received some leads, but nothing substantial. All of a sudden, a transaction came through in which three different members of the group all participated. It was truly a soap opera situation, with none of them even realizing that the others were involved, and it ended up netting Tom a huge commission. To this day, and for obvious reasons, Tom is a hard-core networker. He uses the techniques and is very successful.

Other members, depending upon the types of business with which they are involved, will see business come in quicker and more steadily, especially from fellow members. People in that category would include florists and printers or others with products, goods, or services which are often in demand. Their primary focus should be to cultivate their fellow members, and earn the business of their 250-person sphere of influence as well.

Work the Spheres of Influence

Every so often, I'm asked to observe a networking group and critique its operation. Almost without exception, the first thing I suggest is, "Stop having selling your products and services to each other as a primary goal." Instead, make it your main objective to have the group members serve as your walking ambassadors to their 250-person sphere of influence.

When recruiting or allowing members to join your group, make sure to have them checked out for honesty and integrity. If possible, recruit them by networking with others, including those in your group. Urge your members to invite prospective members—as long as it's in a business category that is presently vacant. The chances are always better that a newcomer referred by a group member will fit the profile of honesty and integrity. You don't want to give a good lead to a bad apple. That won't make you or the other members of the group look good.

In order to get the group off the ground, you may have to do some "babysitting." In other words, you need to call the members the night before the meeting to make sure they're coming. And make sure you hold the meetings early in the morning, before the regular workday begins. Sure, it can be tough getting people to wake up a little earlier one morning per week, but you know what's even tougher? Trying to get people to attend immediately after the regular workday ends. That's a battle royal!

People are normally fresher and have clearer heads in the morning. Besides, if they're motivated enough (which are the type of people you want to network with anyway), they'll get themselves up a little earlier in order to make this very important meeting. And hopefully, when their workday begins, they will get the opportunity to use the leads just received from the morning's meeting while those leads are still fresh in their mind.

To Charge or Not to Charge

People ask if they should charge a fee or dues for belonging to the group. Here's what I've experienced. At first, you won't get a lot of people willing to shell out money—not until they see the value of belonging to the group. In fact, at first, it will cost you some out-of-pocket money in time, stationery, and stamps. Be prepared to absorb those expenses in the beginning. In the long run, you know you're going to come out ahead.

Once you get the group off the ground and it has proven effective, then you can begin charging a token sum. This will pay for any miscellaneous expenses that were initially coming out of your own pocket. I charged a couple of dollars per meeting and had the manager of the host restaurant agree to have a light breakfast served. In fact, he joined our group as the caterer.

I feel it's better to start a group of your own than to join and simply be a member of another one. When it's your group, your baby, your brainchild, you have an even higher personal stake in it. You have a vested interest in making it successful. And you're positioned much stronger within the group. The other members will always have you and your products or services on their mind whenever there is a good prospect out there—and, of course, vice versa.

By the way, if you'd rather not put the effort into beginning your own group, there are plenty of groups already out there which you could join. Although the group's specific agenda may be different from what I've described, the basics are still the same. Simply use the techniques you've learned in order to cultivate relationships with these people. Most cities and towns now have several of these groups, so ask around and you'll find one. Just hope there is still an opening for your business category.

There are people such as Tanny Mann, whom I mentioned earlier, running similar groups in the Massachusetts area, and Eve Peterson, who has developed a number of organizations in both Pennsylvania and Ohio. And many others are spread throughout the country and world. Again, search for them and you'll find them.

Two of the largest with presence in cities and towns throughout North America and even internationally are LeTip International and Business Network International (BNI), both based in California. BNI was founded by a friend of mine, Dr. Ivan Misner, author of *Business by Referral*. Since its inception in 1985, his organization (whose motto is "Givers Gain") has passed over 2,900,000 leads, generating over $1 billion for its participants. To contact them call 800-688-9394.

Most of these for-profit lead exchange organizations charge good money to belong, but the benefits of membership are well worth it. Believe me, the people there work extremely hard to make it worthwhile for their members. I wouldn't want to try doing it on that level.

For most of us, these groups are simply a very effective way to build our network. Without doing it full time, you and I would be hard-pressed trying to make the group a profit center in itself. Of course, that's not our objective anyway. We're there to help each other in our own individual businesses.

Types of Categories

Regarding the actual membership, you can probably come up with a diverse group of business classifications by yourself. Here are some suggestions:

accountant, advertising representative, appliance dealer, attorney, audiovideo production person, automobile dealer, banker, boat salesperson, builder, carpet cleaner, caterer, cellular telephone salesperson, chiropractor, cleaning company, coffee service, computer salesperson, copy machine salesperson, dating service, courier service, dentist, electrician, employment agency, exercise equipment representative, financial planner, florist, funeral director, hair stylist, health club, hot tub salesperson, hotelier, insurance agent, interior designer, jeweler, landscaper, limousine service, massage therapist, moving company, nursing service, office supply representative, pager salesperson, painter, paper products person, party planning service, paving company, pest control representative, photographer, physician, podiatrist, plumber, printer, Realtor, restauranteur, restaurant supplier, roofer, satellite dish salesperson, secretarial service, solar energy salesperson, sporting goods store, storm windows salesperson, swimming pool sales representative, telemarketing service, business telephone systems representative, title company, travel agent, uniform supply service, valet service representative, veterinarian, wallpaper store representative, water cooler salesperson, water purification person, waterbed salesperson, wedding supplier, weight loss center, window tinter...the list goes on and on.

By using your imagination, talking with others, and reading through the Yellow Pages, you'll come up with many more business classifications or categories. I made up a list and that was only about a quarter of it.

Often, where it seems as though two people would be in competition with one another (which you don't want), you can find a way to make them complementary. For instance, there might be two insurance agents. However, one sells life; the other property and casualty. That happened in the group I ran. The two referred so much business to each other, they ended up going into business as partners.

There are also subcategories which really offer no competition. This could include a commercial Realtor and a residential Realtor. Depending upon how big and powerful you wish your group to become, you can start small and work your way up to big.

What about Those Who Have Trouble Speaking in Public?

If you or someone in your group has a fear of standing up in front of the group and speaking, realize that he or she is not alone. Public speaking is considered by many to be their greatest fear. That's understandable. However, that's another good reason to use the same commercial every time. You'll certainly begin to feel comfortable with it, and thus better able to speak before a large gathering.

Beyond that, I'm going to suggest you first visit as a guest, and then enroll in an organization called Toastmasters International. There are local chapters all over the world. Your local chamber of commerce can direct you to a chapter near you.

Toastmasters is an organization of people dedicated to helping you become a better speaker. And, in turn, you eventually do the same for them. It's a very comfortable, win-win situation, and lots of fun. For more information, you can also call their headquarters in Mission Viejo, California, at 714-858-8255.

I've got to confess that, although I speak for a living and am a former radio and television news anchor, I still get that lousy, nervous feeling every time before I present to an audience. Believe me, you're not alone.

Other Important Points

I want to reiterate a point mentioned earlier. Sit next to different people at every meeting. Even in the formal setting you will still get the opportunity to exchange positive words and ideas with someone new, as well as establish rapport. This is a key. Remember, you want these people to know you, like you, and trust you.

Although you will see the same people every week, the little things still count. Send them articles of interest and extend the extra courtesies you offer for your other networking prospects. You can, and definitely should, mail them personalized thank-you postcards for leads. Everyone likes to be recognized, and they will continue to work hard for you if they know that recognition can be expected. Their next lead might be a great one.

Don't be afraid to toot your own horn. Always give your leads publicly. Make sure everyone knows you are working hard to help *their* business grow. That way, they will want to help *your* business grow. And everyone comes out a winner!

Key Points

- When organizing your own networking group, there's a limit of one person for a particular type, or category, of business. Thus, there is no competition within the group.

- Meetings are held one morning per week. Every week!

- The intent of the group is qualified leads, leads, leads, and more leads.

- There are three different types of leads.
  1. General group leads
  2. Individual leads: "Feel free to use my name"
  3. Individual leads: "Don't use my name"

- There is a specific structured setup for the meetings.
  1. *Prenetworking.* Members arrive early to business-socialize.
  2. *Formal networking.* Each member individually stands up to address the group. Develop a vignette, or short commercial, and use it every time.

- State leads and thank-yous out loud.

- Concentrate not on getting these peoples' direct business but that of their 250-person sphere of influence. Cultivate them as you would anyone else in your network (thank-you notes, etc.).

9

Position Yourself as the Expert (and Only Logical Resource) in Your Field

When I say the word "astronomer," who immediately comes to mind? Most people will not hesitate even a moment before answering "Carl Sagan."

When talking about science fiction, and especially robots, what author's name might jump right out at us? Many would name Isaac Asimov.

What about child psychologists? Benjamin Spock. How about Vulcans? Well...Mr. Spock. Motivational speakers? Zig Ziglar, Dr. Denis Waitley, Anthony Robbins, and a few others might immediately come to mind.

What about your line of work? Who stands out in the public eye as the person your community would immediately think of? Is that person *you*? Are you so well positioned in your community that when people either need the products or services you provide or know somebody who does, they think of you—and only you? If they don't at present, they will! That is your goal.

Fellow speaker and author Peter Johnson is a marketing strategist for major corporations and organizations all over the world. A renowned genius in his field, he refers to this concept as "the science of strategic positioning." In his series, *Johnson on Strategic Marketing*, he describes it this way:

> To definitively establish in precise terms the strategic identity, image, and reputation of your specific company, your products, and your services such that in the mind of your targeted market-place there could be no acceptable alternative available any-where...regardless of price.

That definition certainly works for me. When *I* talk about position-ing oneself as the "expert" in relation to networking, however, I'm talking on a much smaller scale—an individual basis. In this case we're talking about positioning the individual as well as (actually, more than) the product or service itself. People need to make an asso-ciation in their minds between who you are and what you do for a liv-ing. After all, they know, like, and trust you. They want to help you succeed and find new business.

Act As If...and You Will Be

In this chapter, I'd like to share with you my ideas on how to attain the position of "expert" and only logical resource in your field. There are several tangible methods, but first you must put yourself in the mind frame of already being there. Imagine you are the person who has already attained success using the techniques we are going to discuss. People now come to you for information, referrals, and advice. You have already begun to use these methods and techniques for your positioning benefit, and it hasn't cost you a dime.

Positioning through the Media

One excellent way of positioning yourself as the expert is to write arti-cles for local, state, and national print media. Let's imagine you're a financial planner and you "help people create and manage wealth." I'm using that profession as an example, but you need to gear this advice toward your own particular field and find a way to make it applicable. Writing articles is a very effective way to position yourself with hundreds or even thousands of people. People automatically regard you as an authority.

Write a weekly column for your local newspaper and position your-self as the expert in your field. It must serve the public interest, so find an angle that will be welcomed by the editor of the newspaper. A consumer advocate is one possibility. Maybe you can share interesting tidbits not known by the average reader. That way people will feel they can rely on you instead of others in your field. For instance, what do you know that the public needs or wants to know about? How about the kind of investment products one should consider? What sort of products should one either be wary of or stay away from altogether? How does one protect one's assets and increase one's wealth without taking potentially catastrophic financial risks (or at least keeping those risks to a minimum)?

A chiropractor could write a weekly column on health and exercise. An accountant could write a column entitled "Tax Tip of the Week." An office products salesperson could give out suggestions regarding how to get the best quality at the lowest price. And so on and so on.

There are many, many topics that financial planners, chiropractors, accountants, office products salespeople, and practically every other person selling a product or service could use to write articles. You can, too, regardless of your profession! Just put your mind to it, and even brainstorm with your family and those in your network.

When writing this article, please keep in mind, it cannot be written as a personal advertisement. It must be kept very public interest–oriented. What you want is a byline, as well as your picture and some information about you (space permitting). You are not using this column directly as a sales tool; instead, you are using it as a positioning tool which will *eventually* turn into a sales and marketing tool. We'll talk more about that after we answer this question...

How Easy Is This to Accomplish?

The challenge you will most likely come up against is this: the editor of the newspaper will probably say something like, "But we've never done this before!" Well, you have to find a way of selling that person on why he or she should do it now.

My friend, author, and former newspaper editor Dean Shapiro also points out some very legitimate reasons why editors are not easily swayed into granting this type of situation. According to Dean, "Newspaper columns about businesses are not an easy thing for an editor to give away. They are *never* free, even when the columnist is not getting any money for doing them. *Someone* is paying for that space, and that's usually the newspaper. If the person writing the column isn't taking out a commensurate amount of paid advertising in the paper, most editors are loathe to give them 'free advertising' even when the column isn't a direct appeal for business. Just putting someone's name out there in connection with what they do is a form of advertising for them. Newspapers need ads to survive and they hate giving *anything* away gratis."

Dean continues: "Editors also have to guard against setting precedents that can come back to haunt them. Give a column to a Realtor each week and you leave yourself wide open to a chiropractor calling and saying, `Hey, you're giving Larry Soandso a column. How about giving me one? I serve more people than he does.' And then the water purification system saleswoman calls and says, `Hey, you're giving a column to a real estate broker and a chiropractor. How about one for me?' You begin to get the picture."

Dean concludes with the strongest point of all, and that is the fact that if a newspaper does give column space away, there has to be a potential tangible gain, such as an increase in paid readership resulting from that column's publication.

So you need to educate the editor on how your column is going to benefit the newspaper, the reader, *and the editor.* Remember, people naturally want to create less work for themselves, and editors are no exception. Therefore, if you can provide them with an article every week at no cost which will increase readership and help them fill a news hole with a valuable public service, they may jump at it. But be prepared for some resistance. Find a way to accomplish your goal, and you'll find the rewards worth the effort.

The $14 Million Woman

One such example is my friend and fellow speaker, Terri Murphy. Aside from being an up-and-coming professional speaker, she is a Realtor—a very successful one. I refer to Terri as "The $14 Million Woman." That's how much real estate Terri sells every year, good market or bad. One of Terri's most powerful positioning tools is her newspaper column, "Murphy on Real Estate."

She had to work for it! According to "Murph," it took her 6 months to convince the editor of her local newspaper to run her column. She says she encountered *lots* of resistance and really had to be imaginative. What Terri did was first write sample articles.

She also offered her column for free until she could prove its worth. Then she pointed out why the paper's use of syndicated columns that applied to major U.S. cities wasn't necessarily in the best interests of those living in her small town.

Terri suggested that the stories needed a local flavor, and that she was just the one to give it to them. With the combination of Terri's determination, sales ability, and logic, her column was accepted. Eventually, "Murphy on Real Estate" went on to become syndicated in 26 newspapers nationwide.

But she didn't stop there. Terri then worked her way in as the host of a weekly radio show. She accomplished this by first sending in someone from her personal network who had connections at the station. She combined the power of her network with the authoritative positioning she already had established as a newspaper columnist.

Yes, she had to work at that one too, but of course, she managed to come through. Terri found a way to succeed. And her sales production continues to soar, in a real estate climate most people feel is cyclical.

The last time I spoke with Terri, she was in the midst of putting together a local cable television show. If her track record is any indication, there is no doubt in my mind it will be as successful as all of her other accomplishments in the media.

Forget about Exposure—It's the Positioning You're After

Once upon a time, before there was the intense competition we now face, *exposure* was all anyone ever really needed. You remember the days when it was profitable to simply hang out your shingle? People would see your sign, be *exposed* to it, and voilà! Business!

And if you or your business ever somehow managed to get mentioned in the newspaper or on television, that was it! People called you. People came to see you. You got great exposure, and that directly resulted in business.

It's a different ball game nowadays. Practically more direct salespeople, insurance agents, Realtors, lawyers, accountants, dentists, chiropractors, and multilevel marketing people are seeking customers, clients, or patients than there are people who can possibly use their services. That's why it is now so important to separate yourself from all the others and be positioned as the expert and "only resource" of whatever it is you do.

Let's get back to our newspaper column. The exposure you achieve from writing that column probably won't bring you enough business to justify the time and effort needed to get and maintain it in the first place. However, you can sure use that column as a very effective positioning tool.

Reprints from your column should be sent on a regular basis to those in your network. In your personal brochure or sales presentation kit, you should highlight the fact that *you* are the columnist on that subject for your local newspaper. Why? What's the point?

It's tremendous positioning! Aren't you successfully implying, without actually saying, that you are the *expert*. You *must* be an expert—why else would the local newspaper choose you to share your knowledge above all of your competitors? That's what Terri does, as well as many others who know the importance of what she calls "power positioning."

Let me ask you a question. Do you think Terri ever tries to get direct listings or sales from her articles and radio talk shows? Absolutely not. That would be both unethical and nonproductive. She simply positions herself as the expert by giving out worthwhile, helpful, sound advice, and it comes back to her over and over again.

What If You Still Can't Get a Column?

Sometimes, entering through the front door is so difficult that walking through the back door simply makes more sense. While waiting for the break that will land you the actual column, Dean Shapiro has some suggestions that make sense.

"Aim a bit lower and shoot for monthly or periodic articles. Submit what are known as 'filler' copy that can fill a given amount of space in a news hole when the need arises. Make sure the articles are not tied to a specific time frame, however, because they may run weeks or even months from the time they are submitted." Dean advises sending a note with your submission saying, "Please run as space permits" or something similar.

Editors, especially at weeklies, pick up on these things, usually in the last few minutes before press run when they have a 13-inch (or whatever size) hole to fill and your column, which fits perfectly, just happens to be close by in the filler file. Be sure and submit a number of them at varying lengths so the editor can have a choice to fill whatever size hole exists in those last-minute press deadline crunches.

Another technique is to "feed" story ideas to an editor. According to Dean, "Very politely (and *not* too frequently) call or write to the editor suggesting a story or stories in your field and make certain these story ideas are broad-based enough to have a wide appeal to readers. Naturally, you, as the story originator, will be quoted in it as the 'authority' and that gives it advantageous positioning strength. Eventually, you could establish yourself as the one (or at least the first) person an editor or reporter calls when a story breaks in that field. That can eventually lead to the granting of column privileges, and for now, excellent positioning."

The fact is, most people, including myself, don't know a whole lot about a lot of different things. I know nothing about financial planning. When you consider the number of financial planners who approach me to invest my money with them, and my level of ignorance, it's a scary situation. All things being equal, don't you think I want an *expert* taking care of my hard-earned money?

I also don't know much about computers, real estate, insurance, automobiles, and most other things in life. Just because salespeople in these arenas are my clients doesn't mean I have actual product knowledge. Far from it. When they know *their* products and use *my* networking techniques, or ones that are similar, that's when they become top producers.

The Truth Is *Not* Necessarily What It Appears to Be

Unfortunately, there are many people who don't have enough product knowledge to actually help their customers and clients (and many who don't care to), yet they know how to position themselves well enough to be perceived as the expert in their field.

In his book, *Direct Mail Copy That Sells,* author and renowned copywriting legend Herschell Gordon Lewis refers to the word, "verisimilitude," meaning "having the appearance of truth." Not necessarily *the truth,* but simply the *appearance* of such. Whether something is actually true, or just seems to be so, people buy what they *perceive* to be the truth. Thus, we could say, "The truth is what the truth appears to be."

Actually, I hope you disagree with my last sentence. The truth *isn't* just what it appears to be. The truth is the truth. Unfortunately, the sentence preceding that one is accurate. In fact, the reason that con artists can fool so many people is that they are experts at making them perceive what they say as being the truth. And, in the short run, they do in fact seem to prosper.

Although it can be frustrating, remember—good guys (and women) *do* finish first. Sometimes it just takes a little while longer to get there. Once there, however, we stay there forever, while the con artist is always looking for a new territory because "Everybody in mine knows me."

The point is this: I know that you, the reader, know your product. You are extremely honest and trustworthy, and will use these techniques for the good of the customers and clients you serve. With that in mind, these techniques will help you position yourself as the expert, the authority in your field.

Another way you can accomplish this goal is to write for your state and national media. Again, citing real estate sales as an example, here's how. Your state board or Association of Realtors® probably has a magazine you can write for, as does the National Association of Realtors®, and other trade magazines within that field. Terri Murphy uses these media as well.

You might wonder what good does that do if other Realtors are the only ones reading it? That may be true, but in your listing and selling presentations it builds credibility with your prospects or customers if they know that you are a published author. You are perceived by your prospects as an expert (which you are). They know that even those in your profession recognize you as an authority; otherwise your article would not have appeared in their magazine.

As a Realtor, Terri also positions herself as an expert to others in her field. Consequently, she receives referrals from her peers all over North America regarding helping newcomers to her area find a place to live.

Now bear in mind that you don't have to be in any of the professions mentioned to write a column or individual articles and position yourself as an expert through their publication. Just as there are always ways to create a market for your product or service, there are ways to create a market for your articles. It is great positioning! I've personally had several hundred articles published in trade and professional magazines, and my efforts have paid off many times over.

Often, these articles are picked up and rerun by other magazines, which increases my positioning even further. Several magazines have asked me to contribute additional articles after running my first one. I get paid for some of them, but most of the time I'm only doing it for positioning.

How to Get Published

When you decide you want to write an article for a trade magazine, simply call and ask for the editor in charge of outside contributing articles or freelance submissions. Tell her your idea as concisely as possible and see if it's a match. If she thinks it is, she'll ask you to submit something, usually a query letter describing what you plan to cover in the article. Sometimes, editors will request the article itself.

I wouldn't submit anything at that point, however. Instead, ask for a set of author's guidelines and a back issue or two of the magazine. You want to see how articles are written, the average length of the articles the journal runs, the slant of the magazine, and, what kind of biography you will be given at the conclusion of the article. Then you tailor your article accordingly.

What you can do if you aim to be published in many periodicals is come up with a couple of generic articles that give good, worthwhile advice and simply gear them to a specific industry or audience and spell out what you're trying to accomplish in your article. You can consult the *Reader's Guide to Periodical Literature* or other reference books in your local library for the names of prospective magazines, or you can look through the racks at the magazines they order. Reference librarians are usually good sources of information on which publications might suit your needs. Don't be afraid to ask them; that's what they're there for.

And whenever you are published, send a press release to your local newspaper letting them know about it. If you're a chiropractor and had an article published in a chiropractic magazine, make sure the editor of your local newspaper knows that. If the local paper prints the release you send or mentions it in some other context such as a "People" column, it's another trophy you can use in order to position yourself as your community's chiropractic authority. A framed copy of a printed article hanging prominently in a waiting room is certainly an effective positioning device to those who are already patients. They can then be referring those in their sphere of influence to a recognized authority in his or her field.

You Can Also Position Yourself through the Electronic Media

Another means of positioning yourself in the community is to appear as a guest expert on local radio and television talk shows. When you call the station, don't ask to speak with the host: ask to speak to the producer. In fact, in a larger market it will probably be a segment producer. Explain to him or her what might be the advantages of having *you* as a guest on the program as opposed to others in the same field. You have to be concise and convincing because producers often get dozens of similar requests every week. You should be prepared with an angle or a hook that will snag the listeners' or viewers' attention.

If you are a medical doctor, for example, you can point out on a radio or television talk show certain practices by many in the medical profession that aren't necessarily ethical. Or you can describe a procedure that doctors should not be doing, even though many of them are. What does the public have the right to know that they're not being told?

I'm not saying you have to engage in yellow journalism or sensationalism, and I'm not suggesting that you need to use those precise examples. What I *am* saying is to "create a reason" why what you have to say is of interest to the show producers and audiences. They want a hook, an "angle." Pretend you are fishing and give them bait they'll bite on.

Remember, make the program match the audience. If you're an accountant, then appearing on a program geared toward teenagers isn't going to do you much good. You'll get exposure, but since your target audience is not watching, you won't increase your positioning. You only need people seeing you who are prospective customers, clients, or, more importantly, sources of referrals.

An excellent manual entitled *How To Get Famous* was authored by Ross Shafer of Woodland Hills, California, a well-known talk show producer, host, and stand-up comic. In this manual, not only does Ross share information on how to get on radio and television talk shows; he also talks about what to do and what not to do once you get there.

Fellow speaker and author Judith Briles of Denver, Colorado, is one of the National Speakers Association's main authorities on, as she calls it, "mastering the media." Judith, who speaks mainly on women's issues, has appeared on all the biggies including *Donahue, Oprah, Sally Jesse Raphael,* and *Geraldo.* She has used the media simply as a vehicle to position herself as an expert to her prospects, and it's worked.

Charles Garcia, a Realtor based in San Francisco, did a superb job of exploiting the media as a positioning tool. He let the segment producers of the local CBS affiliate know he was available for real estate advice and opinion. They eventually took him up on his *kind* offer.

Remember the San Francisco earthquake in 1989? A couple of days after that event a friend of Charles Garcia asked him how he thought this disaster would affect local real estate values. Charles immediately realized that a lot of San Francisco and Bay Area people were wondering the same thing.

He called the station and provided a list of topics relating to the earthquake, its effect on real estate values in different neighborhoods, and projections of what might be expected. He suggested that they wait 7 to 10 days before doing this story in order to give the market a little time to respond.

Meanwhile, Charles began doing his homework. He canvassed his colleagues in the real estate community, interviewing the managers of the major real estate offices in San Francisco and the Bay Area and consumers. He put together an interesting story on the effects of the earthquake on real estate values in the Bay Area.

In this 2-minute segment, he revealed some surprising statistics: very few real estate companies reflected a sharp increase in the number of deals falling out of escrow in the short time after the quake. Most buyers who had been in the process of house hunting before the earthquake were still looking. According to Charles, "Is the home seismically upgraded?" became the question of the day. Charles's status as "real estate expert" was reinforced.

These days Charles's brochure and mailing pieces feature a wonderful picture of him being interviewed by the two anchors. Doesn't that tell his prospects they have the opportunity to work with an expert? And when he sends this to his current customers and clients, they are proud to refer their real estate expert to their own sphere of influence.

As a footnote to this story, the first time Charles appeared on that news program was because the prior Realtor they had been using stood them up. She simply didn't show. The producers then let Charles know they were looking for a dependable real estate agent with whom they could form and develop a relationship.

Still another Realtor, Jim Boyce of Toronto, Ontario, has taken a slightly different tack. A former tennis star, he's now published in a Province tennis magazine in which he gives tennis advice, while highlighting the fact that he is a Realtor. He has also managed to acquire free advertising space in lieu of payment.

Why am I highlighting Realtors as the only examples of people using these techniques in order to effectively and profitably position themselves? Because they seem to be the ones doing it most frequently. But that doesn't mean other professions aren't doing it as well. (In fact, I'd like to hear from those of you in other professions who are also taking advantage of this unique opportunity.)

Are You an Information Resource for Others?

Let's discuss another aspect of positioning yourself as the expert: being an "information resource" for others. In other words, helping people in your community find products, goods, services, or even jobs.

You want to be that person others call to ask, "Hey, do you know a good printer?" Do you know a painless dentist? Do you know who has a good cellular phone and provides excellent service? Be that person who's almost *brokering* the information. Not for a fee, but for positioning.

On one occasion, the editor of a magazine to which I sometimes contribute articles called and asked me if I knew anybody else who could write articles on specific topics for them. Months earlier, I had suggested he use the talents of a fellow member of the National Speakers Association. He did, and that person wrote an excellent article.

When the editor called to ask for more referrals, I decided this was a good opportunity for a lot of win-win situations and excellent positioning for, and with, my other speaker friends. Not to mention the editor himself, who has a lot of pull within the association represented by his magazine.

So I contacted all the speakers within my personal network who I knew could write good articles and relayed the situation to them. By the time I contacted the editor, just a short while later, he had already been deluged with calls from my speaker friends. He loved it because his magazine was in need of a bunch of excellent articles.

That is win-win networking all around. I positioned myself with both my network of speakers *and* with the editor's network. In fact, he came right out and said, "Please let me know if there's *anything* I can do for you."

This type of positioning is actually quite easy to accomplish. Whenever you hear of someone needing something, come right out and match her up with someone who can help her. Do this consistently, and in time, people will know that you are the one to approach for this type of service.

Are You a Referral Source for Others?

When it comes to positioning oneself as a referral source, John Kuczek, president of Kuczek and Associates of Youngstown, Ohio, really has the right idea. He discovered early in his career that positioning yourself as the Big Person on Campus by way of helping others is the key to success, and he continues that practice to this day.

Addressing members of the Million Dollar Round Table at their 1991 annual meeting in New Orleans, Louisiana, Kuczek shared many of his excellent techniques with his fellow insurance sales professionals. Here's one.

According to Kuczek, "I help clients set up loans and mortgages, and they feel indebted to me because they usually dislike dealing with bankers and I help them get what they want. I also advise them on how to handle their earnings and divert some money into savings and remind them never to invest money they can't afford to lose.

"By helping clients structure mortgages and loans," continues Kuczek, "I also build a positive relationship with local banks. When I deal with people growing financially, somebody's always borrowing money. As they pay off loans, new projects come up and they are borrowing money again.

"Over the years," he adds, "I have done more and more business with bankers. By learning to use bankers, I created the ideal situation. The bankers would come to me instead of me approaching them. In the last year or so, banks have come to me and asked for referrals. I gladly oblige as long as my clients who are banking with them are getting the best service available, and that includes getting preferred interest rates on loans.

"Now that my company is comfortably *positioned* with area bankers we also ask *them* for referrals. We ask them to take a look at their customers who have commercial loans and see if they would benefit from our services. Interestingly enough, since we have begun to take this approach, we have actually had situations where banks are now calling us to refer clients. Banks are an indispensable part of my business."

Did you notice the phrase he used? "Comfortably positioned" with bankers. He's a man who knows the meaning of long-term business relationships, which is what networking is all about. No wonder John Kuczek is a qualifying member of the Million Dollar Round Table, Top of the Table, and Forum, which are some of the highest honors one can be awarded as a member of the National Association of Life Underwriters.

Positioning Through the Law of Large Numbers

Even if many of your prospects are currently doing business with your competition, if you feel they are worth your persistence, stay with them. With your excellent, classy follow-up, you'll be ready to step in if your competitor messes up, moves on, or for some other reason loses that person's account and referrals.

In his book, *Swim with the Sharks without Being Eaten Alive,* author Harvey Mackay points out that you should position yourself as the number two person to every prospect on your list and keep adding to that list. He continues that if your list is long enough, there are going to be number ones that retire or lose their territories for a hundred other reasons and succumb to the Law of Large Numbers.

According to Mackay, "If you're standing second in line, in enough lines, sooner or later you're going to move up to number one." I agree totally. Totally! Especially, if you're doing enough things right, such as using the follow-up techniques I've been describing in this book.

Again, if you're the number two person on enough lists, and you're doing the right things, you'll eventually *have* to move up to number one on many of those prospects' lists. And in the networking sense, of course, that doesn't mean being number one just for that person's direct business but for his or her referrals as well.

An excellent analogy has to do with one of my niche markets, the insurance industry. In that profession actuaries are wizards with numbers who can actually predict, almost to the percentage point, how many people in a given area are going to die as a result of traffic fatalities over a certain holiday weekend. Morbid, but true. The only thing they can't tell you is *who* they will be.

Mr. Mackay points out that the insurance industry has basically been built on the Law of Large Numbers. That's why, as Mackay says, if you position yourself as the number two person on enough lists, then sooner or later you've got to work your way up to number one on many of those lists.

What If They Are Already Someone's Customers?

What if many of your networking prospects are currently doing direct business with someone else. Do you realize that you can still get their referrals? Yes, even if you are number two on their list for direct business, you can be number one for their referrals. And position yourself to eventually get their direct business while you're at it.

You may be wondering, "Why would a person possibly refer business to *me* if they're doing business with someone else?" Numerous reasons. All things being equal, they may be doing business directly with your competitor out of a sense of loyalty to that person or maybe even to somebody else—a friend or family member. How many times have you been told by prospects that they *have* to do business with someone because they are somehow connected or related? It's happened to most of us.

If you've impressed this person enough, however, she'll go out of her way to get you referral business. One networking prospect felt so bad that his wife gave some business to a competitor that he actually went on a hunt to find some referrals for me. He was quite successful in that particular venture. Therefore, so was I.

I had earned his loyalty and help by going out of my way for him previously, using my network to assist him with information he needed to help some of his clients. What goes around *does* come around.

So are your networking prospects worth your persistence? If so, stay with them. Position yourself as the number two person on a prospect's direct business list, if that's all the current situation will allow. Position yourself as number one, however, for their referrals. Eventually you may be number one for *both*.

Using the skills and techniques described in this chapter, you will become positioned as the expert, and only logical resource, in your field.

Two Excellent Books on "Positioning"

Two books I highly recommend for those interested in truly mastering the technique of positioning (your business and yourself) are *Positioning: The Battle for Your Mind* (Warner), by Al Ries and Jack Trout, and *Opening Closed Doors* (McGraw-Hill), by C. Richard Weylman.

The first book, authored by advertising mavens and marketing strategists Ries and Trout, is an absolute gold mine of positioning strategies. Although *Positioning: The Battle for Your Mind* is written from the perspective of an ad person, you will find the authors' techniques and strategies totally applicable to the goals you are trying to accomplish.

The second book is written by an extremely successful entrepreneur—now a full-time speaker and author. Weylman has mastered the art of personal target-marketing, also known as niche marketing. *Opening Closed Doors* takes you step-by-step to becoming positioned as the expert in *your* field and shows you exactly how to become recognized by those in your niche market as the expert resource in *theirs*.

Key Points

- Act as if you are already powerfully positioned.
- Position yourself (for free) through the media.
  1. Write columns and articles for local, state, and national print media. These must be consumer-oriented.
  2. Prove to the editor why your information is important for his or her readership.
- Exposure alone is no longer a money maker. Positioning yourself as the expert in your field is the key.
- Verisimilitude is having the appearance of truth.
- Being a guest or resource for television and radio interviews is another excellent positioning tool. You must have a hook or angle that will make you a desirable guest in the producer's mind.
- Be an information resource (jobs, services, etc.) for those in your network.
- Position yourself through the Law of Large Numbers.

10

Customer Service: The Networker's Best Friend

"If you invent a better mousetrap, you can sit back and wait because the world will beat a path to your door." No doubt you've heard that saying. Well, the day of the "better mousetrap" is over, I'm afraid.

You can build the very best mousetrap in the world. You can network yourself and your product to the point where referrals are coming in faster than you can count them. But if you don't provide excellent customer service after establishing a niche in the marketplace, a path *will* be beaten to your door—but by bill collectors, not by customers.

More than ever, we have to earn people's repeat business and referrals by providing the best customer service we possibly can. Nothing will make your newly developed network crumble faster than a stale cookie than not providing proper caring and service.

The Big Eight

I'd like to share with you my eight basic rules of customer service as they relate to networking:

Every Employee Is in Sales

Even those people in your company who are not salespeople are salespeople. What I mean is this. Everyone from the CEO to the lowest person on the totem pole is selling the public every day on why they should or should not be doing business with you.

Studies have shown that each time customers have a positive experience with you or your place of business, they will tell 4 other people. On the other hand, any time they have a negative experience, they'll tell 11 people. And believe me, they'll rush out to tell them! I do it myself!

A surefire way to destroy our newly developed sphere of influence is to forget that we need to *continue* selling people on us. One bad apple really *can* spoil the whole bunch.

Being a professional speaker, I'm always flying, and there's one airline I use most frequently. Practically all the flight attendants representing this airline are absolutely wonderful people, making their passengers feel *great* about flying with them.

But once I had a negative experience—a flight attendant who really was quite nasty. To this day, when I think of that airline, I still cannot help wincing at the memory of that one incident with that one flight attendant, even though it happened years ago.

Yet everyone I have encountered since the incident has been just as helpful and pleasant as the others before it. I'm still loyal to that airline because I realize that this particular flight attendant was an exception. Nonetheless, the seeds of change were planted in my mind, weren't they? Do any of us, or those in our company, ever plant the seeds of change in the minds of our customers, clients, or fellow networkers?

If You Think Your Customers Are Not King, Try Running Your Business Without Them

We need to constantly keep in mind the fact that our customers pay our salaries and commissions. If we own a business, we need to make sure our employees realize the same thing.

A restaurant in my town comes to mind. Since I love to eat, I'm always in restaurants. That's where you see both the best and worst of customer service. This place has decent food, but not the best, and their prices are very high. Nonetheless, they do a great business. They treat their customers tremendously, and it's appreciated. I know whenever I go there that I will feel welcome. They go out of their way to make me feel good. It's worth the price to feel that good.

One of my corporate clients, American Bankers Insurance Group, has a slogan: "The Customer Is the Boss." When they hire somebody or send an agent into the field representing them, that person must be what they call "Boss-oriented."

According to vice chairman Frank Baiamonte, "In our recruiting process, we are only interested in people who already bring a 'boss-oriented' mindset to our company." He adds, "At American Bankers Insurance Group, service is not a department; it's everybody's job."

Don't Ever Tell Customers They're Wrong

This rule can be best illustrated by citing a personal example. One day I had an appointment at the place where I used to get my hair cut. I came in at 1 o'clock, and the receptionist at the desk asked me what I was doing there. The conversation went something like this:

BOB: I have an appointment at 1 with Barbara.

RECEPTIONIST: No, you don't. Your appointment is at 1:30.

BOB: No, I'm sure it's at 1 o'clock. I even wrote it down, right here. (showing my appointment book)

RECEPTIONIST: You're wrong! It's at 1:30.

Well, one of three things obviously happened: either I was wrong, or she was wrong, or there was simply a misunderstanding between the two of us at the time we set the appointment.

In the meantime, however, she really offended me by telling me so emphatically that I was wrong! She insulted her customer. But since I was there already, I took my seat to wait for Barbara. The manager came over and asked, "Bob, what's wrong? You're not your usual friendly, smiley self."

I told her what had happened and that my feathers were just a bit ruffled at being told so emphatically that I was wrong. She replied, "Bob, I feel bad about that, but you have to realize, my people don't make mistakes!"

Well, the manager just made a mistake herself. In fact, she compounded the error made by her receptionist. Three months later, when Barbara left, the manager told me the salon would still like my business, claiming they could continue to serve my needs just as well. I thanked her for the offer, but the incident I just cited was still fresh in my mind.

Now what do you think I did? Did I stay there, or did I follow Barbara 6 miles down the road and out of my way? That's right, I followed Barbara. Why? For one reason, Barbara gives a pretty good haircut; for another, she doesn't tell me I'm wrong.

The owner of the largest dairy store in the world is a most famous customer service success story. For years he has run his business from the base of two rules that are *literally* etched in stone in a huge rock at the entrance to his store.

Rule No. 1:   The customer is always right.

Rule No. 2:   If the customer is ever wrong, reread Rule No. 1.

This very basic philosophy can work for each and every one of us, regardless of our profession.

Deliver What You Promise and a Little Bit More

Again, let me cite another personal example. One morning I went to breakfast at a local franchise restaurant. On the menu they had something which looked very appetizing. I don't remember exactly what it was, but it was something like "eggs with spinach, *smothered* with cream sauce." Now I *love* cream sauce, as indicated by my ever-expanding waistline, and I ordered that particular meal. When the meal was delivered to me, it looked very good. The eggs looked great, the spinach looked tremendous, but with just a *touch* of cream sauce.

I politely called the waitress over and asked, "Could I please get a little extra cream sauce?" I have to say, when I said a little extra, she really took me at my word. She brought me about a thimbleful of sauce. Since I'm really not the type who likes to complain, I ate the spinach and eggs with the little bit of cream sauce.

When she brought me the check, I noticed an extra charge of 50 cents for the cream sauce! Now I'm not cheap, but I had a definite problem with that. When I went to pay my check at the cashier stand, the manager saw me, motioned to me, and asked, "Did you enjoy the meal?" I said, "I certainly did. The eggs were great, the spinach was tremendous, but the only problem I have is that the menu said it was *smothered* with cream sauce. In fact, there was just a little on it. When I asked for more, just a little was brought over. That's okay," I continued, "but I was charged an extra 50 cents for the cream sauce, which turned out to be even less than what was promised on the menu."

With that, the manager grabbed the check out of my hand. He looked at it, looked at me, looked back at the check, and looked at me again. Then he came to his decision. He said, "Sir, I'll tell you what I'm going to do. I'm going to refund your 50 cents, but I've got to tell you, if we were to deliver everything we promised on the menu, we'd go out of business!"

Well, I don't know if they'll go out of business from doing things like that or not, but they certainly will *not* get my repeat business. Nor will they ever get the business of my sphere of influence.

On the other hand, there's the local Chevron station in my town. They call themselves a "Complete Service Station." They are, and more. Never have I experienced a service station that makes you feel as welcome as they make you feel. I wouldn't go anywhere else for gas unless I was 30 miles out of town and puttering along on an empty tank.

The local body shop owner who services my car is the same way. I'm totally ignorant when it comes to cars, and probably considered an easy mark by many mechanics. I have been taken advantage of in the past. But this guy and his crew are great with me, even letting me know when I don't need work I may have thought I needed. You can be sure I've referred a ton of business to them including, at one time or another, everyone on my staff. Jim Dees, of Jim Dees Automotive, is a good man, who delivers on what he promises and a little bit more.

Going the Extra Mile, or Even the Extra Step, Is Worth All the Paid Advertising in the World

One morning before an afternoon program I was putting on in Kansas City, Missouri, I pinched a nerve in my neck. In pain, I called the desk for some ice. Tonya, the front desk clerk, was quick to respond and had ice sent right up. Every 30 minutes after that, Tonya called my room to see if I was okay. Right before I went downstairs for my program, Tonya checked up on me, and again when I finished.

It sure was nice to know somebody cared without anything being in it for her! When I told her superiors about it, they said that was "commonplace for Tonya." I'm sure the Kansas City Marriott is very proud of her.

Another client is the Ritz Carlton. Whenever you ask people on their staff how to get to a certain location within the hotel, they don't just point you in the right direction. They stop what they're doing and escort you there! In fact, both of those incidents exemplify what my friend and fellow speaker Lou Heckler calls "the Wow factor."

Gifford Hampton, manager of the Palm Beach, Florida, branch of the Bank of Boston, told me another great story about going the extra mile.

It seems a woman who had recently moved to Palm Beach from the Midwest came to the bank to discuss the possibility of their handling her account. Before she made any final decision on where to bank, however, she had to go to Boston to visit her daughter. She was going for about 6 weeks and, being a bit elderly, needed a professional to care for her.

Unfortunately, neither her daughter nor anyone else seemed to be able to locate a person with whom they felt comfortable. Well, the

Palm Beach branch cared enough to help. Networking with a sister branch in the Boston area they searched and searched and finally found somebody, actually a husband-and-wife team, to take care of this woman.

The woman was able to enjoy her vacation with a true sense of security. When she returned to Palm Beach, she opened up an account with that branch. Doesn't it make sense? It ties right in with the saying by the great speaker and founder of the National Speakers Association, Cavett Robert: "People don't care how much you know until they know how much you care."

Your Receptionist Is One of Your Most Important Sales People

So make sure he or she is trained to do the job. I hear horror stories from many people regarding the way they are treated on the telephone. I've certainly experienced it myself—and from big, successful, important companies that you'd think would know better.

Even they can't get away with that negative treatment for too long before turning some people off, destroying the company one person (or should I say 250 people) at a time. We can't take the chance of getting away with poor customer service for a second in our own businesses.

Not that we should want to. We need to stress that those who answer the phone know how to make a person feel glad they called. They are the initial contact between our prospects, customers, clients, fellow networkers, and us.

This is what usually happens: companies take their most inexperienced person and stick them on the telephone, not realizing the importance of first impressions. There's an old saying, "You never get a second chance to make a good first impression."

I receive numerous compliments on the way my office staff handles people on the phone. Call my office sometime. They make you feel important—because you *are!*

Here is a tip I first learned from fellow speaker and telephone skills authority David Allan Yoho. When concluding a telephone conversation, let the other person hang up first. You don't want them to hear that cold "click" in their ear, because they may think you're glad to be through with them. Have you ever felt that way when someone hung up the phone just as you finished saying good-bye? That's how it feels to them as well.

Return Telephone Calls Promptly

Some people are just *too busy* to make money. Have you ever had somebody tell you he was just too busy to return your call. We never know who's calling, do we? It could be a prospect or a potential networking prospect.

When it comes to networking, we can't allow people in our network to feel we're being aloof and not responsive to their phone calls. If they feel they're second bananas and aren't on our priority list to return their calls, our network is going to dissolve right before our eyes.

When I was living up north, I was at a chamber of commerce card exchange, hosted and sponsored by a local restaurant. It had just opened and was trying to make a name in the community. The manager announced they were going to offer certificates that we could purchase as gifts for other people to come and eat at the restaurant.

Neat idea. Not long afterward, I felt I owed a networking associate an extra special thank you for some help he'd given me. Wanting to do something nice for him and his family as my way of showing my appreciation, I called the restaurant manager to purchase a $100 gift certificate.

The manager wasn't in, so I left my name and number. I told the person answering the phone that I had met the manager at the card exchange function the restaurant hosted. What I didn't say was why I called. You see, I didn't want to say that I was calling to buy something; I just wanted to call and say I was Bob Burg, to see if the manager thought that was an important enough reason to call back. Was he customer-oriented?

He had met me very briefly and maybe he didn't remember me. Or maybe he thought I was calling to *solicit business*. He never called back. I had been ready to spend $100. Well, actually, I did spend $100, but it was with another restaurant. That one called me back.

It Isn't Necessarily *What* We Say But *How* We Say It

In my business I stay at many hotels. Some are tremendous and the staff is great. Some aren't so tremendous and the staff isn't quite so great. In one particular hotel, the person at the registration desk was saying all the right things, but all the wrong way.

She referred to people as "Sir" and "Ma'am," but very coldly. Soon it was my turn to register. As I was filling in all the information she asked, "Did you fill in this line, sir?" I said, "No I..." and she very quickly interrupted. "Please fill in that line, sir," she said very harshly and coldly. She was saying "sir," but she really didn't mean it! And the customer, and those listening, could tell easily.

A Positive Example

On the other hand, my friend and fellow speaker, Glenna Salsbury, tells the story of a young English teacher who had worked hard all year long trying to help an Asian transfer student master the English language. Understandably, the student was very appreciative.

On the final day of school, the teacher walked into the classroom and on her desk was a single yellow rose. Next to it was a note written by the young man. It read, "Dear Teacher, one day this rose will fade and die, but you will *smell* forever!" Now, the words may not have been exactly right, but do you think she was insulted or complimented?

Of course, she was delighted because of the intention. Sometimes, it isn't what we say, it's how we say it! Our pets know what we mean by the way, tone, and manner we talk to them. It's safe to say our customers, clients, and networking prospects can sense the same thing.

Key Points

- It isn't enough to simply build the network. It must be maintained and advanced by superb customer service.
- There are eight rules of customer service:
  1. Remember that we are salespeople.
  2. If you think your customers are not king, try running your business without them.
  3. Don't ever tell customers they are wrong.
  4. Deliver what you promise and a little bit more.
  5. Going the extra mile, or even the extra step, is worth all the paid advertising in the world.
  6. Your receptionist is one of your most important sales people.
  7. Return telephone calls promptly.
  8. It isn't necessarily *what* we say but *how* we say it.

11

Cross-Promotions: An Interview with Jeff Slutsky

When we think of two people networking with each other, especially as its pertains to referrals, we look at the ideal situation as being, "This person finds leads for that person and that person finds leads for this person." And that, in itself, has the makings of a fine, mutually beneficial, give-and-take, win-win relationship.

Now, let's expand our horizons a bit, and imagine these two people actually going in on a joint promotional venture: two individuals jointly planning the idea and goal of a carryover business. In order to learn how to do this effectively and profitably, I sought the advice of expert Jeff Slutsky, author of the best-selling book *Streetfighting: Low Cost Advertising/Promotions for Your Business.*

In this book, Jeff, a former advertising agency executive, showed retail businesses how to "outsmart, not outspend," their competition.*

We began our discussion by talking about Jeff's streetfighting concept, and then focused on cross-promotions as an extremely effective and profitable way for two networkers to dramatically increase their business with little expense.

---

*A brilliant piece of work, Jeff has been featured in media including the *Wall Street Journal, Inc.* magazine, *USA Today, SUCCESS* magazine, *Entrepreneur* magazine, and on numerous radio programs and television talk shows including *The Sally Jessy Raphael Show.* The latest of his five books is called *How To Get Clients* (Warner).

BOB: What is "streetfighting"?

JEFF: Streetfighting is a descriptive term used to illustrate an attitude toward marketing, promotion, sales, pretty much outthinking the competition, not outspending. When something is considered to be streetfighting, it is usually clever, smart, and effective and done without wasting money. In the best-case scenario, it is something that substantially saves money or gets twice the value for the money. So there are two elements: Number one, it has to get results. And number two, it has to do it for less money.

BOB: Given the incredible and ever-growing competition in today's business and sales environment, how important is it for today's "on-the-street" salesperson to be able to use these streetfighting techniques to get new business without all of the added expense?

JEFF: It gets more and more important every day. Many companies and products have the same advantages and disadvantages. These include product quality, price, and the ability to pay for advertising. Streetfighters must be able to give themselves the edge by consistently being able to outsmart the competition.

BOB: What's your philosophy of building referrals from an existing client?

JEFF: Well, to increase referrals, you must increase the credibility and rapport you have with your client. If you're going to retain the relationship, it's important that you have developed rapport and cemented the relationship along the way. In other words, instead of having gone after the sale right away, you moved the relationship along at the pace best meeting the needs of that particular prospect or client.

All of that includes the first contact, the selling process, and especially after the sale, via great customer service. As you know, it costs a lot more to bring in a new client than it does to keep a current one. It's also more cost-effective to have clients who want to refer business to you.

BOB: What might be one example of a very basic cost-effective streetfighting technique?

JEFF: I'm personally a strong believer in using testimonial letters in the presentation in order to gain credibility. This is a letter in which a third party has said that I do a good job, that my company does a good job, and the product or service is good. So it isn't just my word, it's basically a referral, and it costs nothing at all to get. This is a very, very powerful sales tool. Great client relationships practically assure that you will have as many of these letters or referrals as you want when talking to a new prospect.

Taking it a step further, if you sell to different types of industries, you'll want to have testimonial letters from those specific industries. That tells the prospect you are an expert in that particular field. While many professionals and salespeople use this technique sometimes, a streetfighter uses it all the time.

Any kind of good publicity will also help greatly. After the inbound calls that, hopefully, you'll get, you can reproduce that media exposure, put it into print form, and use it as a positioning tool to increase credibility. (*Note:* This technique is covered in Chapter 11 of Jeff's book.)

Public speaking is also another tremendous opportunity to gain exposure, credibility, and the edge over your competition. Let's face it, when you do a speech for a civic club or organization and can relate it to your product or service, you have literally put yourself on a pedestal in front of your audience. This doesn't mean you have to be a professional speaker, but if you have something of value to offer to the community, a number of different avenues are open to you. A lot of organizations, for example, seek luncheon speakers, and if you present the information to these people, you are looked upon as the expert.

A good example is a cardiologist who gave seminars at retirement homes for senior citizens on the proper maintenance of their cardiovascular system—proper diet, exercise, and so on. Because of conducting these free seminars and because he took the time to meet with people, when they needed a cardiologist, or knew someone who needed a cardiologist, they went to him. This went a long way toward building up his practice.

BOB: What about a salesperson selling a generic product or service? Obviously, they can't simply do a sales presentation.

JEFF: In that case, a salesperson must gear his or her presentation to the consumer's point of view, finding a particular area with specific audience appeal and building on that appeal. How will that product or service be able to solve their particular problem? For example, retirement is always a big issue, so if you sell investments or insurance, you can show people how to retire with a million dollars while making only modest monthly contributions. You are conveying something of value without it being a commercial. You definitely don't want it to be a commercial. Given that caveat, this can be a great venue or means of letting people know what you do.

Cross-Promotions: The Ultimate in Win-Win Networking

BOB: One of the great concepts you developed in your business was the cross-promotion. This, to me, is the quintessential example of win-win networking. Before we delve into its uses by the salesperson or professional, what exactly is a cross-promotion?

JEFF: Cross-promotions have actually been around for a very long time. The oldest cross-promotion I'm aware of was done by Benjamin Franklin over 200 years ago. He ran a special certificate in *Poor Richard's Almanac*. He cross-promoted with Paul Revere, who gave a special deal on his pewter ware if the person bought *Poor Richard's Almanac*. This served to increase the value of the magazine, and the consumer could buy the pewter for 2 cents less. This cross-promotion worked out well for both gentlemen. It was like the first coupon. In my own case, when we started cross-promotions with our retail clients, we found out cross-promoting can go beyond retail sales into direct sales or just about anything.

BOB: How does a retail cross-promotion work?

JEFF: A simple cross-promotion could be nothing more than a fast-food place that is trying to gain more customers. They would set up a relationship with any other type of merchant that reaches the same type of customer base. Let's say the goal of the fast-food place is to go after children to promote their kiddie meals. So they could approach a Toys-R-Us, a kiddie shoe store, a kiddie clothing store, or a children's bookstore and set up a win-win, cross-promotion. The key is to find a cross-promotion partner that targets the type of people you want.

BOB: Let's take the example of a pizza place and a video store. Something like that would seem to go hand in hand. How would that work?

JEFF: That's a classic cross-promotion; pizza, especially if the store does delivery or carryout, and video, which is home entertainment. Both involve an activity at home, so it makes a lot of sense. If you are the owner of the pizza place, you would approach the video store owner and say, "How would you like to provide your customers with something extra—a way they can get a little bit more for their money when they come in to rent your videos, and a great way for you to personally thank them for being your customer?"

You might end up offering a certificate (I don't like to use the word coupon) for $2 off a large pizza that the video store would distribute to their customers. The actual offer is irrelevant as long as it has some sort of value, savings, or freebie attached to it. So it gives the video store an excuse to handle your advertising for you for free.

So all of a sudden a person goes in and rents three videos. It costs them six or seven bucks which seems like a lot of money to them. But, "Thank you for coming in and here is something special for you. When you order your pizza from Joe's Pizza Parlor, you're going to save $3." The video store owner, in essence, is telling the customer: "You really only spent $4, not $7, with us today." The customer then goes away feeling good about doing business with the video store for having gotten something extra.

This is an example of a one-way cross-promotion. All that is required on your part is to provide the video store with certificates. Keep in mind that it's important to put the name of the cross-promotion partner right on the actual printed piece. A nice added touch is to put the video store owner or manager's name and signature—"Compliments of Dave Johnson"—on it as well. This technique works really well.

A two-way cross-promotion, on the other hand, is even easier to set up because it is, essentially, "I'll hand out yours and you hand out mine"—the ultimate networking. The difference is now you have to reciprocate. You have to go that extra mile and actually distribute. In practice, this is fine to do once in a while, but it is difficult to do regularly. When we set up cross-promotions for our clients, we do it on a weekly basis, so we're doing about 50 a year. You might just decide you don't want to hand out 50 certificates all the time. But it might be just the right approach for some really big cross-promotions.

A two-way cross-promotion has another advantage in that you don't have to have an offer on the piece itself for it to contain value. The very fact that you're doing it for them means they will hand out your advertising, and it could be nothing more than a reinforcement of another campaign or just a regular ad, but it doesn't have to be a coupon or certificate of value.

Reverse cross-promotions are totally different. Back to the example of the pizza store. Let's say the video store customers are coming into my store with the certificates to buy my pizza. You might respond with, "Thank you for coming into my store and buying pizza. As a little extra gift I've contacted five other merchants in my area: the ice cream shop, the shoe store, the video store, the car wash, and the beauty parlor. I've created a coupon booklet, and if you use all five coupons, you're going to save $20." So while the customer may have spent $10, she actually gets $20 back. For my part I have a premium of great value to give away. After all, many people often pay $20 or $30 for actual coupon books. This one they get for free just for buying from me. The result is a lot of added value to my business for the mere cost of a little bit of printing.

The other advantage of the reverse cross-promotion is that all 5 or 10 or 15 or 20 of the reverse cross-promotion participants owe me a favor, and now I can set up one-way cross-promotions with them very easily. So essentially, it's really a two-way in disguise, but I'm taking care of all of my two-way obligations in one effective little booklet or packet.

This technique is also good for doing theme cross-promotions, which might be important for a certain type of salesperson. Let's say you have a jewelry store. You want to cross-promote with several other companies which cater to weddings—something very specific. Let's say you approach a tuxedo rental place, bridal shop, limousine service, photographer, musical band, etc. These businesses can't always reach the prospects before they make their decisions on who to hire for these services. Where is the first place people go when they get engaged? They go to the jewelry store.

BOB: And all else being equal, you want them buying their wedding rings from you, not from the jewelry store down the street.

JEFF: Exactly! So the reverse cross-promotion is, "If you buy your ring from us, there is a $250 gift packet of great value for your wedding. It has 20 or more certificates from the wedding cake on up. It not only saves them money but practically plans their wedding for them. So it's a great closing device for someone to make a decision. And again, the promotion is at a very low cost. Reverse cross-promotion becomes targeted by an event or by a specific type of product.

BOB: Now, this was a jewelry store owner or salesperson who set this up. What about the other wedding suppliers who want to get in on the ground floor of the wedding plans?

JEFF: It really doesn't matter which of these businesses you are in. If I was the tuxedo shop, for example, I would go to the jewelry store and try to set up the promotion. I might possibly suggest the idea for the packet as long as I would be assured to get the business for my tux shop. The key point is that I would try to set this up with a lot of jewelry stores because that is where I'll get my referrals and my leads.

So, as a cross-promoter, you pick out any kind of special event and you figure out what else they have to buy. The neat thing about cross-promotion is this: not only does it cost nothing, except for a little bit of quick printing, but it is so targeted. Most advertising is untargeted except for direct mail or maybe telemarketing. With a cross-promotion I can find my customers, if I know who they are, and target by virtue of the cross-promotion partner I use.

I'll share with you one of the biggest success stories in cross-promotions ever. It has to do with a comic book store in Ohio. I had just completed doing a whole series of training programs for Marvel Comics, a big client of mine.

Well, comic book buyers are a very specialized type of audience. Only a very small percentage of the population collects comic books compared to mass media. It's not like eating pizza, which appeals to almost everybody. Video rentals are fairly broad-based as well. But comic books are still fairly specialized.

When the movie *Batman Returns* came out, which was a big, big event, the comic book store owner set up a cross-promotion with the manager of the movie theater that carried that movie. This comic book store, of course, carries *Batman* comic books, *Penguin*, and *Cat Woman* comic books, and all the other related ones.

Naturally, anyone attending that movie *might* be in the market for comic books. But the important thing is, you know that anyone who is into comic books is going to be at that movie. Now you have found your target market. So the cross-promotion is set up and here's what happened.

The theater employees handed out to moviegoers about 10,000 certificates for $1 off of the higher-end, more expensive *Penguin* and *Cat Woman* comic books. The comic book store owner got 150 returns out of 10,000. Although that is not a very high percentage, it doesn't matter. All that matters is the return on investment.

Out of the 150 redemptions, and this is the important part, over 100 customers became regular customers. A regular average customer, according to the owner, spends $10 a week in his store. If you apply the numbers and you've got 100 additional regular customers, that translates into $52,000 in sales the first year alone—all from that one cross-promotion.

Let's take it a step further. Most comic book stores live off referrals from friends. If those 100 new, regular customers refer their friends, then that $52,000 figure is just the beginning.

BOB: When we talk about the sphere of influence of the average person being 250 people, if they can refer just five of those people, what a success!

JEFF: You can still start with these 100 people just bringing in *one* friend apiece. Now it goes from $52,000 to $110,000 in extra income.

That certainly demonstrates the potential power of a cross-promotion when you target the cross-promotional partner appropriately. Not only is a movie theater a good target audience to network with if you have a comic book store, but it was that specific *type* of movie.

BOB: How would somebody more into direct-contact sales, such as an insurance person, Realtor, computer salesperson, or copying machine salesperson, use a cross-promotion? And what about professionals, such as accountants, lawyers, or dentists, who need to bring in new business but can't blatantly sell? How do they begin the cross-promotion process?

JEFF: Here's a good example. This woman is a pharmaceutical representative whose job is to get in front of the doctor and present her case for the drugs that she represents. That is not necessarily an easy thing to do, since there is a lot of competition out there in that particular field.

She knew that a significant percentage of the doctors that she called upon were avid golfers. Not a big surprise. So she asked herself the key question: What other businesses or organizations would also benefit from having access to those same doctors?

One thing that came to mind was one of the big discount golf franchises, and in her city there were four units. So let's say out of all the doctors she calls, 40 or 50 are avid golfers. Doctors are usually not poor, so when they spend money on golf, they probably spend a lot of money on clubs and everything else.

So I suggested that she approach the franchisee of the four stores in this area and say, "Listen, I call on a number of doctors and other golfers. If you'll give me a gift certificate that entitles them to a free sleeve of Titleist golf balls (this being a top name brand), I'll make sure to put it directly in their hands."

Keep in mind, Bob, we are talking about a retail item that is worth about $7 or $8, so it costs the franchise owner $3 or $4. What does it usually cost that retailer to get a potential customer in that front door? They probably spend $20 or $30 per person on mass media advertising to get them in for the first time.

Now here she is offering to go out there to her people and give them a gift certificate that will cost the franchisee only $4. She explained that as she handed these out, she would sign her name to authorize them and require the doctors to appear with the certificate personally to redeem it.

She also used this as an incentive to get the doctors to see her. She had to sign the certificate right in front of them and explain that they needed to take this to the golf shop personally in order to take advantage of the gift.

As far as the golf shop owner was concerned, return on investment was the key. Nobody goes in and just gets the golf balls. Golfers look at the clubs and everything else and possibly become regular customers. At the very least, the retailer gets that doctor's name on their list.

As far as our salesperson is concerned, she now has the ability to distribute, *for free*, these sleeves of Titleist golf balls, which would normally cost her $7 or $8. If she did that 50 times without company reimbursement, it would run into some money. Instead, everybody wins, the ultimate in cross-promoting and the ultimate in networking.

BOB: What is crucial is how she used the incentive to get past the gatekeeper and right in front of the doctor.

JEFF: The doctor had to physically sign it in her presence to validate it. That was one of the techniques that she used to make sure that she got to see the doctor in person. It had to carry both her signature and the doctor's signature and it had a tight expiration date. They had to redeem within 2 weeks. It was just one little thing that allowed her to get in to see the doctors a little more often.

BOB: The next step would be to find something else doctors like and set up a cross-promotion with another vendor, right? After a couple of times, the doctors associate her visit with a free gift, and they see her every time. And in her type of business, frequency is the name of the game.

JEFF: Another example is a life insurance salesperson whose specialty and niche market is helping people build for retirement. You're trying to sell what are known as 10/35 exchanges. It's an equity-to-term conversion of sorts that will benefit older people by giving them necessary cash they can live on.

You're trying to pick up new clients. For this, you could use the reverse cross-promotion approach. Let's say you find someone wanting to save for retirement. Not only are you going to help her save money, but you're going to help her save money for those things she needs for her retirement.

What is it that people need for retirement? Maybe they want membership to a golf club, or money off at a restaurant—an early-bird special anytime they want. In other words, benefits that offer special consideration. So you think it through and write down 10 or 15 of these merchants or salespeople together.

You let them know that you are a life insurance salesperson and will be calling on some very wealthy people who spend money on cars, homes, club memberships, food, and so on. You are giving these people an excellent opportunity to position themselves in front of this very lucrative market.

We are talking about the so-called silver generation, and every time I get new clients or clients that increase their coverage, I would provide them with a thank-you. This thank-you is going to be a packet which almost looks like a wedding invitation containing maybe a dozen nicely printed certificates as a thank-you from me, their agent. It will represent hundreds of dollars of savings. Not only am I helping them save money for retirement, but I'm helping them save money now and it's a nice thank-you. I could use this as a closing device.

BOB: Could you use this as an *opening* device as well? Let's face it—often the toughest part of doing business is getting that first face-to-face appointment with the prospect.

JEFF: As an opening tool, you would maybe not have as elaborate a package. It depends on whether you could get a restaurant to do a two-for-one, which could run into some money for them. In some cases you can get them to do freebies. Or you could offer gift certificates that are worth $25: $5 at this restaurant and $5 at this place. The restaurant owners will do that in a second just for the introduction to those people.

You can use this to get in front of somebody. You can use it as a closing tool. You can use it as a frequency-gaining tool. But the cost is low. Of course, there will be some time invested in setting these relationships up. On the other hand, it also gives you an opportunity to sell your products to the other merchants with whom you are cross-promoting. After all, they have to think about retirement as well. It forces you to network.

BOB: What about those fields in which the salesperson or professional can't come right out and publicly cross-promote? How might that situation be handled?

JEFF: Regarding professionals, one example of a really soft cross-promotion is a doctor who provided hypertension screening as a free service on the premises at a grocery store. It was good for the store because it could advertise the fact that the doctor was going to do this free service. Meanwhile, the doctor obtained the actual test kits free from a pharmaceutical company. It was a great way for this doctor to build up his practice without offending his peers. So it was not blatant advertising, but more like a community involvement project. It was a very effective way of getting him in front of those potential customers, or patients.

BOB: What about professionals, such as a doctor and an accountant, cross-promoting with each other in a very low-key way?

JEFF: An easy way to do a soft cross-promotion is in your waiting room. Let's say you're an accountant, and you want to reach a doctor's patients, to sell your accounting services. If you do a newsletter, that could be put in the doctor's waiting room for patients to read. Simple little things such as that are very effective. Of course, the doctor's newsletter could be put in the accountant's waiting room as well. The same situation could be done with an attorney. You find ways of subtly infiltrating one another's customer base.

BOB: What about doctors suggesting that if their patients called their attorney or accountant and used their name, they could get a few minutes of advice without being charged?

JEFF: Throughout the relationship, let's say you are an attorney and you're networking with an accountant with whom you'd like to cross-promote. You offer an arrangement whereby somebody can call the accountant with a quick question for a limited time for a 30-day free trial. And the accountant's clients can call the attorney and ask a quick question. This way you get each other's clients to actually call. That is your initial lead for converting them to being your clients.

BOB: Let's take one more example and pretend we have a person selling a copy machine. The copy machine sales business is very competitive. We must get at least three or four of these salespeople a month in this office. How could they cross-promote in order to successfully get appointments with the decision makers?

JEFF: One really effective cross-promotion that comes to mind is actually more of an internal cross-promotion, which was done by a copy machine company in my hometown of Columbus, Ohio. At the same time, it crossed over to another area called community involvement. They ran a contest.

The idea was to get businesses to simply fill out a four-question survey. If they did, then $2 would be donated by the copy machine company to a certain charity. Whichever employee got the most questionnaires filled out would win some sort of prize. But all the lead money, the referral fees, as such, were being donated to charity. Here's what happened: A company repair person, not a salesperson, was fixing a copy machine upstairs from us. He went around to a bunch of offices, eventually getting to ours. He told us about the contest and said that if we would simply answer these four or five questions, then $2 would be donated to this charity.

While normally I would not talk to anybody, since this was for charity, I decided to answer the questions. The company had actually managed to get its repair people prospecting for the salespeople. Of course, the questions were basic, designed simply to see if they needed to follow up. Again, most people would answer the few questions because $2 was being donated to charity. So, as you can see, a cross-promotion with a nonprofit organization is a great idea because everybody wins.

The other thing is to develop relationships with those selling noncompetitive items to the same prospects—perhaps computer salespeople, telephone salespeople, and office furniture salespeople. I would develop a networking relationship with salespeople in my territory who were doing that, and what we would do is share.

Let's say I'm in an office on a cold call. The prospect is not interested in a copy machine because she has a brand new one, but in talking with her, I discover a need for a product or service she could buy from one of my networking buddies, and I ask if she'd like to hear from that person. And if it's a situation where I do make the sale, one or two more questions can determine if the prospect is also in need of one of the other products or services. If all of us are doing that for each other, we're getting a four-for-one prospecting deal.

Now, what about you? What can you, the reader, work out with somebody or some business that will be win-win? It isn't always easy to come up with a viable idea, and depending upon your business, it can't necessarily be in the form of a discount certificate. But brainstorm with those in your network, and come up with some ideas. You'll hit upon a winner sooner or later, and, as we learned from Jeff Slutsky, the payoff can be great.

Key Points

- "Streetfighting," according to author Jeff Slutsky, is a descriptive term used to illustrate an attitude toward marketing, promotion, and sales, based on outthinking, not outspending, the competition.

- A cross-promotion is basically a win-win promotion between salespeople or merchants who are trying to reach the same customers. There are different types of cross-promotions.

  1. *One-way cross-promotions.* You will provide certificates to your

cross-promotion partner, who will hand them out to his or her customers upon purchase.

2. *Two-way cross-promotions.* Essentially, "I'll hand out yours and you hand out mine."

3. *Reverse cross-promotions.* Your cross-promotion partner supplies you with the certificates, which you hand out to your customer upon purchase as an added value for buying from you.

■ A huge advantage of the cross-promotion is this: not only does it cost nothing except for a little bit of quick printing but it is extremely targeted to the audience you want to reach.

■ With just a bit of creativity, everyone from the direct salesperson to the professional can use cross-promotions to their advantage.

■ One advantage of cross-promotions to the direct salesperson is that they are an excellent way to get face-to-face with an ordinarily difficult-to-reach decision maker.

■ Cross-promotions are also an excellent closing tool.

■ Professionals (doctors, lawyers, accountants, etc.) can often utilize soft cross-promotions as a way of sending prospects to one another.

■ Internal cross-promotions get everyone else in the company (non-salespeople) prospecting for leads.

12

Home-Based Businesses

Networking for Today's Entrepreneur

Question: What can be the most scary, lonely, risky, difficult, time-con-suming, challenging, and ultimately, rewarding undertaking in the world? That's right—owning your own business. There's nothing like it! Imagine, no one looking over your shoulder telling you what to do and when, where, or how to do it.

No one will decide when your incredible networking skills and determination have earned you too much money (as in more than your boss or manager). Therefore no one will impose a ceiling of income, raising of quota or shrinking of territory. And no one will have the power to keep you from tending to the truly important matters in your life, such as attending your child's baseball game or school play, or *just being there* for your spouse or other family members when you deem it necessary.

As the skilled networker you'll become through learning and utiliz-ing the techniques in this book, sure, you will always be able to find a job in sales. Even if the company you are currently working for goes out of business because of mismanagement or economic factors, you'll always be employable. After all, a salesperson is the only source of revenue a company ever has; basically, everyone else just adds to the company's overhead. In other words, a successful salesperson will never cost a company a penny—he or she will only produce money for that company.

Build Your Future

Yes, you can always find another job working for someone else—but there's more to life than being in someone else's employ, building someone *else's* dream. You can build your *own* dream and the dreams of those you love. You can be a successful business owner!

Surveys throughout the years have consistently shown that the number one dream of most people living in a free-enterprise society is to own their own business. Why? Aside from freeing oneself from the yoke of someone else's rule, there are three main reasons: money, time, and security.

Let's talk about the first reason, making more money. Most people realize that by and large, in order to make a significant amount of money you must be in business for yourself. (There are exceptions, of course, such as Michael Eisner of Disney.) After all, you'll never give yourself an earnings cap, will you? No, as a business owner, you'll be paid (or pay yourself) based on your *production*, not on what someone else believes your production to be worth.

The second reason is to have more time in your life to enjoy the things you want to do. Make no mistake about it, this will not happen right away! In the beginning your own business will take more time, blood, and sweat (and yes, maybe even tears) than any other *job* you've ever had. But sooner or later, if you choose the right type of business and can work efficiently and possibly even duplicate your efforts, you will have the kind of time that most people will never realize for themselves.

Security is reason number three. You will be secure in knowing you can never be fired because of someone else's opinion of you. You'll never be a victim of downsizing, rightsizing, or any other politically correct term today's large corporation uses to tell you "You're history."

Then Why Not?

So why doesn't everyone who wants more money, time, and security do what it takes to own his or her own business? Basically, for the same three reasons but with a *"no"* in front: no money, no time, and no security. There's one other reason as well, which will be the focus of this chapter: no specific knowledge about how to start a business.

Money is a concern for many people because they believe that any business worth going into takes a large amount of initial capital. They believe the only way to get the needed funds is to take a second mortgage on their homes or go begging in front of a bunch of stodgy, grim-faced bankers who will automatically deny their request. In other words they suffer from FEAR (*False Expectations Appearing Real*). Although it will always take *some* money to make more money, we'll look at how, via a home-based business, today's networking entrepreneur can begin his or her enterprise with very little startup capital.

Time, or lack of it, is the excuse many people will use for not starting their own business, when instead, it should be the reason. Many sideline businesses have been started in the garage by already busy aspiring entrepreneurs (Steven Jobs and Steve Wozniak—Apple Computer, Rich DeVos and Jay Van Andel—Amway Corporation, Henry Ford—Ford Motor Company) or literally on the kitchen table (Mary Nesmith—Liquid Paper, Mary Kay Ash—Mary Kay Cosmetics, Lillian Vernon—Lillian Vernon Corporation) and have turned into huge businesses.

How many times has someone said to you, "I'd love to go into a side business for myself and eventually go full time and get out of the rat race, but I just don't have the time. I don't have time for my family, for fun, for a side business, anything." However, if they continue doing what they're doing now, how do they expect to have any more time for their family and for fun 5 years from now? Therefore, if they eventually *want* to have more time, they'll have to *make* the time right now to do whatever it takes to get started on the road to freedom. We'll take a look at several options for today's "already too-busy networker."

Job Security or Job Insecurity?

Security is probably the most insidious reason of all. After all, if being employed by someone else is about the only thing we can be totally secure about, we have no security at all—whatsoever. Just ask all the former employees of "Big Blue" of Boca Raton, Florida. In 1994, a huge number of IBM (once known as the "layoff-proof company") employees, based in that South Florida location, were laid off permanently, and those that were not laid off were given the choice of uprooting their families' lives and moving to Houston, Texas, or Raleigh, North Carolina, to keep their jobs.

In my own Palm Beach County, Florida, 5000 men and women are employed at the United Technologies, Inc. subsidiary, Pratt & Whitney, a major defense contractor that manufactures jet and rocket engines via contract with the U.S. government. Throughout the county, whenever a government contract is about to expire and/or another is being bid upon, masses of well-paid engineers wonder if a short time later they will still be employed. The contract negotiations are front page news in the local newspapers and lead stories on the local nightly news.

The Numbers Are Staggering

Way back in May 1994, *Business Week* reported that there were 192,572 layoffs in the first quarter of that year—averaging over 2110 jobs cut from corporate America every day. The article continued by listing some of the *leaders* in this area and their individual body count since early 1991. The following list should go a long way toward changing the way we look at *"job security"* (the phrase itself is an oxymoron).

Company	Employees Laid Off
IBM	85,000
AT&T	83,500
General Motors	74,000
U.S. Postal Service	55,000
Sears	50,000
Boeing	30,000
NYNEX	22,000
Hughes Aircraft	21,000
GTE	17,000
Martin-Marrietta	15,000
DuPont	14,800
Eastman Kodak	14,000
Phillip Morris	14,000
Procter & Gamble	13,000
PharMor	13,000
Bank of America	12,000
Aetna	11,800
GE Aircraft Engines	10,250
McDonnell-Douglas	10,200
Bell South	10,200
Ford Motor Co.	10,000
Xerox	10,000
Pacific Telesis	10,000

Although the list above from several years back is used by many authors to illustrate the uncertainty of today's job market, the fact is, similar stats appear in the newspaper on a regular basis. As I'm writing this chapter, even the venerable Levi-Strauss has just announced a planned layoff of 10,000 to come in the next 2 weeks.

Believe me, security isn't the reason to *postpone* owning your own business; security is the reason to *start* your own business.

Home or Rented Office Space?

Owning a home-based business has many benefits as opposed to renting office space. The money you'll save on rent and a really short "commute" to your workplace are just a couple of the more obvious ones. There may be tax advantages, more flexibility in your daily schedule, closer contact with your family, and so forth. These days, with the computer technology that is now available and the latest in new office equipment, everything you need to run a business can literally be just a room away.

One word of caution however: Because your business is based in your home and all your equipment is there does not mean that home is where you are going to spend most of your time. Every other aspect of your business remains the same as one based out of a traditional office, including sales and marketing.

This point is brought "home" early in a book that is really a must-read for anyone whose job or business is home-based. Paul and Sarah Edwards are widely recognized as the "gurus" of the "working from home" industry. Their best-selling book, *Working from Home: Everything You Need to Know about Living and Working under the Same Roof* is considered by many to be the definitive book of this genre. In the book's introduction, the Edwards explain that one reason they named their book "Working *from* Home" instead of "Working *at* Home" is to emphasize that the home is simply the base of operations. According to the Edwards, they want "to communicate the importance of going out and reaching out to get business; participating in the broader professional and business community." This, of course, is accomplished in part by applying the principles we discuss throughout this book as well as those in many other books on the subject.

A Couple of Setup Points
Worth Noting

Before you take the big step and actually open your home-based business, you may want to heed the advice of Michael LeBoeuf. A home-based "micropreneur" and author of *The Perfect Business,* as well as six other books, Dr. LeBoeuf strongly advises checking out the legal aspects of your venture. He recommends specifically checking the local licensing and zoning ordinances to ensure that you are in compliance with the law.

As an acid test for determining whether you will likely encounter any challenges in this area, he suggests asking yourself the following question: *"Will the business change the character of the neighborhood in any way?"* In other words, will delivery trucks pull up to your home in the future; will walk-in customers have to park their cars; will noises, appearances, or any other distractions cause neighborhood disruption? According to Dr. LeBoeuf, from a legal standpoint the best home-based business is totally undetectable from the street.

Even in the event that the bureaucrats decide to make life difficult for you and deny you the right to operate your business from your home, one of the many great ideas in Dr. LeBoeuf's book helps you deal with that challenge: Get a business address at one of your local postal and shipping services, such as Mail Boxes Etc. The cost is low, and your business address can look as professional as any large business on Main St., while you acutally do business on *your street.*

Go with What You Know

First let's discuss your home-based business in terms of being full-time. All sorts of good books and magazines in the marketplace (see "Home-Based Business Resource" section at the end of this chapter) have lists of the different types of home-based businesses you can begin. These range from low-cost, one-person operations to well-known franchises. Types of businesses run the gamut from bookkeeping services to graphic design to carpet cleaning to "you-name-it," it's listed.

So what business should *you* go into? The first piece of advice any successful person will usually give is to do both what you enjoy and what you are already good at. Life is too precious to do for a living what we don't enjoy. That could even be one of the main reasons you've deciced to shelve the corporate life and go into business for yourself. Besides, when you do something you enjoy, you're bound to make more money in the long run anyway. We all have talents, knowledge, and abilities, some of which are, yes, actually *marketable!* Determine yours and let that help guide you into choosing your home-based business.

One point well worth emphasizing, however, is *marketability!* If the product or service you wish to market is not marketable (either a ready market or one you feel can be developed), don't even bother. You'll only frustrate yourself and lose money in the process. Even Thomas Edison, after failing to sell a machine that would electronically record votes during assembly (Congress didn't want it because it would lessen the ability to filibuster) vowed that he would never again invent a product that could not be sold.

But there is plenty out there to successfully market! Here are some examples of successful home businesses.

Trish Gardner (a former graphic designer working for a Minneapolis, Minnesota–based corporation) began her home-based business, Creativity Unlimited, Inc., a graphic design and marketing consulting firm, in the basement of her Apple Valley, Minnesota, home several years ago. She wanted to add to the family income while remaining a full-time mom to her two children (now four children). Trish combined her natural and learned abilities in this field with solid networking skills to build a very successful business which accomplished both her financial and family goals. She has since branched out considerably— although by choice she is still based out of her home—and is conducting leadership training seminars across the country.

Jim Puglise and his son Todd had a very profitable home-based computer software development firm called Information Management Systems. This very successful company develops software that provides statistics to hospitals, doctors, and government agencies throughout the United States. Jim's background was first in industrial psychology and then he worked as a personnel and compensation director for a large corporation. Todd was employed by a large firm that did basically what he and his father do today. Jim and Todd began their home-based venture 12 years ago in what was Todd's Miami boyhood bedroom. Their overhead in the business was very low and their income very high—the perfect home-based business for them. Several years ago, they grew so big they were forced to move into more conventional office space, where they continued to thrive. Just recently, Todd moved about 3 hours away to the town of Punta Gorda, Florida and, again, works right out of his home.

Carol Hall is a former administrative assistant for the news director of a West Palm Beach, Florida, network-affiliated television station. Sick of the normal hassles of the workplace, the less-than-sufficient paycheck, and the day-to-day commuting, she came up with a great idea based on a need she noticed in the marketplace, her knowledge of the business, and her desire to work out of her own home.

The employees in her station's news department often received telephone calls from viewers, attorneys, public relations people, and others requesting video copies of news stories in which their children, clients, etc., were featured. Since the station did not want to set up an internal department for charging a fee to duplicate and send these stories, Carol, who had an excellent relationship with her boss, as well as with other local stations, thought it was an idea she could successfully take on.

Based out of her spare bedroom, armed with six televisions and VCRs, and an ability to cultivate a network of endless referrals from two distinct television markets, Carol was able to quickly develop a successful news story duplication and sales business. She has now expanded into several out-of-area and out-of-state markets by networking with other media contacts she has developed, and she is on her way to making a lot of money while enjoying a nice lifestyle.

Ron Stahr, originally from Edmonton, Alberta, was a successful salesman for a commercial cleaning company in Dallas, Texas. After marrying Pam, however, and knowing that they would want to raise a family together, he realized that if he ever wanted to provide his loved ones with the comfortable lifestyle he envisioned, he would have to be in business for himself.

Ron and Pam moved to Florida, where Pam's parents resided, and the two entrepreneurs began Sunbelt Janitorial Services out of their bedroom. Eventually, Ron and Pam's *little* home-based business grew so large that they were forced to rent a huge office space to house their enterprise.

After several years of huge success (among the plaudits they received, Ron and Pam were featured on the cover of *Home Office Computing* magazine, which highlighted their business accomplishments), they sold their business, cashed out, and have moved to the country, to live "the good life" with their three children.

Gloria McCall was the number two sales producer nationally for AT&T when she decided to take her business private and home-based. She is now the proud owner–operator of TelAmerica U.S.A., Inc., a management and consulting firm dealing in long-distance network communication services all over the world and earning a very healthy six-figure income. However, shortly after opening her home-based business it was discovered that Gloria had cancer. She bravely fought back and is now serving as an inspiration to other women both in entrepreneurship and cancer recovery. Gloria plans to "cash out" her business over the next few years for well over several million dollars and she will be set for life. Even now she is writing a book about recovering from cancer. All this from her home-based office.

I began my speaking and writing business in my living room with the help of a telephone, file folder, and directory of associations to which I could market my services. Being a one man show allowed me to grow my business without the hassles of unnecessary overhead. As my business began to thrive, I eventually needed office space for my staff and for the many products that needed storing. However, my next goal is to buy a larger home and move the entire operation back to where I want to be...home sweet home!

The above are just a few examples of taking personal aptitudes, a desire for freedom, and a good potential marketplace, and creating the desired situation.

We Need the Following Three

Years ago, my Dad told me, "Whether you go into business for yourself or not, it is vital to have three professionals in your life that you absolutely know you can trust; a lawyer, an accountant, and an insurance agent." There are others as well that we could mention—a banker, financial advisor, mechanic, and so forth—but I believe what Dad said is correct. The first three can go a long way toward helping us achieve our financial goals as well as keeping us out of serious financial trouble.

So as you begin to research, organize, and form your business, start to ask others with whom you have a "know you, like you, trust you relationship" for referrals to qualified lawyers, accountants, and insurance professionals. (For the purpose of discussing your home-based business, we're talking about insurance in the form of health and other *business*-related matters; however, it's also important to be sure you have coverage on your entire estate and to set up a good long-term financial plan.) A good idea is to make sure all the above-named professionals have experience working with small or, even better, specifically *home-based* businesses. Remember, we are living more and more in an age of specialists.

After you have narrowed your choices to just a few candidates, get references and *call* those references. It's better to discover problems now than in the future. You can, of course, switch to someone new if the need ever arises, but by that time the costs in both money and time can be devastating.

One more thing. Before retaining someone's services, let her or him in on your personal business goals and what you want to accomplish. Be as certain as you can that the person's general philosophies meet yours and that he or she will prove to be an asset to and extension of your business. Remember, *you* are the potential client and have a right to get as much information as *you* deem necessary.

Home-Based Office Equipment

Running a business involves two main areas—the *urgent* and the *important!* The important areas are those that produce income. These areas include sales, marketing, networking, and doing the technical work (i.e., the graphic artist doing the actual artwork) made possible by the previous three. However, the urgent areas include anything that *must* be done—and usually within a specific time frame—yet which does not go directly toward bringing in the income.

This would include, but is not limited to, bookkeeping, sending out correspondence, and other types of office management. In a traditional, larger business there is a support staff of secretaries, bookkeepers, etc. who are employed to handle those specific tasks. The home-based business owner, who must keep overhead as low as possible, usually will need to handle these matters, at least at the beginning. Fortunately, modern technology has made it possible to accomplish all this solo, if necessary, as long as that person is willing to work smart.

Thus, understanding the equipment necessary to begin operating your home-based enterprise is important, and many outstanding books and tapes (several listed in the resource section at the conclusion of this chapter) address this subject. It's obvious to almost everyone, however, that the first piece of equipment we must purchase and learn to use is a computer. This was once a very scary thought for me, as it is for others, but it's vital to get over that fear and proceed with the learning.

The Computer Is Here to Stay...Make It an Asset

With the help of someone who can teach you and with a bit of practice, practically anyone can learn enough to use this tool to their advantage. I say that because if *I* can learn enough about how to use a computer to get by, *anyone else can too.* Best of all, the further advanced our technology becomes, the more user-friendly the computer becomes as well.

As a home-based business owner, whether you are alone, or even if you have an assistant, most of the organizational work is going to fall into your hands. With working knowledge of your computer, you won't become so dominated by the paperwork (the urgent) that you are kept from doing what you are supposed to be doing—selling your products/services and/or doing the work that actually produces the income—(the important).

Jim Barber is a home-based business owner who writes, speaks, and consults internationally on computer technology and personal development. Although Jim is an extremely humorous and interesting speaker, I asked him for some "straight to the point" answers regarding questions the home-based business owner/novice computer user might have:

BOB: How important is the computer to today's home-based business owner?

JIM: Bob, without an effective computer system, it's doubtful that any small or home-based business could even function. Granted, in the past it was a luxury; but today, the computer is as indispensable as a telephone or a stapler.

BOB: What can a computer do for the home-based business owner?

JIM: It offers a wide range of opportunities, and its uses are continually growing. For example, computers are incredibly effective in organizing data, so one major use is information management. You can organize information on clients, prospects, employees, inventory, sales, projects, finances, or almost anything else you can think of.

BOB: You mentioned finances. Is accounting still an important use of computers?

JIM: Absolutely! Computer-based accounting has been a fundamental use of computers since their earliest days. But the next major step will be in electronic fund transfers, paying for all types of items by computer. There are still some security issues that are being worked out, but the computer will revolutionize how we buy products just as credit cards did a couple of decades ago.

BOB: What are some of the other uses that most of us don't naturally think about?

JIM: The computer is rapidly developing into a research tool of unprecedented power. Today's business people can keep entire libraries of information at their offices. And information that they don't have is easily accessible from remote locations. A person no longer needs to be physically close to the source of information. We can do research halfway around the world *more easily* than going to our local library.

BOB: That's fascinating on the inbound side—that is, getting the information we want. How does the computer strengthen our capacity for communicating with others?

JIM: Communication is becoming very exciting! E-mail (electronic mail) is generally cheaper and faster than its alternatives. And the extra capabilities that e-mail offers, such as transferring pictures, sound, and video, are only just starting to be used. Other forms of technology, like the telephone and fax machine, probably won't be replaced by the computer, but they will be controlled by tomorrow's computer systems.

BOB: It all sounds great, Jim. Is there a downside?

JIM: Computers not only offer undreamed opportunities to the home-based business person, they also bring unexpected difficulties. Among the problems at this time are loss of data and attacks by viruses. Probably the biggest challenge though, is in keeping current with the rapid advances in technology.

You see, today's "cutting edge" computer system will be merely adequate within a couple of years and totally obsolete within 5 years. Software requires upgrading, sometimes more often than the actual hardware. But that's not the biggest problem. As a computer's hardware and software become obsolete, so does the user's knowledge of how to use them.

BOB: So, what's the solution?

JIM: Training! A computer, like any other tool, is useless unless you know how to use it well. The computer is a marvelous tool, and it offers many opportunities and capabilities to today's home-based business owner. But knowing how to use those capabilities requires almost continual training. The smart businessperson recognizes the need to become—and stay—computer literate.*

Take That First Step

What we did at Burg Communications was to find an excellent computer consultant (through referrals of course) and let that person take us from A to Z, helping us to choose and buy our computers, printers, the needed software, etc., and then train us to use the entire system. It wasn't always fun, but definitely worth it, in how it has added so positively to our business.

What other equipment is needed to help your business flow? Besides a workable desk, chairs, filing cabinet(s), and other standard items in addition to anything specific to your particular business, a copying machine and fax machine has now become a necessity in order to be able to communicate at as fast a pace as your competition.

Again, whether through a local consultant or by reviewing information from some of the resources at the end of this chapter, be sure that the equipment you choose is well in line with your current (and

---

*Jim Barber has authored 16 books on computers, which have been sold in over a dozen countries. Useful information about home-based businesses can be found in Jim's on-line newsletter *The Barber Shop* (http://www.thebarbershop.com).

future) needs and budget. Also, whether to lease this equipment or buy is a decision to be made by both you and your accountant or financial advisor.

Telephones, Answering Machines, and Voice Mail— Your Most Important Links

In her wonderful book, *Working Solo,* Terry Lonier had this to say about telephones and answering machines:

> These two basic pieces of office equipment are at the heart of your solo business. They have an impact on every facet of your business, including the image you project, the quality of your daily operations, and your abilities to expand and grow. When right, they let the world know you are a professional, in control of your business, and able to deliver a quality product or service. When wrong, they give the impression that your business is in disarray or may not be serious or trustworthy...potential disasters for your business.

Earlier in this book we talked about using the telephone as an important prospecting and networking tool. As a home-based business owner, you'll most likely discover that your phone skills will become a driving force in making your business a success. According to Edna Sheedy, author of *Start and Run a Profitable Home-Based Business,* "Statistics show that *Homepreneurs* conduct 90 percent of their business by telephone." That figure may not pertain to your particular business, but the importance of mastering your skills in that area cannot be overestimated.

Telephone Technique—a Key to Your Home-Based Business Success

One key technique when using the telephone as a relationship-building tool is voice intonation. This is a relatively simple concept but, like many of the simple things in life, not always easy. This goes beyond just using voice inflection so as not to sound monotone. We already know that boring a prospect to death is *not* good. Basically, we are talking about varying your voice in order to correctly respond—and show respect—to the other person. For instance, although we usually want to be positive and upbeat over the telephone, there are times when, based on the other person's challenges or situation, we need to sound more subdued. If they speak softly we want to tone down our volume a bit. If your prospect or client is very relationship-oriented, then adjusting your tone from very businesslike to more touchy-feely is definitely a good idea.

Effective voice intonation is a skill worth cultivating into a habit, as are many other aspects of using the telephone effectively. I recommend that you invest in books, tapes, newsletters (see the resource section at end of chapter) and seminars on telephone skills in order to learn more about this vital home-based business "tool" as well as to continually "sharpen your ax in this area." To continually refine and improve your telephone skills, you may want to subscribe to Art Sobczak's "Telephone Selling Report," an excellent newsletter dealing with all aspects of this topic.

By the way, as with any effective tool, the telephone is meant not to replace but to work hand-in-hand with other techniques and technologies. Make sure your picture appears on any correspondence you send. If your prospect or client knows you only by voice, it's imperative that they see your face as much as possible, in a natural way such as on postcard notes and scratch pads as discussed earlier in the book (Chapter 4).

In The Age of Communication, Still *More* Tools

Answering machines, voice mail, and other forms of professional telephone answering and message taking are vital components of your business. After all, your business probably requires travel and being away from your home office; in addition, if you are your only employee, what happens if you're on the telephone with a prospect or client and another call comes in?

I must say that, personally, I am not a fan of live answering services. Please excuse the generalization, and surely, there are many excellent ones in operation today providing very good service. I myself, however, haven't come across more than just a few. And it makes sense when analyzed. Remember that in Chapter 10 regarding customer service, it was explained why the people who answer the phone are so vitally important to your company; they, in fact, represent your company to anyone who calls and are your company's ambassador to all callers— especially those first-time callers who may not know you, and will judge your company from that first call.

Now, imagine a person who is making a fairly low wage, who may not have had a lot of training, and who isn't even *your* employee, answering your phone. Do you think they will feel motivated to ensure that you look good to the caller? Probably not! Should it be that way? Of course not; everyone should do their best at all times. We are talking about the real world, however, and cannot leave our company's fate to chance.

Two Workable Choices

So, let's consider the alternatives. Answering machines are still the best known. Although new features with great benefits are being added continually, the purpose of answering machines is solely to take messages for you when you can't pick up. The only negative is that answering machines may make you appear to be the small company you are. This is not necessarily bad, unless you feel, as a positioning tool, that you should appear bigger, which is often a good idea.

Voice mail is another approach. The right system can make you look very professional, well-established, and large. It gives you and your caller many options, usually by having the caller continually *punch in numbers.* Can you tell by the italics that I personally do not like being answered by voice mail and having to punch in numbers to get to the right people or information?

Well, that's the negative. Many people don't like it. It can be a very frustrating experience for a prospect or current client to be unable to get a warm voice on the telephone. Thus, while voice mail provides you with a very professional image, you need to be very careful to make it as user-friendly as possible. But in this case "user-friendly" doesn't mean easy to use...it means pleasant to use!

In *Working Solo* (see resource section at the end of the chapter) Terry Lonier gives a rundown of the various types, features, benefits, and uses associated with today's telephones, answering machines, and voice mail products, as well as practically every other piece of office equipment you may ever need.

One Last Thought
Regarding the Computer
(and Other Technical
"Stuff")

It's probably worthwhile advice for any of us (especially yours truly) who have been resistant to letting the computer intrude too much into our lives to stay as updated as possible regarding this technology and the related networking and marketing trends. This so at best, we can have use of the same tools as our competitors, and at worst, we don't get left in the dust.

Choosing a Company Name

In Chapter 9 we discussed how to position yourself as the expert (and only logical resource) in your field. Every technique discussed in that chapter, of course, will also work for you in your home-based business. The only new thought I want to introduce is choosing a name for your company.

Remember, as a home-based business owner, you'll want to accomplish the most possible with your available, if somewhat limited, resources. Do you recall the benefit statement you created to describe how what you do will either help your prospects to get something they want or solve a problem they have? In the same way, your business name should convey the nature of your business and, if possible, its benefit to the prospect.

A supplier of mine, as well as dear friend, Janita Cooper, is CEO of Master Duplicating Corporation. Her company duplicates audio and video tapes, and packages them, for some of the most successful speakers in the world. Although her business is not home-based (it's large, with lots of employees and large duplicating machines that wouldn't fit too well inside a home), something she once said to me explained very simply and effectively why the name of your business is so important.

I asked her how she came up with the name Master Duplicating. She replied, "I could have named it `Janita's company,' but no one would have known what line of work I was in." Good point. By the same token, the name "Master Duplicating" tells anyone in her niche market, mainly professional speakers, exactly what she does.

To Use, or Not to Use Your Name...That Is The Question

There are two schools of thought regarding the use of your own name as part of your business name. Some people say that it is simply ego and will only take away from the message you want to convey. Others feel that putting your own name on the masthead inspires trust. In other words, "Hey buddy, I'm gonna treat you right because my name is on the line." Go in whichever direction you feel comfortable.

So, depending on the nature of your business and how specific you can get, think of a name that is recognizable, memorable, and carves as much of a niche in your prospects' or potential referral sources' mind as possible. One example might be Dave Smith. He is about to start a residential cleaning service.

Dave could name his business "The Dave Smith Company." That, of course, wouldn't work any better than the aforementioned "Janita's Company." A better name might be "Smith's Residential Cleaning Service." But this name does nothing to separate Dave's cleaning service from anyone else's cleaning service. Let's take this one more step and call it, "White Glove Professional Residential Cleaning Service."

What does this name accomplish? First, it tells what the business does. Second, it paints a picture of a job well done. After all, can't you just picture your home being so clean that it passes the "white glove test"? Yes, the word *professional* is overused, but so what? It still adds to the message.

An excellent book that deals with both company names and benefit statements is *Seven Second Marketing*. In this book, networking authority Dr. Ivan Misner teaches, by way of hundreds and hundreds of various real-world examples, what types of names can work best for whatever business one happens to own or be involved in. Many of the names either provide their own effective benefit statement or naturally tie in with one. I found it very helpful.

Use Every Advantage to Your Advantage

No, I didn't take that saying from Yogi Berra, although it does sound like something he might say. The point is, most home-based business owners don't realize the incredible advantage they have over the huge, big-budgeted corporations. *What?* you might be thinking. *How can you say I have an advantage over companies that are so much bigger with a lot more money to spend?*

In their book, *Guerrilla Marketing for the Home-Based Business,* Jay Levinson and Seth Godin make a very interesting point. Because of the size and inherent bureaucracy of a big business, it can't possibly offer the flexibility and accountability of the CEO like your business can. The authors also mentioned the importance of personal service: "When a company hires ad agency Ogilvy and Mather, it doesn't get to work directly with master ad man David Ogilvy. But your clients get your full attention. That's a key selling point for a home-based business."

Take Care of Those Who Take Care of You

As a home-based business owner, and most likely on a smaller budget than most larger businesses, every relationship-building advantage you can cultivate will help you get an edge on your bigger, fatter, and better established competitors. Here's one idea that bucks convention but will come back to you in a positive way throughout your years in business: Pay your suppliers on time, especially other small businesses that depend on immediate cash flow.

It's one thing to wait until the last minute to pay your electric bill. As long as it's paid on time, you're okay, and you can be sure the person opening the envelope isn't going to take it personally. It's quite another thing to hold off on paying your local small printer, graphic designer, or secretarial service which quickly produced a big job for you.

First of all, paying these people on time is the *right* thing to do. They need their money on a timely basis in order to pay *their* bills. Second, you can bet they'll be more likely to go out of their way for you in the event you need something done fast or extra, if they know you consistently pay on time. From personal experience, I can tell you that we at Burg Communications get special treatment from our vendors and suppliers because of our "quick pay" policy. And whenever we've needed credit references, they were only too pleased to give us a fine recommendation.

And yes, there were times, especially in those first few years, when things got tough and the money just wasn't in the coffers. But we always made it a point to keep communication with our vendors totally open, pay as much as we could, and always show them the proper respect (such as returning their phone calls or, usually, calling them first to apprise them of our situation) while paying off our debts.

Treat Everyone with Respect...It Will Pay Big Dividends

One more thing—and I believe so many business owners, both large and small, "miss the boat" when it comes to the following, mainly through a combination of ego and just plain not thinking—treat your suppliers or potential suppliers with the same courtesy and respect that you would treat your customers and clients. How many times have you witnessed this situation: The person taking the call has the most pleasant voice in the world, ready and eager to serve. Until, that is, he or she realizes the person on the phone wants to, yes, *sell them something.*

Suddenly this person's mannerisms, body language, and voice change to become almost rigid, maybe even snooty and standoffish, just waiting for the opportunity to sternly communicate that he is not interested or is "too busy" to speak right now. Does it really feel good to treat someone disrespectfully?

I was horrified recently while in the office of an acquaintance who owns a very successful real estate firm. In the middle of our conversation, he was buzzed by his assistant who told him he had a phone call. He took the call, listened for all of about two seconds, and then, to my shock, barked, "not interested," and, with a disgusted look, slammed the phone in the person's ear. He then said to me, "those salespeople are just so annoying."

I'm thinking to myself, *Pal, what exactly are you...a salesman!* Here's a guy who makes a great living for his family as a salesperson. He's a man who on his way to success and now as the owner of a business surely has had a lot of phones slammed in *his* ear, and now he's doing the exact same thing to some other guy who's working just as hard to make a living and support *his* family. Aside from just not thinking things through, I believe ego truly comes into play as well in many of these situations. Let me explain.

For years we as salespeople have been put off, rejected, and had phones slammed in our ear by our prospects. It can hurt emotionally. Now, however, we are the one—the special—the unattainable—the prospect! Finally, we have the *right* to be just as rude to this poor salesperson as our prospects have been, and maybe continue to be, to us. Of course, having the *right* to do something and doing the *right thing* are often entirely different.

Certainly, I don't agree with that philosophy, and I'm not even sure that rationalization is conscious. But it happens every day, doesn't it? Well, not only is this the incorrect way to treat another human being, it is also bad business. We never know when that person, or someone that person knows, may be in a position to introduce us to someone with whom we can do a lot of business. Please keep this in mind as your time becomes more and more sought after by salespeople.

What about dealing with a supplier? Yes, at times you may have to send some work back because it did not meet your standards. Or, maybe the estimated price or time of delivery just won't work for you for a certain assignment. We deal with those situations all the time. But always with respect! In fact, it's a joke now at our printers that the people at Burg Communications can be the "finnikiest" clients they have and sometimes a real "pain in the neck" (probably not their exact words), but that we're so polite, they never really mind.

How to Afford to Start Your Own Home-Based Business

Before moving on to discuss a couple of excellent home-based business opportunities that you can start with very little capital, I want to bring up a question we touched on earlier in the chapter. That is the question of money, and how to come up with enough of it to begin a more traditional type of business even though it will still be run from your home. Obviously, most people cannot afford to simply give up the job they now have to strike out on their own. There are options, however, even though the gratification of full-time home-based business ownership may have to be delayed for just a bit.

The following advice and options are taken directly from Paul and Sarah Edwards's excellent book/resource, *Working from Home* under the heading, "Six Plans for Starting a Home Business" (my comments are in parenthesis).

1. *The moonlighting plan.* Keep your full-time job and develop your business as a sideline. When it takes off, you can go full-time. Be sure to work at least 8 hours a week on a sideline business. (*Or whatever it takes.*)

2. *The part-time plan.* Work a part-time job to provide a base income while you're building up the business. When your business equals the base income, drop the part-time job.

3. *The spin-off plan.* Turn your previous employer into your first major customer or, when ethically possible, take a major client with you from your previous job. (*That's one great reason to be the best employee you can possibly be while having to work for someone else.*)

4. *The cushion plan.* Find a financial resource to support yourself with while you start your business. Your cushion should be large enough to cover your base expenses for at least 6 to 12 months. Time can be another cushion. You might start a business while on sabbatical or leave.

5. *The piggyback plan.* If you have a working spouse or partner, cut back your expenses so you can live on one salary until your business gets going.

6. *The have-your-clients-finance-you plan.* If you have sufficient stature in your field, you might obtain retainer contracts with clients for the first year that provide you with assured revenue in exchange for offering them services at 25 percent less than the billing rate you establish.

Sure, maybe none of those options are as inviting as just going for it right now. In fact, none of these suggestions by Paul and Sarah might be something you *want* to do. They are good suggestions though. And, if one of them is your most viable option, and your dream for home-based business ownership is big enough, you'll make yourself do it.

Meanwhile, two businesses in particular are most definitely better off begun on a part-time basis, and won't cost much to begin, but in time can provide you with an income and lifestyle that most people will never know.

Nontraditional, Home-Based Businesses That Can Work for You!

Network marketing (also known as *multilevel marketing* or MLM), and *mail order* (or *direct marketing*) are two great part-time home-based businesses that can eventually lead into very lucrative, full-time businesses. Both, however, often are associated with two false notions. One is that the businesses are get-rich-quick opportunities (they're not). The other is that success is limited to only those lucky few (it isn't). Both, however, do take hard work, ability to learn specific success systems, and lots of persistence. Which sounds only fair, doesn't it?

Over the next couple of chapters we'll look at each of these two dynamic home-based businesses. We'll destroy some myths, build a foundation, and then lead you in the right direction to making either of them part of your successful home-based business future, if you so choose.

Key Points

People dream of owning their own businesses for three reasons: to have more money, more time, and more security. It may be scary, but owning your own business can be the most rewarding undertaking in the world.

- What business should you go into? Go with what you know. Ask yourself:
  1. Is it something I enjoy doing?
  2. Am I good at it?
  3. Is it marketable? Will others pay for my product or service?
- It is vitally important to have three professionals you absolutely trust: a lawyer, an accountant, and an insurance agent.
- Check out the legal aspects of your venture, particularly local licensing and zoning ordinances.

- Name your business something that is immediately and easily identifiable. Even better is if the benefit to your prospect is within your name.

- Choose equipment in keeping with your needs and budget. A computer is essential. You'll also need a desk, comfortable chairs, filing cabinet(s), copying machine, fax machine, telephones, and answering machine, as well as anything specific to your particular business.

- Treat everyone with respect. Treat your suppliers or potential suppliers with the same courtesy and respect that you would treat your customers and clients.

- If you cannot afford to leave your present employment to set up your home-based business, consider options such as starting part-time.

RESOURCE GUIDE

The following resources are a partial list to get you started. I suggest that you seek out additional resources continually.

Books

Arden, Lynie: *The Work at Home Source Book*. Boulder, Colorado, Live Oak Publications, 1996.

D'Arcangelo, David: *Wealth Starts at Home*. New York, McGraw-Hill, 1997.

Edwards, Paul, and Sarah Edwards: *Working from Home*. New York, Tarcher/Putnam, 1994.

Edwards, Paul, and Sarah Edwards: *Finding Your Perfect Work*. New York, Tarcher/Putnam, 1996.

Edwards, Paul, and Sarah Edwards: *Secrets of Self-Employment*. New York, Tarcher/Putnam, 1996.

Edwards, Paul, and Sarah Edwards: *Best Home Businesses for the 90's*. New York, Tarcher/Putnam, 1997.

Edwards, Paul, and Sarah Edwards: *Making Money with Your Computer at Home*. New York, Tarcher/Putnam, 1997.

Edwards, Paul, Sarah Edwards, and Rick Benzel: *Teaming Up*. New York, Tarcher/Putnam, 1997.

Edwards, Paul, Sarah Edwards, and Laura Clampitt-Douglas: *Getting Business to Come to You*. New York, Tarcher/Putnam, 1998.

Edwards, Paul, Sarah Edwards, and Walter Zooi: *Home Businesses You Can Buy*. New York, Tarcher/Putnam, 1997.

Goss, Frederick D.: *Success in Newsletter Publishing, a Practical Guide*. Arlington, VA, Newsletter Publishers Association, 1993.

LeBoeuf, Michael: *The Perfect Business*. New York, Simon & Schuster, 1996.

Levinson, Jay, and Seth Godin: *Guerrilla Marketing for the Home-Based Business.* New York, Houghton Mifflin, 1995.

Lonier, Terry: *The Frugal Entrepreneur.* New Paltz, NY, Portico Press, 1996.

Lonier, Terry: *Working Solo.* New Paltz, NY, Portico Press, 1994.

Mancuso, Joseph R.: *How to Write a Winning Business Plan.* Englewood Cliffs, NJ, Prentice Hall, 1990.

Matusky, Gregory, and the Philip Lief Group: *The Best Home-Based Franchises.* New York, Doubleday, 1992.

Other Publications

Entrepreneur Magazine, 2392 Morse Ave., Irvine, CA 92614 (714-261-2325); also by *Entrepreneur Magazine: Starting and Running Your Homebased Business* (800-421-2300).

Entrepreneur's Home Office Magazine, 2392 Morse Avenue, Irvine, CA 92614 (714-261-2325).

Home Business Magazine, 9582 Hamilton Ave., Suite 368, Huntington Beach, CA 92646 (714-968-0331).

Home Office Computing, 411 Lafayette Street, New York, NY 10003 (800-288-7812).

Success Magazine, 733 Third Ave., New York, NY 10017 (800-234-7324).

Telephone Selling Report, 5301 S. 144th St., Omaha, NE 68137 (402-895-9399).

Wealth Building, 15738 South Bell Rd., Suite 200, Lockport, IL 60441 (708-429-4444).

Working at Home (published by *Success Magazine*), 733 Third Ave., New York, NY 10017 (800-234-7324).

Working Solo Newsletter, P.O. Box 190, New Paltz, NY 12561 (914-255-7165).

13

Network Marketing... The Last Bastion of Free Enterprise?

(And Definitely *Not* a Pyramid)

There are still plenty of people here in North America and around the world who are not familiar with network marketing. There are even more people who at one time or another were exposed to this industry and, because of the circumstances (an unqualified person who showed their company's marketing plan to them, a next door neighbor with an opinion based on hearsay, etc.), don't really understand how it works, but *think* they do. By the way, I'll explain a bit later in the chapter why network marketing is *absolutely not* (according to the Federal Trade Commission) a pyramid.

One of the advantages of choosing network marketing as a part-time business is that it is very inexpensive to become involved. Usually, for somewhere between $100 and $500, you can be on your way with enough initial products and business building tools (tapes, books, prospecting literature, etc.) to get you off to a good start. Don't let the low financial investment fool you, however. To be successful in this venture, you'll need to treat it as though you invested hundreds of thousands of dollars to get started. In other words, train yourself to see the "big picture" from the very start.

People get into this business for the same reason they would involve themselves in any other home-based business—freedom! They'd like to make more money, have more time to enjoy it, and develop a sense of financial security. And for those willing to do what it takes to achieve that lifestyle, it's very possible. What distinguishes network marketing from other businesses, however, is the opportunity for *anyone* to be able to build a residual-based income.

Residual income, also called *passive* income, is simply money that continues to roll in *after* the work is already done. Alan Alda has probably made more money from his M*A*S*H syndication residuals, or royalties, than he was paid while the show was in production. It's reported that singer-songwriter Paul Anka was paid $1000 per week in passive, residual income during the 25 + years the *Tonight Show* starred Johnny Carson. Why? Well, it seems Mr. Anka composed a little tune that was played at the opening of every show, while Ed McMahon introduced the guests, and continued through "Here's Johnny!" If you've ever seen that show, you're familiar with the tune called "Johnny's Theme."

Network marketing is one of the few businesses which allows someone other than an entertainer or author to earn money long after the original work is completed. Yes, there are other businesses in which there is a certain amount of passive income involved, but not usually to the extent of network marketing.

Network marketing is based on three concepts: personal consumption, merchandising, and duplication. Let's look at all three:

1. *Consumption.* Since any network marketing company needs products and/or services running throughout the organization in order for the company and its independent distributors to make money, consumable items are a key to long-term success. Depending upon the company, this will include, but certainly not be limited to, vitamins, supplements, cleaning products (household and personal), cosmetics, and, of course, much more.

A product line based on consumable products ensures that the distributor doesn't have to spend extra money in order to consume the products; they will simply redirect their already fixed expenses to purchase from their *own* business. (Depending upon the company, ordering is typically through catalogs, the Internet, and soon, directly from the television.) Doesn't that just make sense? If you can buy plastic bags, shampoo, makeup, paper towels, etc., from your own business, why support the local supermarket? Depending upon the company's accounting system, dollars the distributor spends on these items may be translated into points and a monthly bonus paid according to the percentage earned by that distributor.

2. *Merchandising.* Simply another word for selling. A distributor has a choice of whether to merchandise a little or a lot. While this is a good way to earn money while developing your organization, and is always a good source of added income, it's not the way to build a profitable, long-term business based on residual income: The reason is that if you sell to a person once, your income from that person is based on whether she or he continues to buy from you after that one purchase. Most successful network marketers are not as interested in that as they are in the next concept.

3. *Duplication.* This is where, as they say, "the rubber meets the road." Duplication simply means showing other people how to do exactly what you're doing; consuming, merchandising a little or a lot, and duplicating your efforts by sharing the opportunity with others.

When you *sponsor* people (they don't become your employees, but, like you, they are independent contractors) into your network marketing business, it is now your responsibility to teach them the steps discussed above. As they consume (by simply redirecting their already fixed expenses) the products or utilize the services provided or brokered by the parent company and merchandise a little or a lot, they will earn points and a monthly bonus similar to yours. The good news is that since you introduced them into the business, the parent company rewards you by adding their volume to yours, thereby upping your total point volume, increasing both your bonus percentage and the amount of the bonus check you receive.

Now, teach them how to sponsor other people into the business, just as you sponsored them. As they sponsor people who consume from their own business (again—simply by redirecting their already fixed expenses), the company will reward them by adding their distributor's volume to theirs, increasing both their bonus percentage and amount of the bonus check they will receive. More good news: All that new volume also gets added to yours, increasing both your bonus percentage and the amount of the bonus check you will receive.

Keep personally sponsoring new people, while helping those in your organization to sponsor others. And teach those distributors throughout your organization to continually teach this pattern to the people throughout *their* organization, and in time you can develop an absolutely huge residual income, while helping others to do the same. In fact, probably the greatest service this business provides is that the only way for you to be successful is to help others become successful along the way.

This is the basic concept and setup of a networking marketing organization. Different companies deal in different products and services, are set up differently in organizational structure, and offer different compensation plans, ideally leading to where the distributor will begin to earn residual income. It's up to you to decide which will work best for you. Research some of the companies that have been in business for awhile and have a *proven* track record. Also, attend several company or distributor-sponsored opportunity meetings and see what kind of a feeling you get regarding the people involved with that company or particular distributor organization.

Network Marketing Tools (Books, Tapes, Seminars, Major Events, Voice Mail, Prospecting Literature, Etc.)

Fortunately, business-building tools for the network marketing business abound. When researching a particular company, learn about its inventory of these types of resources. Some companies produce their own training materials or distribute those produced by others. They will then, through their lines of distribution, teach you how to effectively use these tools in order to profitably build your business.

Certain companies are more effective at providing the infrastructure (including, but not limited to, establishing licensing with international and state governments, warehousing, and shipping products, handling accounting and paying bonus checks), and their distributor organizations provide their own tools and training system. Most notably, Amway would fall into that category. The Amway Corporation, over the years, has become more of a servicing corporation to its distributor affiliates, providing access to major manufacturers and most of the *Fortune 500* companies, as well as setting up a business infrastructure in over 80 countries.

From Humble Beginnings to a Vast Empire

Amway, founded in a garage in 1959 by budding entrepreneurs and boyhood friends Rich DeVos and Jay Van Andel, has always been, and almost certainly will always be, a family-owned-and-operated business. Over the last couple of years the day-to-day operations of the company has been placed in the hands of the next generation. Steve Van Andel is now Chairman of the Board and Dick DeVos is

President, and most of the other offspring are also involved. The two families run their operation with class and pride.

Whereas the Amway Corporation provides a phenomenal infrastructure from which its distributors can benefit and does provide some company-sponsored events, most of the successful distributors look to their "upline" (ancestry of sponsorship) leadership for continuing business-building information. In this setup, several major distributor organizations have expertly set up their own training "systems" complete with every type of business-building tool imaginable to help their distributors grow their business. Within these major "system" organizations are hundreds and hundreds of "Diamond" organizations, many of whom I have the pleasure of working with as clients, and each one will follow with a slight variation the proven success system they "plug into."

It's an incredibly effective system which has resulted in Amway being the leader in its field ($7.4 billion in sales worldwide in 1996).* People currently joining these Amway "system" groups are building their businesses faster and more profitably than ever before in the company's history.

Other Companies Produce Their Own Tools

In contrast, another client of mine, a network marketing company called The Peoples Network (TPN), provides its own training tools as part of its product line. Interestingly enough, the main product line was originally based on a complete schedule of motivational, informational, self-improvement, and financial television programming, featuring many of the top authorities in each of those fields. And the company's founders, Jeff Olson and Eric Worre, provide training seminars once a week that their distributors can watch and enjoy in the comfort of their own homes.

How is that possible? Because TPN, which at the time of this writing had recently formed a joint venture with PrimeStar Partners, provides its distributors with a satellite dish with access to over 160 channels. The main channel features TPN's very own productions, which include 24 hours of the type of positive programming mentioned in the last paragraph, and distributor training. Most of these programs are produced at TPN's own studios. Although these shows are still a significant part of its product line, the company is continually devel-

---

*Michael S. Clouse, "Business Is Booming!" *Upline,* 1996.

oping and distributing more and more consumable and durable goods.

Aside from the actual televised sessions led by Olson and Worre, distributor training is accomplished through teaching tools produced by the company itself, which distributors can order through a tool catalog, by attending conventions called "Masterminds" (based on a chapter of the classic *Think and Grow Rich* by Napoleon Hill) and, again, via TPN's own channel on PrimeStar.

I've featured just two of the many excellent companies representative of this industry, discussing their relationships between company and distributor training. In researching other companies, you'll notice that some provide training internally and others don't have any set "system" of their own but direct their distributors to where they can purchase the needed tools.

The Unofficial Newsletter of the MLM Industry

Upline is the best-known independent magazine/newsletter in the network marketing industry (there are others as well—see Resources at end of chapter). Each month it is filled with information on how to build your business, tools you can use in order to more effectively prospect, and resources of books and tapes from authors both within and outside the industry that can help you achieve your goals.

Upline's team, including Founding Editor John Fogg, author of *The Greatest Networker in the World*, Publisher Randolph Byrd, Chief Executive Officer Graham Anthony, and Editor-in-Chief Michael Clouse, have done a marvelous job in building the image of network marketing, and creating alliances with magazines such as *Success*, which have further publicized this growing industry.

Network Marketing Myths

Because of the dramatic changes that have taken place in this industry over the past 40-odd years as well as the general confusion among the public as to what this industry truly is and does, network marketing myths abound regarding what types of companies and what types of products and/or services are best to become involved with. The following are just a few of the major myths you'll want to keep in mind as you do your due diligence and fact checking.

Myth 1. It's best to get in on the ground floor. This is probably the most outrageous and most believed of all the fallacies of network marketing. Although, in all fairness and before analysis, the myth would seem to make sense. After all, isn't it the people on the ground floor who make all the money? The answer is no for a couple of reasons.

First of all, such an infinitesimal number of these ground floor opportunities ever actually get off the ground (never mind making it long-term) that the chances are you'll never make a significant amount of money with such a company anyway. And if you do make a bunch at first, once the company goes out of business you'll be back to square one. The only residual you'll see to that opportunity is a lack of confidence, if not distrust, in you by all the people whom you were able to involve in your organization.

Second, if the biggest selling point regarding your opportunity is that "it's ground floor," how are you going to interest people after the ground floor factor is gone? In other words, the benefit of the ground floor opportunity cannot be duplicated. As Amway Crown Ambassador Tim Foley says: "It's not *when* you get in, it's what you do when you get in."

Myth 2. Network marketing has reached the point of saturation. Actually, due to the number of people 18 years old and older entering the workforce and the growing number of foreign countries open for business (125 as of this writing!), the network marketing industry seems less saturated now than it ever has been. In addition, as network marketing continues to create success stories, more and more people who just a few years ago would never have even considered becoming involved in this business are now eager to get started and create the lifestyle they want. The biggest reason, however, that this industry can never become saturated, is that to succeed it takes hard work and persistence, and many people simply aren't willing to put forth these two traits.

Myth 3. The prices of products for consumption should be significantly less expensive than those I can buy from the store or as inexpensive as the discount stores. Actually, the more one understands about how network marketing works, the more one realizes that, although prices should be competitive with retail store prices, substantially discounted prices on your products would do more harm than good to your overall business. Allow me to explain.

Traditional distribution entails a manufactured product being sold through several channels before reaching the consumer. For example:

Manufacturer → Manuf. Rep → Jobber → Wholesaler → Retailer → Consumer

---

As you know, every link in this chain is in business to make money (which is as it should be). Thus, while the quality of the product stays the same throughout its journey, the price rises significantly as each "middleman" makes a profit while also paying its overhead. By the time the product gets to your local supermarket, department store, etc., you are paying a significantly higher price than its manufactured price. Again, I'm not saying there is anything wrong with that; it's just that there are options to work this system into a lucrative business of your own, should you choose to take that route.

Network marketing eliminates the retailer and most of the middlemen, thereby granting you more direct access to the actual product or service.

Manufacturer → Company → You
or
Manufacturer → You

Now back to the original question: *Why aren't the prices to the distributor heavily discounted?* The reason, plain and simple, is that the more profit your parent network marketing company makes, the more money it can pay out in bonus checks to you and those in your organization. Sure, the company could discount the prices so dramatically that it made just a little profit while you saved some money. Then, you'd be part of a discount buyers club.

Is that really what you want? Or do you want to be part of a money-*making* organization? It just can't be had both ways. You can either save a little or make a lot. The successful network marketers have learned to look at the "big picture."

Ask yourself this question: "Is my goal, as a home-based network marketing business owner, to save $500 or $1000 a year, or is it to make more money than I've ever had before, have more time to enjoy it, and develop security for me and my family?" Only you can answer that, of course. Also, how many people do you know who actually became wealthy by saving a few dollars on the products they buy? Maybe Sam Walton, but you know what he did with those products— he sold them to others.

And one more question: "If you were to pay retail prices or, in some cases, even a few cents more for your consumable products through your own company, and then made, say, a hundred dollars extra a month through the products consumed by your organization, how much extra did your products actually cost you?" Of course, nothing. You made money!

Myth 4. I should research this business by seeking counsel from people who tried it and were unsuccessful. That way I'll get the real story. If you wanted to become a lawyer, would you seek advice about that profession from someone who quit law school? Or, if you wanted to be a doctor, would you ask someone who flunked medical school how to be successful in that profession? Then why on earth would a person check out the network marketing business from someone who was unsuccessful or quit after talking to one person who didn't want to get in and stole their dream at the same time? My point is, get your information from those who already are where you want to be.

Myth 5. Within three months, I should be rich. Although I know you don't actually believe that, you'd be amazed at the number of people who do. And I'm talking about otherwise intelligent, rational, business-minded people. No, any legitimate network marketing opportunity will promote a 2- to 5-year plan of success. Success, as you measure success, may take more time; it may take less. I know of many people who, within a couple of years, and sometimes even less than that, were making a terrific income from their network marketing business. But 2 to 5 years is a very legitimate time frame to focus on.

One of the things that hurts the reputation of this industry is people quitting after 3 months because "I'm not rich yet." Then, not willing to take responsibility for their own impatience or lack of discipline in sticking with it, they tell everybody within earshot that "network marketing doesn't work." Of course, they are somewhat correct. Network marketing only works if you are willing to work it.

Myth 6. It's a pyramid. Please understand that "pyramids" are illegal. Network marketing is not a pyramid. Although every traditional business (as well as any religious, charitable, or social organization) takes on the shape of a pyramid (see the illustration on p. 168) the fact is, according to the Federal Trade Commission [in a 1977 decision (FTC v. Amway Corporation)], "Network Marketing is not a pyramid." The two reasons cited were:

1. Distributors do not earn income by sponsoring people into their organizations. Income is only earned based on products and services flowing through the organization.

2. A distributor can make more money than his sponsor. Income is not determined through placement in the organization.

Myth 7. The product is the key. I hate to burst anybody's bubble with this one, but the fact is, what propels people into the network marketing "business" (those who plan to build an organization as opposed to simply being a consumer who has a distributor number) is not the product but the opportunity itself. When joining a network marketing company, realize that you are not in a product business— you are in the distribution business, and mainly, you are in the "people development" business.

Dr. Joe Rubino, who joined network marketing as a financially successful but "time-poor" dentist and is now a Master Instructor and top distributor with Oxyfresh Worldwide, describes it this way in his wonderful new book, *Secrets of Building a Million-dollar Network Marketing Organization from a Guy Who's BEEN THERE DONE THAT:*

> Sure, there have to be great products—and they usually are. Sure, those products must give great benefits—positive results that enhance the consumer's quality of life—and they usually do. But there's more—much more. And the *more* is—people. Network marketing is about people. At its best, network marketing is about people getting control of their lives, following their dreams, living their values, *and* supporting others to do the same.

As Dr. Rubino indicates, whatever products or services are involved must be good—that is a given. Build an army of *people,* however, and mainly through personal consumption, as well as some merchandising, the product will move. Leaders in the industry will tell you: "Products don't move people—people move products!" That's another good reason that the more consumable products your company provides, the more long-term, residual income you can potentially earn. One important point I must make is that there are some tremendous products that are marketed solely via network marketing. Many successful distributors originally became involved after a dramatic, life-enhancing experience with a product and then felt compelled to share its benefits with others (and thus joined the business). Two of my clients in particular fall into that category.

Kathy Jackson joined Nikken, a company specializing in magnetic wellness and other natural health products, after her daughter Nikki's debilitating fatigue vastly improved as a result of trying one of the products. Feeling passionately that she should share this success with everyone she could, Kathy, in a relatively short period of time, has built a huge international business. One of the people she shared the products with was Nikki's best friend, Lisa, the daughter of Jack and Shirley Maitland. Lisa Maitland had suffered from excruciating headaches for years. After a product experience in which her headaches all but disappeared, Jack and Shirley began doing the same thing as their new sponsor, Kathy, and have already put together an extremely successful Nikken business. Actually, Shirley is much more oriented toward the product side of the business, while Jack concentrates on building the organization. Together, they are a very effective partnership.

There are many who, like Jack, found a great product and decided to build a huge organization by focusing on the product's benefits and utilizing the company as a vehicle to help them do so. Although this may seem to contradict what I said earlier, the point is that success in any network marketing opportunity is still based primarily on the *people* involved.

Myth 8. I don't have the money or time to start my own network marketing business. Go back to the beginning of this chapter and read it again. Remember why you wanted to be in business for yourself in the first place. Two of the reasons are to make more money and have more time to enjoy it. Build a successful network marketing organization, and you'll eventually have both.

Actually, the financial startup costs will be minimal. You can probably afford that part now. If not, save some money and reinvest it in your business in order to get it off the ground. You'll find a way. The man regarded by many as the "king of network marketers", Dexter Yager, says, "If the dream is big enough, the facts don't count!"

Regarding time, you're right, you don't *have* time...you *make* time! And, if you don't have time now, and you keep on doing what you're doing, what makes you think you'll have any more time 5 years from now? Amway Executive Diamond Bubba Pratt (who had neither time nor money when he started and is now among the most successful network marketers in the world) says, "If you want to make some changes in your life, you first have to make some changes in your life."

Who's Getting In?

What do the following have in common: doctor, accountant, construction worker, lawyer, nurse, teacher, banker, laborer, insurance professional, realtor, land surveyor, architect, musician, professional athlete, and we might as well include just about every other profession or job classification in the world? What they have in common is that they are all finding the network marketing opportunity to be a very positive addition to their lives.

You might ask, "Why would someone like, say, a doctor, who's probably earning a lot of money and is already very busy, take on a project such as building a network marketing business?" First of all, with all the changes taking place in health care nowadays, many doctors aren't making the money they were just a few years ago (yet they still have their high overhead and huge loans to pay off), and they are wondering just what the future of their profession holds.

But let's assume we're talking about people who, regardless of their profession, are earning a lot of money and are already very busy. Why are they building a network marketing organization? To get the time they want back in their lives. To have more control of their days. As we discussed at the beginning of this chapter, to once again be able to do the things that are truly important, such as spend time with their family. The general consensus is, the more successful and the busier a person is, the better a network marketing prospect they make. Why? Because they already believe in and have experienced success but still want to make some changes in their life that very few businesses other than network marketing can provide.

Then Why the Bad Rap?

Let's set the record straight. The fact is, network marketing has received a bad rap. And there are several reasons. One is that people confuse it with *illegal* pyramids. You may ask, why bother putting the word *illegal* before the word *pyramid*; aren't all pyramids illegal? Not at all. In fact, let's look at a typical *legal* pyramid known as a large corporation. The following is a table of organization for a fictional U.S. corporation:

Chair

President / CEO

Vice President   Vice President

Asst VP   Asst VP   Asst VP   Asst VP

Reg. Dir   Reg. Dir   Reg. Dir   Reg. Dir   Reg. Dir   Reg. Dir   Reg. Dir

Div. Mgr   Div. Mgr   Div. Mgr   Div. Mgr   Div. Mgr   Div. Mgr   Div. Mgr   Div. Mgr   Div. Mgr   Div. Mgr

everyone else everyone else everyone else everyone else everyone else everyone else everyone else ever

That may be a very simplistic look, yet it is the basic structure. And it's a pyramid, pure and simple.

The point is, there is nothing wrong with an organization emulating the shape of a pyramid. A pyramid stands for strength and support. Look at the ones still standing from thousands of years ago. Also, the chances are good that the leadership of your local church, synagogue, mosque, temple, charitable organization, civic organization, law enforcement agency, and every other organization that has a plan for success takes on a pyramid structure as well.

A typical network marketing organization never actually forms the shape of a perfect pyramid, yet, it strives for the same basic format.

Let's note, however, the basic difference between a corporate pyramid and a network marketing organization that was able to take the exact same shape.

			Distributor				
			Distributor				
		Distributor		Distributor			
	Distributor	Distributor	Distributor	Distributor			
Distributor	Distributor	Distributor	Distributor	Distributor	Distributor		
Distributor	Distributor	Distributor	Distributor	Distributor	Distributor	Distributor	Distributor
Distributor	Distributor	Distributor	Distributor	Distributor	Distributor	Distributor	Dist

1. *Top-heavy corporation.* Guess who is guaranteed to make the most money as a result of the corporate pyramid setup? That's right, the chair and president/CEO. Who makes the most after that? Yes, the vice presidents. Next, of course, would be the assistant vice presidents. And, you can take the rest from there. Totally predictable.

2. *Network marketing organization.* The people producing the most make the most money. Yes, a distributor can make significantly more money than the person who sponsored her or him. Happens all the time. That's one of the beauties of network marketing—you get paid based on what you produce, not based on what your boss thinks you're worth.

Another reason for the bad reputation associated with network marketing is the lack of personal responsibility taken by people who have previously joined a company, worked (or played) at the business for a relatively short time, faced a couple of rejections, and then quit. That, of course, is a choice everyone has the right to make.

What hurts the industry as a whole, however, is that, instead of taking responsibility for not sticking with it or for not following a proven system, people will try to place the blame elsewhere. ("The company wasn't good, the business doesn't work, etc.) After all, isn't it human nature to blame outside circumstances for lack of accomplishment than to look "inside" where it really counts? So these people, instead of becoming ambassadors for the industry, try to "poison" everyone else. It's really a shame.

And, I hate to say it, but one more reason for the somewhat negative reputation of the industry is a result of misinformed and uncaring media more interested in ratings and readership than in presenting the facts. How many articles have you read or TV news programs have you watched talking about the MLM companies and distributors that have failed. Not that this hasn't ever, or could never, happen. It does—it happens in *every* business, doesn't it? But I've been privileged to know the other side of the coin as well; yet I have rarely seen that side highlighted in a media report. The fact is, negative stories sell. In researching this business, it's your job to get the facts.

Getting Past the Dream Stealers

One potential stumbling block you'll encounter the very moment you begin checking out the network marketing business is the negativity you'll receive from the people around you. I said *potential* stumbling block because it doesn't have to be that. You'll only stumble over negativity if you allow yourself to.

Why do people, including loved ones, friends, and others try to discourage people from beginning a network marketing business? Often, well-intentioned ignorance is the chief reason. Dream stealers come in two varieties—those who are well-intentioned and those who don't want you to succeed because of their own lack of success.

You see, as human beings, we all tend to make major decisions based on very limited information. Combine that with the fact that most people doubt that which has not yet happened, and you've got the recipe for a lot of negativity before you.

First, let's realize that if everyone decided to listen to history's naysayers, we would still be living on a planet that is flat, a planet, by the way, circled by the sun, watching *television* in the dark because electricity would not have been discovered (I think that last part was a joke). I believe it was in 1898 that the U.S. Patent Director General made this brilliant statement: "Anything that can possibly be invented, already has been." Now there's a guy who I imagine believed in the wisdom of a big bureaucratic government.

Does anyone really think that Alexander Graham Bell was encouraged by the masses to invent the telephone, or that the Wright brothers were encouraged to master flight ("If man were meant to fly he'd have been born with wings"—that from their own father!), or that Ray Kroc was encouraged to develop his McDonald's franchise concept ("Ray, c'mon, be serious; no one wants to eat 'fast-food')?" Oh, and by the way, in the '60s the U.S. Congress came within 11 votes of declaring the franchise industry illegal...some considered the industry a sort of "illegal pyramid." Now, of course, that industry accounts for over a third of our nation's gross national product.

Base Your Decision on Facts, Not the Uninformed Opinions of Others

Once you decide to own a distributorship and get started, plug into the success system suggested by your upline. As you learn more you'll become more knowledgeable. As you become more knowledgeable your confidence will increase. And, as your confidence increases, it will be harder and harder for the dream stealers to accomplish their mission. If you listen to others' opinions and let them discourage you, you'll need to live with the results, or lack of results.

The best thing to do is to politely thank the negative person for his or her opinion, and then do what you have to do for you and your family. If that person does not offer to pay your bills and send your kids to college and take care of you financially in your old age, then their opinion shouldn't really count, should it? As war hero, minister, author, and motivational speaker Clebe McClary says, use the F.I.D.O. method—Forget *It* and *Drive On!*

Networking/Prospecting for Your MLM Business

In this business, your *inventory*—your most important asset—is the names on your list. The names of people you can call and, based on your standing with them or the people through whom you met them, you'll have an opportunity to share with them your business opportunity. That doesn't necessarily mean they'll decide to become a part of your organization or even a customer; that part is mainly a "numbers game," but no matter. As long as your names list doesn't run out, you are in business.

The good news is that, since this entire book is about the subject of effective and profitable prospecting and networking techniques, you already know how to accomplish this for your MLM business. You'll never have to run out of names of people to show your business opportunity to because you know how to meet and develop relationships with new people on a daily basis. I do, however, want to provide just a few additional techniques you can use that are somewhat specific to this industry.

In network marketing you begin with a prospect list of people you already know. From Chapter 2 you know that list will be somewhere in the vicinity of 250 names. I suggest listing everyone, even those people you are just positive will have absolutely no interest at all in learning more about your opportunity.

Why? First, because you don't really know that they won't have interest. That's known in the business as "prejudging" your prospect. You never know what reasons a person will have for being open to a new business idea, but the three we've already mentioned (money, time, and security) are good for starters. Let them make their own decisions regarding whether they are interested. You'll eventually hear horror stories from distributors who did not prospect a person because they assumed he or she would not be interested only to see this person show up at a meeting as a guest of someone else, and then become a very successful distributor *in that other person's group.* Ouch! Also, just having those people's names on your list will trigger the names of other people for you that you might be ready to share the business with.

How to Make Your List

Just as there is a way to ask people for referrals which helps them identify and single people out for you, there is also a way to do that for yourself when making your initial prospect list. First, simply write down the names of people who naturally come to your mind. Don't worry if there aren't too many at first—that is natural, just as when you ask a potential referral source if he or she "knows anyone who...". It's difficult to single people out.

Next, go through your personal Rolodex, holiday card list, high school and college yearbooks, and any other similar resources that come to mind and write down everyone's name. Even those people who at this time, for whatever reason, you know you won't call. It's okay—write down their names anyway.

Now, take out your local *Yellow Pages.* That's right! The *Yellow Pages.* What I want you to do is turn to the page which lists every single occupation beginning with the letter *A.* Simply start with the first occupation and go all the way through to the end, at each individual occupation asking yourself, "Who do I know who does this?" By the time you go through every single occupation listed, you'll find your list becoming huge. After all, who do you know who's an *a*ccountant, a *b*anker, a *c*hiropractor, a *d*entist, an *e*lectrician, etc.?

It is time to now pick up the *White Pages* telephone directory. Take your time and just look through the names, letting both the first and last names listed remind you of people you know with those same last names. Who do you know named Smith, Jones, Anderson, Bevilaqua?

Who do you know named Bob, Susan, David, Linda, Marcia, Jan, Cindy, Moe, Larry, or Curly? Limitless, isn't it? You won't have a real big challenge coming up with your initial list of names.

This is also a good way to help your new distributors make *their* lists as well. Hint: If you find your new distributor saying, "I just don't know anyone," then realize that she or he is really saying, "I don't yet have enough confidence in either this business or in myself to contact people, so please help me gain that confidence."

Time to Start Calling

Typically, you are either going to invite a person to see your company's sales and marketing plan in a one-on-one setting (or any combination of them and their spouse and you and your spouse) or a group setting, such as a home meeting. For each of these settings, keep in mind that because of the preconceived notions most people have about MLM, it's important that you don't make your sponsoring presentation over the telephone. It must be done in person.

As is the case even with many traditional businesses, the only reason for your telephone call is to set up the appointment, or meeting. If you let their questions ("What is it?," "What do I have to do?," etc.) intimidate you into giving your presentation over the telephone, you'll end up telling them just enough so that they can make a "no" decision based on very limited information.

Let's say your sponsor has agreed to present the opportunity for you via a home meeting at your house. He has asked you to invite as many people as possible to attend the meeting. He's also told you that you need to get attendance commitments from *twice* as many people as you plan to have show up. In other words, if you want 15 people to attend, you must get commitments from 30. And it's true; people can disappoint you if you let them. So how do you correctly invite someone over the telephone? Let's say, in this case, you're going to call people you already know well.

Your First Sale Is Just to
Set the Meeting

Terry McEwen, an Amway Executive Diamond, suggests first "clearing the night." In other words, "Hi Joe, this is Terry. What are you and Karen doing Wednesday night besides watching TV?" Joe replies, "Nothing. Why, what's up?"

What this does is commit Joe to the fact that he really doesn't have any significant plans for this Wednesday night that should keep him from attending a business meeting, if in fact he has interest in the first place.

At this point, if you are the one setting the appointment you might say, "Joe, Marcia and I are expanding a business project with some other very successful business people in the area, and we'd like you and Karen to come over Wednesday night and take a look. Of course, we can't promise you anything, but it looks real good. Can you guys be here just before 8 p.m.?"

What we did there was to casually, and with *posture* (the attitude of "I care...but not *that* much"), offer him the opportunity to find out more about this project, without telling him too much so that he could form an incorrect opinion.

Joe will most likely respond in one of three ways: He could say "No, I'm not real interested." In that case you could either try to find out his objection by asking questions or just think "NEXT" and go on to your next prospect. Or, Joe might respond by saying, "Yes, we'll be there." In that case, just tactfully make sure he realizes you expect him to keep the appointment. The following words will usually work just fine: "Joe, I'm only having a limited amount of people there and I know you're a person of your word who always keeps his appointments. I can count on you for that, right?" Joe says, "Uh, yeah." Then you can respond, "Great, just write down in your daily planner for this Wednesday the 19th at just before 8 p.m., okay?"

The third way Joe might respond is to say, "What is it?" This is where you have to make sure you've rehearsed your responses so you don't get caught off guard. Remember, say too much and Joe will disqualify himself—say too little and Joe will wonder to himself, "Hey, what's he hiding?" Your response might be somewhat dictated by the type of products and services your company represents and/or distributes, as well as company teaching. For instance, even if you mention the type of products you represent, you need to ask yourself if you can still effectively describe the opportunity over the telephone. The answer is probably not. In network marketing, it's much more advantageous to both of you if you present your opportunity in person.

A generic response to his question could be, "Joe, are you familiar with the concept of in-home, or home-based distribution?" Joe replies, "No, what's that?" You can then say, "It's a very interesting concept that seems as though it could be quite lucrative. It's really a visual presentation so instead of even trying to explain it over the phone, I'd like to have you and Karen come over and see for yourself." At that point, close the appointment and go on to your next call.

Inviting a person to see your business opportunity in a one-on-one setting is a bit easier since you're not locked into a specific meeting time. "Hey, Joe, I'm expanding a business project and I'd like to run the idea past you and Karen one night this week." If Joe is interested in knowing more about it, you can let him know, "I've got Wednesday or Thursday night open; which night is better for you?"

Prospecting Those You've Never Met

Some successful network marketers really enjoy getting lists of people they don't even know and simply calling and inviting them to see their business opportunity—for instance, a directory of business owners, club members, or whatever they can find. Business cards that are stacked on a counter at a luncheonette might be another option. There are lots of options for the truly resourceful. Here is a sample, very generic opening that works: "Hi, Sandra? My name is Marcia Gunderman. We've never met. I'm expanding a business in your area and I'm looking for some people who are looking to make more money or diversify their income...would that include you?"

Sandra can now respond by saying no, yes, or what's it about? You'll then have your answers prepared and attempt to set the appointment. Since she doesn't know you and may be worried about wasting her time, you can phrase your appointment close by saying, "Why don't I pop by for a quick 15-minute cup of coffee? I'll run the idea past you and if you think there's something there, great—if not, great!" That's about as nonthreatening as can be, isn't it?

While 15 minutes won't necessarily give you time for an entire presentation, it is enough time to qualify her interest and set up a longer follow-up meeting or invite her to one of your company's larger open-opportunity meetings where she can get a chance to see a bigger picture. You'll probably also want to leave her with some tapes or company literature which will help her to become more familiar with the benefits of your opportunity.

By the way, realize that this technique is about as much of a "numbers game" as can be. You simply know that by making enough calls you'll turn some into appointments and some appointments into distributors or customers.

Endless Referrals, Too!

And, of course, regardless of the circumstances that put you in front of your prospect, you are now in a position to ask for additional referrals from those who, for their own reasons, aren't interested right now but can possibly lead you to someone who may be. John Terhune, a former prosecuting attorney, found his last two qualifying "legs" for his Amway Emeraldship (he called this his Freedom Pin as he was then able to retire from his job) as a result of referrals from two people who declined the opportunity for themselves. He is now a Diamond.

One final note: Some companies have an array of prospecting videotapes, audiotapes, and literature you can use to make the prospecting process even easier.

Follow J. Paul Getty's Advice

Billionaire J. Paul Getty, in his autobiography, *How to Be Rich,* presented six guidelines for success in business. To many people, they describe the network marketing opportunity:

1. Be in business for yourself.
2. Market a product or service that is in great demand.
3. Guarantee that product or service.
4. Give better service than the competition.
5. Reward those who do the work.
6. Build your success upon the success of others.

If the opportunity you are checking out meets these criteria, and your dream is big enough to keep doing the work until you make it happen, then go for it!

Key Points

- Advantages of choosing a network marketing business:
    1. It is very inexpensive to start.
    2. It can be started on a part-time basis.
    3. It provides the opportunity for practically anybody to build a residual-based income.

- Network marketing is based on three concepts: personal consumption, merchandising, and duplication.

- In choosing a company, look at some that have been in business for a while and have a track record of success.

- When you sponsor a person into your network marketing business, he or she is an independent contractor (not your employee) and it's your responsibility to teach what you have learned, in order to begin the process of duplication.

- Training and business-building tools for the network marketing industry abound. Certain companies provide training while others mainly offer the infrastructure. Tools include books, tapes, voice mail, seminars, major events, prospecting literature, etc.

- There are also independent companies that specialize in training and tools for the MLM industry. They include *Upline Magazine* and a host of others listed in the Resource Guide.

- Three reasons why the network marketing industry has received a bad rap:
  1. People mistakenly confuse it with illegal pyramids.
  2. People sometimes get involved and then quit without putting in the necessary effort and blame their lack of success on outside influences.
  3. Media can be misinformed and uncaring.

- Your most important asset is the names on your list. As long as your names list doesn't run out, you are in business. (Fortunately, since that's what this book is about, you are covered in that area.)

- There is a simple, very effective way to come up with names for your initial list. There will be around 250 names if you list everyone. After you sponsor someone, teach her or him how to do the same thing.

- A big part of your success depends on how well you get past the dream stealers. Dexter Yager says, "Don't let anybody steal your dream."

Resource Guide

The following is a partial list. I suggest continually seeking out additional resources as well.

Books

Andrecht, Venus: *MLM Magic*. Ramona, CA, Ransom Hill Press, 1993.

Brooke, Richard: *Mach II with Your Hair on Fire*. Charlottesville, VA, Upline Press, 1998.

Butwin, Robert: *Street Smart Networking*. Charlottesville, VA, Upline Press, 1994.

Clements, Leonard W.: *Inside Network Marketing*. Rocklin, CA, Prima Publications, 1996.

Clouse, Michael S.: *Business Is Booming*. Charlottesville, VA, Upline Press, 1996.

Crisp, Robert E.: *Raising a Giant*. Charlottesville, VA, Upline Press, 1998.

Ellsberg, Sandy: *Bread Winner/Bread Baker*. Charlottesville, VA, Upline Press, 1997.

Failla, Dan: *Basics: How to Build a Large Successful Multi-Level Marketing Organization*. Charlottsville, VA, Upline Press, 1996.

Fogg, John Milton: *The Greatest Networker in the World*. Charlottesville, VA, Upline Press, 1992.

Gage, Randy: *How to Build a Multi-Level Money Machine*. Miami Beach, FL, GR&DI Publications, 1998.

Hedges, Burke: *Who Stole the American Dream*. Tampa, FL, INTI Publishing, 1992.

Hedges, Burke: *You Can't Steal Second with Your Foot on First*. Tampa, FL, INTI Publishing, 1995.

Hirsch, Peter L.: *Living with Passion*. Charlottesville, VA, Upline Press, 1994.

Kalench, John: *17 Secrets of the Master Prospectors*. Charlottesville, VA, Upline Press, 1994.

Nadler, Beverly: *Congratulations You Lost Your Job!* Charlottesville, VA, Upline Press, 1992.

Natiuk, Robert: *Your Destiny*. Miami Beach, FL, GR&DI Publications, 1994.

Poe, Richard: *Wave 3: The New Era in Network Marketing*. Rocklin, CA, Prima Publishing , 1994.

Poe, Richard: *The Wave 3 Way to Building Your Downline*. Rocklin, CA , Prima Publishing, 1997.

Quain, Bill: *Reclaiming the American Dream*. Wales Publishing, 1994.

Ruhe, Jan: *Fire Up*. Charlottesville, VA, Upline Press, 1995.

Ruhe, Jan: *MLM Nuts and Bolts*. Charlottesville, VA, Upline Press, 1997.

Schreiter, Tom: *Big Al Tells All*. Houston, TX, KAAS Publishing, 1985.

Schreiter, Tom ; *Big Al's How to Create a Recruiting Explosion*. Houston, TX, KAAS Publishing, 1986.

Schreiter, Tom: *Big Al's Turbo MLM*. Houston, TX, KAAS Publishing, 1988.

Schreiter, Tom: *Big Al's How to Build MLM Leaders for Fun & Profit*. Houston, TX, KAAS Publishing, 1991.

Schreiter, Tom: *Big Al's Super Prospecting*. Houston, TX, KAAS Publishing, 1998.

Stanmeyer, William A.: *The Best Kept Secret in America*. Bridgewater, VA, Good Printers, 1996.

Rubino, Joe: *Been There Done That*. Charlottsville, VA, Upline Press, 1997.

Yarnell, Mark, and Yarnell, Rene Reid: *Your First Year in Network Marketing.* Rocklin, CA, Prima Publishing, 1998.

Organization

Multi Level Marketing International Association (MLMIA), 119 Stanford Ct., Irvine, CA 92612 (714-854-0484).

Industry Publications

Big Al's Recruiting Newsletter, KAAS Publishing, 1199 Nasa Rd., 1 Suite 104, Houston, TX 77058 (713-280-9800).

MLM Insider Magazine, 3529 NE 171st St., N. Miami Beach, FL 33160 (305-947-5600).

Money Maker's Monthly, 6827 West 171st St., Tinley Park, IL (708-633-8888).

Network Marketing (published by *Success* magazine) 733 Third Ave., New York, N.Y. (800-234-7324).

Profit Now, P.O. Box 4245, Barboursville, WV 25504-4245 (800-229-1717).

Upline, 106 South St., Charlottesville, VA 22902 (888-UPLINE1).

14

The Mail Order/
Direct Marketing
Business

Money in Your Mailbox

Although mail order—which is now mainly referred to as *direct marketing* because of the variety of media involved in the process—is quite a different business from network marketing, there are several similarities. One similarity is the eventual fortune and freedom you can achieve for both you and your family after first building a very strong foundation.

Another similarity, however, is somewhat negative: Direct marketing is just as misunderstood as network marketing by the general populace, who thinks of direct marketing either as a "get-rich-quick" type of business (or even scheme) or as a business which has already peaked in its profitability. Neither is correct.

Can You Say "a Hundred Million"?

From the Sears catalogs of the 1800s to E. Haldeman-Julius's sales of 100 million of his "Little Blue Books" in the 1920s, it works. From Lillian Vernon's kitchen table to riches and fame, it works. From Gary Halbert's $7.5 million worth of cash orders for family crests and Ted

Nicholas' spectacular sales of his book, *How to Form a Corporation for $75*, to Joe Sugarman's millions and millions selling expensive, bulky, portable calculators when they first came out, this business works.

And, from the current successes of huge catalog companies to the catalogs of the home-based business owner, mail order/direct response is a business that most definitely works. In fact, practically anyone can get into this business and profit from it, so long as that person is willing to learn and do the work required to make success happen.

Although, as you can tell from the last paragraph, mail order/direct response has been utilized as a business or at least one element of a business for quite a long time, only relatively recently has it been considered a somewhat mainstream business that *anyone* can do.

The Dean of Mail Order

Melvin Powers of Wilshire Books is one of the pioneers of the genre of the "How anyone can get rich in mail order" books and seminars. In fact, Mr. Powers's book, *How to Get Rich in Mail Order* was the first book I ever read on this topic, and the wisdom included has proved invaluable even though direct response has thus far been only a small part of my business. In his book, you'll learn the fundamentals about starting this type of business, be provided with tons of specific examples, and be exposed to many other resources you'll need to get your business off to a profitable start.

In a nutshell, mail order/direct response (from this point on, I'll use the two terms interchangeably) is simply a way to sell your products and/or services directly to the consumer—bypassing the intermediary—as a result of advertising, with most of your sales presentation through mail and various other media.

Let's Begin with a Best-Possible-Case Example

Let's imagine you create beautifully crafted wooden eagles that make wonderful house ornaments or gifts. You plan to sell them for $29.95. You then decide that instead of trying to sell your eagles to a wholesaler, distributor, or even directly to retail outlets, you'd rather market it yourself through direct response, have total project control, and keep the majority of money instead of giving most of it away in the distribution chain.

As a very basic example of the mail order process, you take out an advertisement in a magazine to offer your product; a 1/6-of a page display ad. You create your attention-grabbing, benefits-oriented headline, write compelling copy, give a 100 percent money back guarantee, and include ordering information.

In a perfect world, your mailbox will soon be filled with more checks (for $29.95 plus $5 shipping) than you can possibly imagine, your telephone will "ring off the hook" with people begging you to charge their order to one of their major credit cards, and your fax machine will spend the morning hours spewing out paper with orders on them.

RRRrrriiiinnnnngggggg! That's the sound of your alarm clock going off because you have just been dreaming. That's right, it isn't quite that easy, despite what the young fellow on the infomercial tries to tell you. (Yes, he has become wealthy through direct response, but not from taking out one-shot, classified ads.)

Actually, the chances are that your advertisement probably will not draw enough orders to even come close to paying for the ad. However, that doesn't mean you can't make a fortune from marketing your eagles and related products through direct response. You can, it just takes a lot more work than most people think.

One-Step, Two-Step

The above is an example of a one-step ad: You plan to sell your product in one step. You place the ad; the reader sees the ad and orders. Unfortunately, today's readers get hit with so much advertising that they are not as likely to buy from just that one ad. That's not to say it *never* happens, but it is the exception rather than the rule. Most mail-order experts will tell you those days are pretty much gone.

A two-step ad will often prove much more effective: The first ad you place—probably a classified ad—is utilized strictly to elicit a response from the reader for you to send more information (this is also known as a "lead generation" ad). This is usually free information, which will be your sales letter, your written sales presentation.

This gives you an excellent opportunity to now send as much information as you'd like to the reader, who by virtue of the very fact he or she took the time and made the effort to send for the information, is most likely a qualified prospect for your product. By the way, even if the reader doesn't buy your eagle after the first letter, she or he might after one of your next two letters, or even more, if that's what your marketing plan determines.

You are, at this point, going through the process of building your list. Most mail order experts agree that the list is *the most important* element in your direct mail campaign. There are list brokers all over the United States (consult your local *Yellow Pages* and local library's *Standard Rate & Data* directory) that can rent and sell mailing lists to you ranging from the general to the extremely specific, but we won't delve into that here. The *best* way to build your list is to keep adding customers. That's your ultimate best mailing list.

Back-End—Where the Real Money Is Made in Direct Response Marketing

Let's take your eagle project a step further. Say a woman buys one of your beautiful eagles; she is now the best prospect you have for any of your other related products. She is in your database, you have her mailing information, and she has already shown a propensity to buy this type of product. Now, when you come out with your eagle calendars, eagle coffee mugs, or, if it's animal sculptures she's more interested in, your hand-crafted rhinoceros sculpture, your elephant sculpture, your lion sculpture, etc., you simply send another letter, maybe now with a catalog, and you might have another sale. And it's win/win—she's getting a chance to buy something along the lines of her interest, and you have her name and address for free, since you no longer have to advertise for it.

How far can you take this? As far as you want. Your two-step ads might become display ads, getting bigger and bigger as you're able to reinvest a portion of your profits back into advertising for more and more qualified prospects. Going back to the home-based business chapter, your knowledge of the computer will certainly prove to be very worthwhile. In fact, with decent computer skills in the area of mail order, you can be a one-person show for a long time while bringing in a lot of money.

Meet an Expert in This Field

The chances are very good that you either know of, or have been directly or indirectly influenced to buy something from, a man named

Dan S. Kennedy. A truly knowledgeable and in-demand marketing consultant and president of several companies of his own in Phoenix, Arizona, Dan is a friend of mine and an expert in the field of direct response. He has been quoted and featured often in magazines such as *Success* and *Entrepreneur* and is a major consultant for Guthy-Renker Corporation, one of, if not the most, successful infomercial/direct response companies in the world. (In fact, if you've bought just about anything from a television infomercial, including Guthy-Renker products like Vanna White's Perfect Smile tooth-whitening system, Pro-Active acne treatment, any DirectTalk™ product, and on and on, you've been persuaded to purchase, at least in part, by Dan Kennedy.) Dan is also an internationally-known speaker who has shared the platform with former U.S. presidents, hundreds of celebrities such as Bill Cosby and Larry King, major speaking legends such as Zig Ziglar and Tom Hopkins (and, I'm proud to say, lesser-known speakers such as yours truly), and he is the author of numerous books on free enterprise, entrepreneurship, and of course, direct response marketing.

His book, *How to Make Millions with Your Ideas* is an absolute "must read" for today's home-based business owner, especially if you are seriously considering investing in the direct response business. And he has a monthly newsletter that applies to practically any business or profession imaginable.

As you can tell, I have a lot of respect for both Dan and his wisdom. With his permission, I am happy to share some of that wisdom throughout the remainder of this section. Several of Dan's products will be listed in the resource section at the conclusion of this chapter; I suggest calling his office for more information.

Dan's first piece of advice is to become a dedicated, determined student of this field. He says to read dozens of books, go to seminars, join several associations, and otherwise immerse yourself in direct response self-education. He believes that in this business, where the idea is not to reinvent but to duplicate what's already been invented and successfully applied, constant and continuing education is an absolute must.

One of the first lessons Dan teaches for the beginning direct response marketer is to completely own the product or service you are selling, as opposed to simply distributing it. The reason is that between advertising and the actual cost of the product, unless you own it, there may not be enough of a markup for your business to be profitable.

An Excellent Product to Sell Via Direct Response

According to Dan, the best type of product to sell via direct marketing is an information-type product. That's because the money you can charge has absolutely nothing to do with the cost of the product itself—only the value it provides the customer. This information might be in the form of books, large manuals, audio or videocassettes, and these days, even software programs and CD-ROMs.

Some of these cost very little to produce. And, even the ones that might be somewhat expensive to originally produce, once the initial cost is paid for, your only expense will be in the duplication. I can tell you first-hand that information products are very lucrative products to market.

Your question might be, "What type of information product am I qualified to create and market?" Here's the good part: Remember in Chapter 12 we outlined three parameters for your home-based business? To paraphrase, they were to do what you enjoy, what you're good at (or have knowledge in), and what is marketable. So how can you take those criteria and turn them into a saleable information product?

Turn Your Interests into Dollars

Do you have a hobby in which you have acquired a good bit of knowledge? Maybe you are a bird aficionado. Could you market a manual on the care and feeding of birds? Or maybe a guide to breeding exotic birds for great profits or a how-to manual on how to be a champion bird exhibitor. And why stop there? Can you develop audio and video products on these same topics or others? I don't know much about birds other than eagles (I love them and collect sculptures of them), but if *you* do, I'll bet you could come up with a lot more ideas than the ones I just named.

Are you a gourmet cook? Wow!—just think of all the prospects you have for exciting new recipes. Maybe you'll gear your books, manuals, video's and newsletter on this topic to a particular niche of buyers (low-fat food eaters, natural food eaters, athletes, romantics, etc.). You might wonder, "But aren't cookbooks a dime a dozen? Aren't there tons of them out there?" Yes, there are. And, why do you think there are tons of cookbooks out there? *Because people like them and buy them!* In other words, don't be intimidated because others are already doing something. Use that as encouragement that a viable market has already been discovered, at no cost to you for research.

Although I speak and write on networking for business, I've also written a book on how "single" people can network in order to meet people to date—*Network Your Way to Endless Romance: Secrets to Help You Meet the Mate of Your Dreams.* I market this book via mail order, as well as through bookstores, but I've also created ancillary information products on this topic including a series of special reports, audios, and, as of this writing, a video is in the works.

There is so much out there, including an almost infinite number of niche markets and special interests, that coming up with a series of information products is a very doable idea for you. Are you into photography? How about an information product on how to effectively market your photographic services or advice on a more technical aspect of that art in which you are already proficient? Where would you advertise your information product with either a one-step or two-step ad? How many trade magazines are there for various types of photographers?

Are you a speech pathologist? How about an information product instructing parents how to teach various techniques to their children at home to speed up their progress and increase their confidence? Where would you advertise this particular information product? How many parenting magazines are there out there from which to choose?

You've Got Your Product— Now Let's Sell It!

Now that you have your product, be it information-type product or a more traditional product, it's now time to begin the advertising process. If you're like I am, you will begin by trying something almost guaranteed to fail; I did it, because I had not yet studied direct response and it seemed to make sense. And that is—ta da—putting a one-step advertisement for your product in a major magazine and thinking, "Wow, there are 3 million people reading this magazine and, as Dan Kennedy says, `if just one-tenth of 1 percent of those readers order, I'll be rich, rich, rich!'"

According to Dan, "That particular dream has destroyed more fledgling mail order entrepreneurs than I can count in this lifetime." He explains that first of all, you can't make money from that ad by paying anywhere near the rate that medium is going to charge you. The fact is, there are services most people don't know about (which, of course, Dan lists in his book, *How to Make a Million with Your Ideas*) that can get discounts of 50 to 80 percent and that certainly helps.

The other challenge is that, depending on your product, its price point, and the readership involved, one-step advertising is generally a losing proposition. Personally, I was blown away the first time I tried this with my very first information product, advertising to 3 million readers and receiving all of four responses. And believe me, my product was not nearly expensive enough to even come close to breaking even with four sales.

So, maybe you invest in a classified ad or small space ad asking people to send for more information on how to...whatever it is you are going to help them accomplish. You can offer the information for free or even charge a dollar or two in order to discourage those who just want to get their hands on "any" freebie available. Remember, if you offer to provide the information for free, you will probably get more responses than charging a token something, but possibly those responses won't be of as high quality. (Caveat: that statement does not *always* hold true.)

Dan is a pioneer of offering a 24-hour-per-day free recorded message for people to call in order to listen, and then if they want, to leave their address for you to send the free information. He says this will increase calls because people will not be defensive, thinking that a salesperson will try to "sell" them something. And, they have an out...they can always hang up at anytime during the message if they don't want to receive the information. If they do listen throughout and leave their mailing information, they are most likely a very qualified prospect for you.

Testing One, Two, Three

Also an important element in this process is to *test*. The mail order greats such as Ted Nicholas, Gary Halbert, Melvin Powers, Dan Kennedy, Jay Abraham, and all the others stress this constantly in their writings and teachings. Test! Test! Test! One of the great benefits of direct response marketing is that unlike traditional advertising (an old advertising axiom is: 50 percent of my advertising works perfectly—the only trouble is, I don't know which 50 percent that is), direct response results are totally measurable.

This is accomplished by what is known as *coding*. Simply explained, let's say you are running an ad in two magazines read by the same niche market readership—chiropractic physicians. One of your magazines is *Chiropractic Today* and the other is *Healers*. You'd like to know which magazine pulled a better response, wouldn't you?

To code your ad, simply add a letter or department after your address. For instance, 3456 Maple Way, Dept. C. The C on the incoming envelope would clue you that the response was from the first magazine. *Dept. H* would signify the other. If you're asking them to call for a free report, you might use a particular extension number as a code. This was a very basic explanation, of course. As you study the masters in this field, you'll learn more and more ways to measure your responses for lots of different elements of your advertisements and letters.

The Sales Letter

Okay, you've got a bunch of prospects from your two-step ad. You're now ready to go after them. What's next? Again, we are taking a complex issue with many variables (type of product, price point, etc.) and boiling it down to a very elementary example. Nonetheless, this will get us off to a good start with a basic understanding of the process. The next step is to send our sales letter.

Dan Kennedy explains in detail how to write a sales letter in his phenomenal book, *The Ultimate Sales Letter* (see the Resource Guide), but right now, let's take just a few ideas. Dan is a big believer in writing in conversational tone without getting too hung up on perfect grammar—conversing with the reader and establishing genuine rapport. The following are just a few of his thoughts:

1. *Is your letter fully personalized?* Of course you can get by with "Dear Neighbor" or "Dear Valued Customer," but not if you want real impact.

2. *Does your letter touch the reader's emotions?* If it doesn't, don't bother sending it.

3. *Does your letter tell a story? Does it describe for the reader how you solved a problem or came up with a solution for a similar person?* Stories are a powerful way to bring your message to life.

4. *How long is your message?* Keeping a letter to 1 page is acceptable if that's what it takes to tell the story. Don't be afraid of a long letter—3, 4, 5 , 8, or even 32 pages—if the pages are interesting and compelling. And include testimonials. Lots of testimonials from ecstatic buyers.

5. *What's your offer?* There must be a meaningful offer to move the customer to action. Do you show the prospect that you have the solution to his or her problem: that you can make his life better with your product/service; that her pain will continue or get worse if she doesn't get your product/service; that he can buy easily from you; that she can pay in affordable terms with a no-risk better-than-money-back guarantee if, for any reason she doesn't like your prod-

uct or service? If you can't say all the above about your offer—you're losing business you should be getting. Make it absolutely irresistible to do business with you—and the prospect will do it.

6. *Do you have a P.S. at the end?* After the headline, the P.S. is the most read part of the letter. The P.S. should, in and of itself, be compelling enough to send the reader back to read the actual message. The P.S. can make or break your letter!

7. *Are you going first-class?* First-class postage creates the impression that the sender wanted you to receive the mailing. Whenever possible, go first-class.

And Dan adds that repetition is key when it comes to sending your letters. Prospects may not buy from the first letter, so determine how many follow-up letters you are going to send in that particular sequence. How will you know how many to send for maximum, and most profitable, response? Test! Test! Test!

And, as mentioned earlier, the people who do buy from you are your very best prospects for all your back-end, related products and services. Dan calls this TCV, or total customer value (how much will they buy from you over the long haul?). Keep advertising, building your database, establish great, continuing relationships, study the industry, and Test! Test! Test! and you can develop a nice little (or big) money machine that brings you closer to your dream.

Key Points

- Mail order/direct response is simply a way to sell your products and/or services directly to the consumer—bypassing the traditional intermediaries—as a result of advertising, usually through the mail.

- A one-step ad plans to sell your product as a direct result of one ad. It is usually difficult to make a one-step ad even pay for itself.

- A two-step ad (also known as a "lead generation" ad) elicits a request from the respondent for more information. Now you have the opportunity to send as much sales information to your prospect as you want, as well as adding a new name to your database for future campaigns.

- Mail order experts agree that the list is *the most important* element in your direct mail campaign.

- The back-end is where the real money is made. After a person buys from you once, he is your very best prospect to buy related products and services from you in the future.

- The idea is not to reinvent but to duplicate what's already been invented and successfully applied, so constant and continuing education in your field is a must.

- When possible, own the product or service you are selling or there may not be enough of a markup to make your business profitable.

- Some hints from Dan Kennedy regarding your sales letter:
  1. Is your letter fully personalized?
  2. Does it touch the reader's emotions?
  3. Does your letter tell a story, describing how you solved a problem for a similar person?
  4. Don't be afraid of a long letter if it is interesting and compelling. And include lots of testimonials from ecstatic buyers.
  5. What's your offer? There must be an irresistible offer to move the customer to action.
  6. Place an intriguing P.S. at the end of your letter. (After the headline, the P.S. is the most read part of the letter!)
  7. Are you going first-class? First-class postage creates the impression that the sender wanted the recipient to read the actual message.
  8. Repetition is often the key to success. Determine how many follow-up letters you are going to send.

- Test, test, test!

Resource Guide

This is a partial list. I recommend continually seeking out additional resources as well.

Books

Haldeman-Julius, E.: *The First Hundred Million.* Mesa, AZ, Encore Publishing, 1995.

Kennedy, Daniel S.: *The Ultimate Sales Letter.* Holbrook, MA, Bob Adams, 1990.

Kennedy, Dan S.: *How to Make Millions with Your Ideas.* New York, Penguin, 1996.

Kennedy, Daniel S.: *The Ultimate Information Entrepreneur.* Phoenix, AZ, Empire Communications, 1996.

Lant, Jeffery: *How to Make a Whole Lot More Than $1,000,000.* Cambridge, MA, JLA Publishing, 1990.

Nicholas, Ted: *Magic Words That Bring You Riches*. Indian Beach, FL, Nicholas Direct, 1995.

Ogilvy, David: *Ogilvy on Advertising*. New York, Vintage Books, 1985.

Peery, Jason: *Response Booster*. Palo Alto, CA, Peery Publications, 1998.

Powers, Melvin: *How to Get Rich in Mail Order*. Hollywood, CA, Wilshire Books, 1997.

Powers, Melvin: *Making Money with Classified Ads*. Hollywood, CA , Wilshire Books, 1995.

Stone, Bob: *Successful Direct Marketing Methods*. NTC Publishing Group, 1994.

Straw, J. F. (Jim): *Own Your Own Mail Order Business*. Cleveland, TN, Phlander Company, 1996.

Newsletters

Dan Kennedy's No B.S. Marketing Letter, 5818 N. 7th St., #103, Phoenix, AZ 85014 (602-997-7707).

Mailorder Marketing, P.O. Box 5385, Cleveland, TN 37320 (706-259-2280).

Association

Direct Marketing Association (DMA), 1120 Ave. of the Americas, New York, NY 10036 (212-972-2410).

15
Inter-Net-Working

Or—Endless Referrals:
Network Your Everyday (Internet)
Contacts into Sales

As a person who speaks and writes on business networking, I'm constantly asked about "networking by way of the Internet." After all, we can all have access to an e-mail address and a Web site. And whenever a new technology, such as online marketing comes along, especially when it has the essence of major change surrounding it, naturally lots of people want to hop on the bandwagon, including those wondering if it is the "magic pill" that will lead to fast, easy riches.

Daniel S. Janal, speaker and author of *Online Marketing Handbook: How to Sell, Advertise, Publicize, and Promote Your Products and Services on the Internet and Commercial Online Systems,* one of the most highly regarded books in this genre, defines online marketing as "a system for selling products and services to target audiences who use the Internet and commercial online services, by utilizing online tools and services in a strategic manner consistent with the company's overall marketing program." Notice the final part of the definition: "a strategic manner consistent with the company's overall marketing program." That's the key; not looking at this as a "quick fix" or as the "one thing" that's going to bring you unlimited wealth, but as part of an overall, long-term strategy.

Part of the Overall
Marketing Plan

Two basic conclusions I've come to regarding marketing via the Internet:

1. Online marketing can work, is currently working for many, and will work even better in the future once marketers and consumers alike become more "cyber-savvy." And those marketers who are willing to learn the correct ways of implementing these strategies can profit greatly as we head into the twenty-first century.

2. Online marketing is not an end in and of itself but instead is another excellent tool to be utilized in the overall marketing of your product or service.

An analogy to the second point comes from my background as a television news anchor. I once asked the news director of another station what he thought of the TelePrompTer—the technology which allows news readers to read the words directly off the camera making it appear as though they are, in fact, not reading, but simply looking at you, relating information they have stored in their head—and his answer surprised me. I thought he would either describe it as the *worst* thing to happen to news broadcasting (i.e., "it's fake, phony, false, etc.") or the best thing to happen to the industry since Walter Cronkite (i.e., "has changed the entire way we can bring news to the viewers").

What he said, plain and simply, was, "Bob, it's just another communication tool. The information still has to be procured, processed, written, and conveyed, all with the same effort and high quality. The TelePrompTer just adds a warmer, friendlier way of communicating that same information. I like it."

"Just another tool." To me, that was a good answer, from a man who understood the "principles" of broadcasting yet was open enough to the new ideas and technologies that would help both him and the end user, the consumer. The same holds true for those in the world of marketing; those who understand the principles of successful marketing will simply take that wisdom and apply it in a positive way to this new *tool*, the Internet, to help both them and the end user, the consumer.

The Networking Parallel between the Cyber World and the *Real World*

Just as our intent in the real world of networking and prospecting is to *find* the right people, *meet* them, and then *win them over* through effective followup and follow through, the same is true in the virtual world of sales and marketing. According to Patrick Anderson and Michael Henderson of Adnet International of Atlanta, a company specializing in Internet design and marketing, "The Internet is a big world and rather confusing at first. However, once the methods of prospecting are understood, you'll be in a position to increase your profits substantially."

Make a Good System Even Better

If, as part of your overall sales and marketing plan, you already utilize referral-based marketing, direct response advertising, outbound calling and telemarketing, introductory sales letters and brochures, and/or any of the principles and techniques discussed throughout this book, the Internet will provide a wealth of new prospecting leads, networking contacts and strategic alliance partners. In this chapter, we'll cover various Internet techniques to use with each of these strategies.

From a technical perspective, the Internet is an interrelated network of computers. From a business perspective, it is a way to interact with people who share similar interests. When the principles of this book are applied to the online world, it becomes, according to Anderson and Henderson, "Inter-Net-Working."

So, Who Is Online?

By and large, people use the Internet when they are alone at their computers and have set aside time to explore, communicate, research, or relax. This is a very opportune time to connect with them. Whatever is on their minds at this very moment is what they will search for. Whatever intrigues them or interests them in the next moment is where they will go to next. They will remain in, and return to, the areas which interest them the most.

As Henderson and Anderson point out, "Look at what your fellow business people are doing on the Internet. They are spending time and money creating Web sites that tell us who they are and what they are interested in. They are leaving notes and comments in public discussion areas. They are telling us something about themselves and their needs and then they are asking the Netpreneur, or seller, to get in touch with *them!*" And the general online consumer is actively searching for what interests them as well.

Because of this, the Internet allows us to do something truly unique. It allows us to target and prequalify our prospects in a very different way—not by demographics, but by actions! In other words, as an online marketer, we are able to target our audience by finding people who, by their very actions, have already demonstrated that they are interested in our products and services.

This leads to a very interesting observation made by Anderson and Henderson: "By looking through someone's Web site, and/or listening in (observation through public chat rooms) on their online conversations, you can learn quite a bit about them. People will reveal several things about themselves and their business or wants that make it easy to predict their level of interest in what you have to offer. You can read their personal stories, look for things you both have in common, and quickly strike up a mutually interesting conversation. This doesn't happen in any other medium. Don't ignore it! Anyone who catches on to this idea will never have to make a cold call again!"

The Principles Remain the Same

Know you, like you, and trust you becomes more critical than ever while establishing yourself on this new medium. After all, there is still lots of uncertainty by the general populace over who can be trusted on the Internet. The media fuels the fear of Big Brother practically every day with stories of credit card thieves, hackers, and viruses all somehow invading our computers and getting access to our personal information. However, such an extreme amount of unverified information sometimes makes it difficult to determine which sources can be relied on. For these reasons, mistrust is the single most important obstacle to overcome in order to establish an opening dialog with a new prospect.

And that's okay, because those who can overcome this challenge will profit greatly. And Anderson and Henderson explain that it is actually very easy to set yourself apart from the crowd. They describe this as the biggest secret to Internet success, and it is simply, "Don't act like a computer! That's all. Interact with people on a personal level." The two explain that although it seems obvious, most people try to rely on automatic ways to contact people "en masse," and it makes their prospects suspicious. "Remember," says Anderson, "that they are alone at their computer, willing to visit with another human—but not another machine."

No Tech-Talk, Just Marketing

I'm going to assume that you already understand the basics of being online, such as some of the lingo and the major terms heard everyday. Thus, I won't be investing time in *definitions* of words such as *e-mail,* the *Internet, chat rooms,* etc., unless it's important to clarify some aspect of that from a marketing point. Instead we'll just talk about the benefits of each and how to make them work for you. I'm also not going to go into incredible detail regarding any of the marketing strategies highlighted, as that alone would take an entire book. In fact, I will reference lots of other resources for you to investigate on those topics should you wish to do so.

This chapter, then, is designed only to highlight some of the effective ways that today's online marketers are utilizing this new technology to more effectively position themselves and their products and services through this medium.

The Advantages of Networking through E-mail

E-mail, or electronic mail, is the most basic tool of online marketing, yet it is also among the most important. Aside from simply being an easy and effective medium for people to send letters and other communication instantly, it's also the primary way the online marketer can stay in touch with their prospect, customer, or client.

E-mail authority Jim Daniels, author of the book, *Internet E-mail! Beyond the Basics!* (InfoFree@mailback.com) says e-mail is *the* most powerful marketing tool born from the Internet. According to Daniels, "E-mail is even more important than the World Wide Web. Although a great Web page can be a very effective tool for online marketing, without E-mail the Web would be far less effective for business."

Anderson and Henderson agree. "The most important tool for Internet prospecting is e-mail. Learn to use it well, as it will get you in the door and become your primary followup system." They suggest providing full contact information with your e-mail, just as you would with all of your other business correspondence. This helps validate who you are and builds trust.

Create a short benefit statement, quote, or comment that intrigues and informs. Add this tag line to the end of every piece of e-mail you send. Most e-mail programs have something called a signature file that allows you to automatically add this text at the end of your message. Include more than your name and contact information. Make it easy for people to understand why they might want to do business with you or refer you to others.

The following is an example of Patrick Anderson's signature file:

(770) 936-8308	(800) 701-8176
patrick@adnetintl.com	http://www.adnetintl.com

FREE Internet Business Newsletter
newsletter@adnetintl.com

"We show professionals and entrepreneurs how to develop
a constant source of new leads and referral business!"

The conviction that e-mail is a vital marketing tool is shared by many online marketing experts because, contrary to what the general population thinks, personal relationships are an absolutely essential aspect of online marketing. As explained earlier, the know you, like you, trust you aspect of business networking is key to success not only in the regular world but in the virtual world of the Internet as well.

Acknowledging that the general public still does not yet feel totally comfortable with consuming online, if they don't totally buy into the online marketer, and their relationship with him, they won't do business. Through e-mail, you can correspond often with your prospect or client, and quickly. In fact, quickness is important in this new medium. Even those who already are comfortable purchasing in this capacity, want "speed of response," and that can definitely be provided by e-mail.

Dan Janal emphasizes the importance of speed for online marketing. "One of the greatest benefits of e-mail is that it gives the online marketer a tremendous amount of flexibility. You can automatically respond to customers' e-mail requests for information 24 hours a day. You won't lose sales, because your e-mail operator is always on duty."

The Common Denominator

Janal sees e-mail as the "common denominator" for reaching people and one of the key tools people use to build relationships with one another. He lists the following benefits of e-mail use:

1. Prospecting for leads by introducing consumers to your product or service.

2. Converting prospects to customers by providing them with requested information, such as company overviews, product backgrounders, press releases, reports, surveys and media reviews.

3. Building relationships and developing brand loyalty by informing consumers of new products or services, sales, discounts, seminars, events and the like.

4. Conducting market research by reading consumers' messages.

David Arnold, author of numerous books on computers and marketing and president of Eugene, Oregon-based Seth Network International, presents programs on networking in the information age. David is a big believer in using e-mail as a proactive marketing tool. He explains: "Electronic messages via computer is truly a phenomenon. E-mail is acceptably chatty but gives you time to compose your thoughts. It arrives in seconds and costs absolutely nothing in postage or paper. And recipients can read and reply at their own convenience."

David points out several rules of etiquette for e-mailers, including:

1. *Keep your messages short.* People who e-mail regularly get flooded with messages, and they appreciate those they can read, digest, and answer quickly.

2. *Check your e-mail regularly and reply immediately.*

3. *Don't use all capital letters.* They're harder to read and will be interpreted as shouting.

David, like most other online authorities, is quick to stress that networking through E-mail and the Internet simply supplements ability; it doesn't replace it. That is a very important point! We need to avoid getting so caught up in any one "new" way of doing things that we forget what, as they say, "Brung us to the dance in the first place." Instead, let all the different tools and techniques work together for ultimate success.

By the way, since e-mail is now becoming an everyday happening, be sure to include your e-mail address—as well as your Web site domain, if you have one—on all your business stationery and marketing tools. It isn't a requirement yet but probably will be soon. Arnold comments that "In the 80's people asked *if* you had a fax machine. In the 90's it's, `What is* your fax number?'" Arnold further points out that as of now, people still ask, "do you have e-mail?" "Soon enough," he says, "the question will be, 'What's your e-mail address?'"

Using E-mail to Schedule Appointments with Your Prospects

A number of businesses have discovered that they are able to generate leads with an e-mail message but still need to move people off their computers and start a dialogue in order to close the sale. As with practically anything else being marketed, unless you have an impulse type of product (direct-sale catalog business or such), people will not typically purchase from you on the first contact. They either need more information or motivation to buy. You must get them on the telephone to continue the selling process, if your product or service can be sold via the telephone, or set an in-person appointment. (However, there certainly are exceptions to the rule.)

So how do you get cold prospects to reply to your e-mail or, better yet, pick up the phone and call you? Anderson and Henderson suggest treating your e-mail messages as though they are voice mail messages, which will move them to an entirely different level. Give people a reason to e-mail you back or call. State your name, the purpose of your correspondence, and a quick benefit informing them what they would derive from knowing more about you, your product or service.

According to Henderson, "The biggest advantage to beginning with an e-mail correspondence is that people are still curious about e-mail and they look forward to reading their messages. And they usually read it at a time they can concentrate on it and reply to it. In fact, if they want to respond, they can do so immediately."

Anderson reminds that this is not a bulk e-mail or obvious broadcast advertisement. Not only would that run contrary to networking etiquette (netiquette) but it is also very ineffective. "We get an overwhelming response because our message is treated as an important personal note."

Much of the time, the person you are contacting checks his own e-mail so there is no one to intercept your correspondence. In the event there is, however, using these methods will also provide a legitimate way around the gatekeeper. They are trained to restrict calls, but Webmasters are not. They will trash "spam" (bulk e-mail) and obvious solicitations, but they don't take a chance with anything that seems personal. Michael Henderson says, "In most cases our e-mail goes to a Webmaster who feels compelled to forward it directly to the person in charge. This further enhances our message, because now it looks like internal mail that is necessary to read."

What about e-mail tag? After a message, there is a phone call, but the person isn't there, so an e-mail must be sent telling the person they couldn't be reached. Isn't that frustrating, and a turnoff to your prospect? Ironically, no. In fact, just the opposite. By e-mailing each other several times, a bond is actually formed between the two of you. Then, when your call finally succeeds, it's somewhat exciting. "Somebody I met on the Internet actually called me." I don't know how long this will necessarily last, but for now it makes that first actual conversation a lot of fun and is a great way to create instant rapport.

Your Own Personal Library

Terri Lonier, author of *Working Solo*, suggests that you can use the Net not only to market your business but also to get information to help market your business. She says to just put out word in the right places that you have a question, and you'll receive answers. She adds that, "The Internet can even the score for the budget-conscious home-based business owner in order to outgun the *bigger guys* who seem to have all the resources."

Regarding the information aspect and how it can help you to market your products and services, it seems as though every special interest group and profession has daily or weekly "chat sessions" in which anyone interested can join, converse, and share information.

Several members of my own professional association, the National Speakers Association, began a weekly chat session; lots of members participate—sharing information, asking questions on marketing their services, and generally benefiting all concerned.

Don't Let Fear Stop You— Begin Learning about This Right Away

Although until recently I had not invested a lot of time working the Internet, I'm steadily learning more and more on a consistent basis.

Technological genius that I am—please note the italics—it was scary at first. Now it's not as bad. The fact is, even though change can be uncomfortable for some—myself certainly included—we realize that change is constant and, if not embraced, will probably run us over. Fortunately, there are enough good books and teachers on this subject that we can all work our way through the trepidation. Just keep in mind…if *I* can do it, you can too.

And, until you are knowledgeable enough to market online, you can find a way to work with and through others who can market your products on their site for a percentage of sales. My books, and several of my tape programs, have been marketed through the Internet for quite a while by others who were already "up and running." (Yes, I am now online myself—even have a Web site, http://www.burg.com.) Depending on your type of business, there's no reason you shouldn't do the same. And then, when the time comes that you do have your own Web site and marketing strategy, do the same with others.

Of course, knowing the fine art of business networking as you already do, you've figured out how you and others can engage in mutually beneficial, give and take, win/win relationships. Many of Jeff Slutsky's techniques in Cross-Promoting, discussed in Chapter 11, can be applied online for the benefit of all concerned.

Again, relationships are the key! Please be careful not to get so infatuated with the virtual world of the computer and all that it can do, that you forget the actual ingredient to success…work and relationship building!

Speaking of relationships, one excellent opportunity to establish the mutually beneficial, give and take, win/win relationship so vital to successful business networking can be found online through the use of links.

Inter-Net-Working with Others—The Phenomenal Power of Links

Online marketers discovered long ago the incredible power of advertising for other people and promoting them on your Web site—or mentioning their business and saying nice things about them on the Internet. The fastest, most remarkable way to solidify the goodwill of a relationship is to refer business to someone by pointing people to their Web site. This is called "adding a link" to their Web site from yours.

Links are a way to click your mouse and move to another Web page—they are the hidden power of the World Wide Web.

Trading links is the fundamental spirit of networking on the Internet. It gently pulls people into your Web site. It gives people a reason to like you and makes them want to refer business to you.

There are two benefits to exchanging links. One is the immediate increase in traffic to your Web site from people who are thinking of networking with you. This can quite often lead to sales. The second benefit, and most important in our minds, is the ongoing funnel of new, prequalified prospects it brings to your doorstep.

Use search engines, such as Yahoo and Infoseek, to find Web sites selling noncompetitive products to the same prospects. Send them a short note, by e-mail, that offers to add a link to their Web site. Mention that you feel they provide a good product, service, or resource that your customers are interested in. Make it very easy for them to come to your site and exchange links. Let them know to feel free to come by your site anytime and add their link. Inform them that your database marketing research suggests that your customers would be willing buyers of their products. Remind them to say something really nice about themselves when they add their link.

The sure-fire way to make this even more effective is to add a link to them beforehand! Say something wonderful and glowing, give them a tremendous endorsement, mention the reasons that people would want to visit their Web site. Then send a note that asks for permission to add their link. Tell them that you want to be sure you have correct information for copyright notices and contact information. Will people click immediately on your site? Will they look for their link? Will they beam when they read what you said about them? Will they tell other people about *your* Web site? Will they add a link to their Web page cross-promoting *you?* Will they be open to discussing joint ventures and other cross-marketing opportunities? You bet! In fact, they will do anything you suggest that is easy for them to do.

This is tremendously powerful and can generate more business than you may realize. Follow up with the most influential people and ask them if they would like to be placed on top of your link list. What can they think of doing that would make you want to promote them even more? Ask the question...you'll be very pleased with the answers!

The beauty of this approach is that everybody wins. Even if they don't buy anything from you or never place a reciprocal link on their site—your customers have you to thank for providing such a useful resource!

Active Referral—a Program
You Can Use or Duplicate

A while back I was contacted by two men mentioned earlier in this chapter, Michael Henderson and Patrick Anderson of Adnet International (http://www.adnetintl.com), based in Atlanta, Georgia. They told me that after reading the original edition of *Endless Referrals,* they began basing the marketing and referrals aspect of their Internet marketing business around the philosophies of that book. Their company is a cutting-edge Internet design and marketing company that develops custom business applications for their clients specifically for Internet marketing.

I was especially fascinated not only with the way they had automated—actually systemized—the follow-up process but, more important, with their innovative method of sharing links to make people want to see them succeed and *want* to help them find new business. Sounds familiar, doesn't it?

They actually developed a marketing program specifically designed to elicit referrals via the Internet community. What impressed me (and maybe surprised me) at that time was the magnitude with which they both recognized and capitalized on the fact that regardless of the physical reach of the computer, the actual business being transacted was still based on personal relationships. I asked them to explain their system, called "ActiveReferral":

> We really feel that the relationship-building strategies in your book are timeless and can be applied very naturally to the Internet. The following is an outline of the strategies that we've been using to apply your networking principles to successfully marketing oneself via the Internet.
>
> Over the past 3 years we have produced and promoted over 150 business Web sites. We quickly discovered the incredible power of advertising for other people and promoting them on *our* Web site— or mentioning their businesses and saying nice things about them on the Internet. If somebody has a Web site of their own, and you provide a way for people to "link" to their site from yours, it's the fastest, most incredible way to solidify the goodwill of a relationship. Links are a way to click your mouse and move to another Web page—*they are the hidden power of the Internet.* Trading and sharing links is the golden hook that pulls people into your Web site and gives them a reason to like you and want to talk to you some more.
>
> With this in mind, we have designed a Web site strategy that incorporates several of the techniques that you talk about in your book. The following can be utilized with someone you meet locally or with someone thousands of miles away whom you meet first through the Internet. One of the best ideas is the follow-up post-

card. As you teach, with a postcard, you're able to show people your picture and add a quick little note—then drop it in the mailbox. Here's how we've taken that idea and enhanced it just a little bit more.

We use the Internet to send the postcard note by simply typing in someone's first name and e-mail address. If they don't have e-mail we can convert it to be sent to a fax number. This is the instant follow-up step that automatically sends a personalized note reminding them of your meeting. Unlike the postcard, however, we send a full-page reproduction of our Web site with a color photograph of ourselves. The letter is designed to make them feel good and underscore the positive tone developed in the meeting.

Of course, the letter can be written in any way. However, within that letter, we use some of your questions that are a "successful networker's most valuable ammunition," if we didn't get to that during our meeting. In other words, we want to keep the "you-oriented focus" we've already established. Then we also say, "By the way, I really enjoyed meeting with you. I think I have a pretty good idea of who a good prospect is for you. In fact, I appreciated your character and your experience so much that I wanted to tell other people about you and so I took the time to put you on our Web site. You should read the glowing testimonial I wrote about you. Take a look at our Web site at http://www/whatever.com to see the comments I made about you. Hope that it turns into some more business for you!

P.S. I might need a couple more of your business cards. We'll be in touch."

Now the "hook" is set. When people get something on their fax or in their e-mail that tells them you've put them on your Web site, the first thing they're going to do is go look at the Web site. If they're online at all or they can get access, they'll do that immediately. In fact, if they're reading their e-mail, they'll just click directly on the e-mail "link" and be taken right away to your Web site. The first page of the Web site is designed like your postcard idea. It's got someone's picture and business logo (but now it's in full color). And it can be laid out and designed very nicely with animation, video, and sound by using the multimedia ability of the Web.

Now that you have cemented the goodwill of the relationship (by promoting them on your Web site), you can move right into the next important idea you discuss in your book, which is, "how to help your referral partners know who would be a good prospect for you." The first page of the Web site will let them know who you can help. It also gives you a chance to give a little bit more of an overview of your products and services and then present your personal benefit statement. This is the presentation that people see after getting the personalized follow-up letter from you. They get a chance to find out more about you.

The reason they will read through it is that they want to read what you've said about them. At the bottom of the first page you have another link which says, "Click here to meet some of my associates or my referral partners." Or "Click here for additional resources." Or, "Click here to meet people I recommend you work with." When they click on the link, they see a Web page that shows their name, the information off their business card, and the warm glowing things you say about them. They read the third-party endorsement you put on your Web page to help promote them. They appreciate the fact that you are helping to promote them. And you know the power of that!

This works every time. And it works in the "real world" even with people who've never been on the Internet and don't have Web pages, as well as in the online world with people you've never met who do have Web pages.

In a sense, the purpose is the same as the networking organization you talk about developing in Chapter 8: (1) to develop and maintain a give-and-take relationship with as many other business people as possible, (2) to train each of these people to know how to prospect for you, and (3) to know how to match you up with their 250-person sphere of influence.

We developed this strategy 2 years ago, and the premise for us, with all the Web sites we have designed since then, is that they must have an effect in the real world—even if nobody ever looks at your Web site! We found that by telling people we gave them a "link," or that we mentioned them on our Web page, that we established and began the cementing of goodwill even if they never looked at the Web site.

And, if they didn't have a computer, the other thing that they would do is go to their good friend's house (a computer owner) who does have a computer and they'd say, "Let's pull up this person's Web page, because he told me to take a look at it because I'm mentioned." Now you have two people looking at your page, they're talking about you—and the networking has already begun, because they are feeling good about you!

Here are a couple of other things we do. One is add a feedback form, a place where people can send information, such as their name, address, and phone number. And with this interactive form (sort of a questionnaire), we ask them "questions that make the sale." We also ask for referrals, but not in person. We let people add their referrals to our Web page, which then gets sent to our e-mail automatically. We do this with an interactive form that allows them to type in the name, address, and phone number of people we should contact. We utilize some of your thoughts for helping them figure out who a good referral would be and make it easy for them to type in the names of referrals while they're looking at our Web page. We have found that this approach shortens the networking process significantly. It creates a fun, interactive, online world that's kind of like playing a video game, combined with all the networking hooks in your book. People will fill in a name just to see what will happen next!

In the past, this would have been difficult for people to be able to do. They would have to learn a lot about HTML programming or they would have to hire a full-time Web programmer. To be proactive about adding endorsements and links to a Web site has been costly and time consuming until now.

We've recently completed development of a software program, called ActiveEdit, which lets people instantly update their Web page without any knowledge of HTML or FTP. They simply type right into their browser (Internet Explorer or Netscape), press a button, and immediately their Web page gets updated. It is as easy to use as a word processor.

The way people use the program is simple:

At the end of the day they sit down with their little stack of business cards and enter the name and contact information from everybody that they bumped into during the day. They then write up something really nice about them, something they liked about them, something about their business, etc. They then hit the update button and immediately all those people are now on their Web site. No programming. No coding. And anybody can do it!

The next thing they do is enter the person's name and e-mail address (or fax number), and the followup letter is ready. They can change and personalize the prewritten letter if they want. Press a button, and immediately the letter gets sent via e-mail, or it gets converted through the Internet to a fax machine. And that's all they have to do.

These simple steps can be repeated every day. They help to quickly create the "know you, like you, trust you" feelings upon which the success of your networking system is based. And they've gone to the next level of making people feel extra important, and even indebted to them because, in actuality, you have advertised for them. Here is the reason we call our system *ActiveReferral:* Introducing people to other potential prospects, of course, is very effective. But if you "actively" promote them and prospect for them (by advertising for them on the Internet), they will think of ways to help promote you and refer business back to you every time. There's nothing passive about this—it's active!

Position Yourself Online as Well

Just as we discussed in Chapter 9—positioning yourself as the expert and only logical resource in your field—the same holds just as true on the Internet. How do you get the word out as efficiently as possible to carve a niche in the mind of your potential consumer or networking partner? Anderson and Henderson explain:

One way for online marketers to position themselves as the expert in their industry is by publishing articles and testimonials on their Web page. As you point out, it's a challenge to get newspaper editors to allow you to have an article or column in their newspapers. Not so in this case. One can immediately put up articles on the Internet. And now you're "published on the Net." This offers much of the same kind of credibility.

The next step is to take your articles and get them published on other people's Web pages and in other electronic magazines or "e-zines" on the Internet. And, there are libraries on America Online (AOL) that give you the same kind of positioning as being published in magazines or newspapers. These methods are much more immediate and accomplishable for most people.

The automated follow-up page is used to publish your articles onto a Web page and send them to Internet publishers. Having the HTML code already written makes it easy for publishers to "print" your article. Because it is so easy to use, automated followup is also excellent for sending articles of interest and personalized thank-you notes to those who gave you leads, continually putting your smile in front of your referral partners so they begin to look forward to hearing from you again.

These techniques work extremely well for professionals and entrepreneurs who want to build more local referral business. They prospect in their local area, then use Internet technology to automate their follow-up procedures. The entire purpose of their Web site is to further the referral process. Everyone they meet becomes an important addition to their "Web" as they continually internetwork. First they add their employees, then their favorite suppliers, then their best customers. Soon they add everyone with whom they come into contact inside the community. The goodwill value compounds significantly.

The national and global marketplace apply just as well. There are ways to identify people who want what you have to sell, who have already demonstrated "by their actions" that they want your products and services. This gives you a very powerful sales advantage. All of a sudden, you're not working off a cold list because you've been able to use the Internet to quickly do research on people and qualify them and also find out a lot of things about them both personally and about their business.

So when you make that first introductory call, they respond more positively, because you already know the topics that are of interest to them. You can create a common frame of reference to discuss ideas with them. They are interested! In addition, if you've been able to justify plugging them on your Web site (even before you meet or talk to them) you have an instant goodwill builder. They are predisposed to "like you and trust you"—even though they *don't* know you! You can move right into the networking process without ever having met them. The success rate with this has been absolutely phenomenal.

I appreciate the time Michael and Patrick took to explain what they are doing. They have provided some excellent, usable information to duplicate. They've also taken what the novice online marketer sees as two *seemingly* separate ideas (the Internet and relationship building) and brought them together. It just affirms that the two are not mutually exclusive. Check out Michael and Patrick's Web site at http://www.activereferral.com. They also have an excellent e-zine (Internet magazine) called *Hits to Sales* at http://www.hitstosales.com.

Where to Prospect on the Internet

One of the main pieces of wisdom regarding Inter-Net-working is the realization that although countless millions of people are now online, they are not necessarily your prospects for marketing online any more than they were before you got online. Instead, think target marketing, or niche marketing. Your intent is to find the ones who are predisposed to want what you have to offer.

There are several different places to start your prospecting efforts. Fortunately a lot of things that we are familiar with in the real world, such as *Yellow Pages* and business directories, have an online alternative. Patrick Anderson suggests, "Don't forget to ask other people who you meet online for their favorite prospecting spots. It is amazing how helpful people are in cyberspace."

The four primary Internet technologies are Web sites, newsgroups, mailing lists (listservs), and chat rooms. Each of these areas has a different method to search for topics and specific interest areas. There are also online services, such as CompuServe, Prodigy, AOL, and BBSs (bulletin board services) that provide access to groups of people who are not on the Internet.

Search Facilities Are Key

And, when it comes to finding your prospects to target, learning how to use the different search facilities on the Internet and online services will be a major factor in your success.

It is just as important as learning how to use the card catalog in the public library. You will find that people tend to be attracted to newsgroups for entirely different reasons than those who visit chat rooms, or surf on Web sites. With a little research you will find the places that yield the most responsive prospects. Here are the places to start (again, realizing that between the time this is being written and the time you read it, many things in the "amazing world of cyber" will have changed):

Web Sites
http://www.search.com/
http://www.hitstosales.com/
  searchlinks.html

Business Directories
http://www.inter800.com/
http://www.citysurf.com/

Yellow Pages
http://www1.bigyellow.com/
http://www.bigbook.com/

Newsgroups
http://www.dejanews.com/
http://www.liszt.com/news/

Chat Rooms
http://www.liszt.com/chat/
http://www.excite.com/channel/
  chat/

Mailing Lists/ListServs
http://www.neosoft.com/
  internet/paml/indexes.html
http://www.liszt.com/

Classified Ad Sites
http://www.uran.net/imall/
  mother.html

National Chambers of Commerce
http://www.uschamber.org/mall/
index.html

Many of the above references will be discussed later in this chapter.

How Are These Used for Ultimate Marketing Effectiveness?

Some of these sites will take advertising and some won't. Some are open to self-promotion and others aren't. The point is, thinking only of those two options is totally missing the big picture with regards to what you can accomplish through the proper use of these vehicles. Throughout the remainder of this chapter you'll learn from several "netpreneurs" what is working for them. One idea from Henderson and Anderson is to find one or two well-positioned businesses who want to advertise for you and refer their existing customers to you! Their suggestion for using the lists is as follows:

> Decide in advance who your networking prospects are. Look through each of these search areas to see how they make it easy to identify your target audience. Try to determine which people are the centers of influence in their group, which Web sites get the most traffic, and who the movers and shakers are.
>
> Find a name and an e-mail address and send a personalized introductory letter that explains what your customers have in common and how you propose working together to share leads. Follow up with telephone calls for maximum response. Read the chapters

on How to Work Any Crowd and Cross-Promotions for more ideas of ways to persuade business people to desire win/win relationships with you.

Direct Marketing Via the Internet

In the previous chapter we discussed the mail order/direct marketing business. The basic principles in that chapter apply to the online version of this type of marketing as well. As with direct marketing, it is very difficult to make money through one-step advertisements. In other words, the most efficient way to advertise and/or promote is to use the first ad simply as a means to get those with interest to respond. Then, a very targeted letter can be constructed and sent in order to make the sale. Then, the database aspect for the back-end part of the marketing process would apply.

Utilizing the various Internet technologies, search facilities, and other ideas to draw interest to your site discussed within this chapter, then, please note the following:

The 12th Commandment—Thou Shalt Not Spam
or
To Spam or Not to Spam...There Is No Question

Spamming is the unsolicited sending of e-mail advertisements to consumers. Also called bulk e-mail, it is to the online community what junk mail is to the rest of the world. Oh, by the way, the 11th commandment is "Thou Shalt Not Kid Thyself." Anyway, depending on what you desire to sell through direct marketing over the Internet, the same one-step and two-step philosophy holds true. Because of the massive amount of people they can reach at virtually no cost, many Internet marketers send out lots of bulk e-mail advertising messages to massive amounts of people—names lists they acquire through someone else's e-mail advertisement offering sometimes millions of e-mail addresses for very little money.

First of all, remember, you usually get what you pay for. Second, this kind of advertising, known as Spamming, aside from being generally quite ineffective and a total breach of "netiquette," is quite looked down upon by the Internet community, can get you "flamed" big-time (which means you'll get lots of nasty messages sent to you), and most important, can elicit having your online privileges being taken away.

That's right. And, as this chapter is being written, new federal laws are in the process of being enacted prohibiting this type of marketing.

Henderson and Anderson say, "Forget bulk e-mail....Impersonal advertisements yield an impersonal response and an unqualified prospect. It is the exact opposite of Inter-Net-working." They add, and I love this, "Here's a novel idea—send me a personal note and I'll respond to it personally!" Approach people in a way you would like to be approached. Otherwise your message will be treated like "junk mail" and tuned out.

What's much more effective is, just as discussed in traditional direct response advertising, to systematically go about acquiring a list made up of targeted, qualified prospects. This can be done by renting, purchasing, or trading for already good lists or by one-step advertising and publicity which will attract those you are targeting to respond and request additional information.

Still Another Reason to Avoid Spamming

Some people may think it is great to send a million bulk e-mail solicitations in order to receive a thousand unqualified leads. But wouldn't it be much more profitable to know how to send one effective e-mail that will generate one referral partner who will send you prequalified leads for life?

Keep in mind that bulk e-mail may be cheap, but follow-up time is expensive. If you don't have qualified leads, you will waste a lot of time with hundreds of people! The goal is to spend more time with fewer people—more quality time developing relationships with more qualified prospects.

Still another point mentioned earlier in the book holds just as true online: The people we are looking for are not intended to be only our customers or buyers. They are much more important than that! They will become our advocates, our promoters, our third-party endorsements, our referral base...our personal walking (or typing) ambassadors. Try to identify a group of people who know how to reach your target audience.

How to Work Any (Virtual) Crowd

Many people who begin marketing online are anxious to jump right into the various newsgroups, chat rooms, and listservs in order to promote their various products and services. Not only will that strategy prove ineffective, it would rank right up there with Spamming when it comes to irritating, if not downright offending, the very people they want to have as customers.

Remember, people are *not* actively searching out ads and brochures to read. Most of the information is readily accessible and free, just like the information at a public library. So how would people at the library respond if you put your business card in the middle of several library books? What feelings would you elicit by walking up to someone and saying, "Since you're looking at books in this aisle, you need my brochure"? How many people would you irritate by sticking flyers on the windshield of every car in the parking lot?

Would you be asked to leave if you repeatedly interrupted people who were having quiet discussions, then jumped right into a sales presentation and walked away? Not to mention, in following the principles of business networking in this book, you certainly wouldn't even be that aggressive at an event designed for business networking. The very last thing you would ever do is approach a person or a group of people and immediately begin talking about yourself and your business.

Just the idea sounds kind of crazy, doesn't it? But, people are doing the online equivalent every day. They forget how to be polite, introduce themselves, and adjust their behavior to the particular group situation they are in. What works at a business after hours function will seem strange at a baseball game. You would approach a younger crowd at a weekend party differently than an older group of civic club members. Try very hard to identify and observe these different online segments if you want your prospecting efforts to be successful.

Newsgroups, chat rooms, and such are specific areas where people discuss their common interests. There are over 15,000 newsgroups where practically every special interest group imaginable is represented. Mailing lists (listservs) are like newsgroups, segmented by special interest, but articles arrive via e-mail.

Newsgroups and chat rooms are basically just a crowd of like-minded people. A group of people like any other group. Try not to see the Internet as one large network of computers but instead as several different communities, ongoing conversations, and meeting places for people with similar interests.

The good news is that, just as in the real world, within these cyber groups are centers of influence. These people can be determined by the fact that they are very vocal (lots of posts) and, *more important, they receive lots of responses.* This indicates they are respected by others.

Many experts suggest that, when researching a particular market, finding its related newsgroups and chat rooms and "lurking" is a good idea. This way you can monitor the conversations and gain a deeper understanding of the wants, needs, likes, dislikes, etc., of their participants before jumping in. It's a good form of recognizance, and that is an excellent start. Let's take it even a step further:

Let's set a goal to identify the centers of influence within those groups and then propel the relationships with those people using the information in Chapter 3—how to work any crowd. Also, refer back to the section in this chapter on linking.

A Great Example

Patrick Anderson noticed in one of the local Atlanta newsgroups that three people seemed to fit the category of center of influence. One was an artist. Patrick checked this person's Web site, really enjoyed what he saw, and felt there might be some way he could use his work for his own Web site, as well as referring him to others. So he called the artist, whose name is Joe, on the telephone (note that he didn't e-mail him— he called him!) to introduce himself. He then related to Joe his thoughts about the artist's work.

Understandably, Joe was delighted, and right away suggested someone who could use Patrick's Web site design and marketing services as well. Another 250-person or more sphere of influence was now part of Patrick's life, and Joe's as well. We can only imagine how far this new network beginning with Patrick and Joe will extend and how many lives and businesses will be affected and influenced positively.

Now let's talk a bit about "time leveraging." The typical newsgroup prospector, in order to attain a large number of valid leads, must basically become a newsgroup *junkie*. The fact is, most of us don't have that kind of time to devote to this one avenue of prospecting. As Patrick points out, however, "when you make a great Inter-Net-working connection with someone who *is*, in fact, a newsgroup junkie, she can become your personal walking ambassador to the news room community. You are then benefiting as though you've invested the time there yourself."

Here's a great example illustrating this point: Michael and Patrick were able to generate over 2 million hits for the Country Music Association Award's webcast with just ten days to promote! One person commented to them afterward, "I can understand how you pulled that off, I saw your promotions regarding the event all over the newsgroups." What's so amazing about this is that I personally know Patrick and Michael *never posted one message to any of the newsgroups themselves*. Not one! They simply enlisted the help of several of the centers of influence they had cultivated prior to the promotion, and those persons' natural cyber conversations and fantastic "third-party" endorsements resulted in a simply outstanding cyber turnout.

When prospecting through newsgroups and such, Michael Henderson advises that the rules of the game are clearly outlined. Unfortunately, some individuals will ignore that and try to push their way into the process. He says that it is much more effective to ask questions of those in the know, in a very humble, unassuming manner. "You'll find the newsgroup veterans who will be only too glad to help."

When it comes to establishing mutually beneficial relationships, the rules that apply to real-world organizations basically apply to the virtual world as well. That's why I suggest that before you begin to prospect via the Internet that you again review and internalize the information in Chapters 2 and 3.

One more important point: Although this particular section really focused on newsgroups, please do not overlook the fact that the exact same approaches and techniques will work just as well in chat rooms, discussion forums, and listservs.

Classified Ads

This part may surprise you because the reason for using the classified ads is *not* to put in your classified ad. "What's that Burg? Now you've really flipped your lid!" I can understand your feeling that way, however there is actually a much more effective usage of this Internet tool, and that is for prospecting.

For purposes of clarification, we're not talking about taking a classified ad in an online newsletter, e-zine, or traditional print medium, but the "classified ad" section of your online provider.

Let's face it, unless you have a product or service that is so in demand that people will purposefully search the classifieds for the express purpose of finding your ad, the chances are you're not going to see enough of a return to make it worth your while. And I'll bet you and I both don't deal in that particular product or service. However, the people who are doing the advertising, depending upon what it is they're advertising, may be wonderful, qualified prospects for either your product or service or for establishing a networking relationship. So pursue that relationship in exactly the same manner you would any other, by utilizing the information in this book, and specifically, in this chapter.

More Ideas on Promoting
Your Web Site

Many of the techniques and tactics discussed throughout this chapter are totally applicable to this section as well. We're just going to explore several more ideas that can help you generate increased response.

Of the thousands of tips and bushels full of advice available for promoting your Web site (which of course would be a book in itself), the following are a few you can immediately apply. After finishing this chapter, peruse the Resource Guide for a listing of some of those places you can search for even more information on this topic.

According to Internet marketing authority Jonathan Mizel, president of CyberWave Media (http://www.cyberwave.com), a common misconception about the Internet is that just having a Web site will bring people to it. "Nothing could be further from the truth," says Mizel. "In fact, if you have a Web site, the truth is that you are one of tens of millions of people who also have a Web site. As is generally the case, if you want to get people to your Web site, you'll need to take proactive steps to get them there. It doesn't matter how great a site you have if nobody visits. Without the leads and traffic, you are out of the game before you even start."

The bottom line is that generating traffic should be your first priority in establishing a business presence on the Internet.

Mizel, like many online authorities, is very big on taking linking (discussed earlier in this chapter) as far as possible for the benefit of all concerned. "Obtain reciprocal links from similar businesses that are already on the Web," he advises. "You can trade links with virtually anyone, even your direct competitors. Create strategic alliances. While online, we must work with our competitors to normalize the consumers' experience of spending money on the Internet. *Our biggest competition is the fear of online commerce in the mind of the prospect.*"

He suggests purchasing and bartering links from proven traffic zones. This is a very sound idea, and scores of Web sites will sell (or trade) you a link in the form of a banner ad. A banner ad is one of those graphic ads that show up in many commercial sites like search engines. When you see existing advertising on a site that you think would complement yours, ask for the rates. You'll find that many smaller sites will sell you a link for as little as $250 per month.

Placing paid ads in e-mail newsletters that are read by your target market can also be an effective means of generating response. Online marketer Gary Christianson states that just one of his ads in the online newsletter *DEMC* (demc.com) brought in over 170 responses. Gary is another netrepreneur who makes very effective use of "free reports"—brief reports filled with helpful information to the reader created by the marketer to sell a product or service as the next step. Even if you don't specifically market an information-type product, you can find a way to bring free reports into your marketing strategy.

For example, a friend of mine, Joan Waldner, just began a management consulting firm that provides assistance in reorganizing all aspects of one's personal and business needs. She is currently in the process of writing a free report entitled "10 Secrets Today's Ultra—Busy Professional Can Use to Reorganize Their Life and Improve Their Life Style." She'll advertise this free report in the local Palm Beach County business magazines and any other media those in her target market follow. And you know that to order their free report, prospects will need to either call her office or visit her Web site.

Your free report gives your prospect a reason for visiting right away. And as you've seen, this holds true for when you advertise your Web site with a traditional medium as well as online. Free reports are a proven method of generating response and serve two purposes: Again, one is to give you an opportunity for the immediate sale because the report, although it will contain excellent information, is basically a sales letter asking for the order. And two, you now have another name to add to your database for future sales letters, back-end products, etc.

Publishing online articles is another method of generating high response with no capital outlay. Jonathan Mizel says he has received more free publicity from just a few articles he's written and placed in online file libraries than had he sent out 500 press releases. One nice break was when a writer from *Entrepreneurial Edge* saw an article of his in one of CompuServe's file libraries. And a friend of Jonathan's wrote an article on America Online that has been downloaded over 15,000 times (and has generated thousands of inquiries).

Another suggestion by Mizel is to create publicity-generating articles and press releases and submit them to established, traditional media sources such as "real-world" magazines and newsletters. These articles should provide good, solid information that will inform and be appreciated by readers, but will also let them know that there is much more viable information to be gained by visiting your site (which naturally, will be mentioned in the tag line).

And don't forget the other media as well. Keep plugging away to those producers of television and radio programs. Whenever you manage to be interviewed on radio or television, be sure and mention your Web site. With a lot of effort and the right timing, your site could get featured in a traditional media source and derive lots of traffic.

One idea that computers have made feasible for anyone regardless of budget is to produce an online newsletter. Create a newsletter with useful information that will result in people who visit your site to get additional information you have on their topics of interest. A sale may then result. Having a newsletter also puts you in the position of being able to create mutually beneficial, win/win relationships with other newsletter publishers. You can list their newsletter (and provide a link to it) and vice-versa.

Online information marketer and newsletter publisher Gary Christensen (http://www.homeincome.com) reports that a number of new subscribers to his newsletter found him through his listings with other newsletters. According to Gary, the *Opportunity Digest* e-zine alone has brought in 20 new subscribers.

And one final suggestion from Jonathan Mizel is that your Web site and e-mail address should be on the following:

- Business cards and letterhead
- Print and display advertising
- Broadcast advertising such as radio and TV
- Direct mail and brochures
- Press and publicity releases

Again, the bottom line is this: Generating traffic should be your first priority in establishing a business presence on the Internet.

And I've saved the vehicle you've been waiting to hear all about for last....

Search Engines, Directories (Yahoo, etc.)

A search engine is designed to help you find Web sites that are highly relevant to the keywords entered as search criteria. If you have ever searched for something in a computer database, you will understand the idea. Think of a computerized card catalog at the library that helps you find all the books on whatever topic you are interested in.

When the Internet was largely noncommercial the search engines were a research tool for academia—and they worked quite well. Now, however, they have become the target of business-oriented Web sites who all have one goal in mind—and understandably so—to have their site listed at the top.

In a recent survey, 86 percent of the respondents reported they discovered Web sites through the search engines (primarily Yahoo, Infoseek, AltaVista, Excite, Lycos, WebCrawler, and Hotbot). The high visibility and ability to instantly generate traffic to a Web site from a global marketplace is what makes the fight for the top spot so competitive, and often ruthless.

So, the question is, "How do you get that top spot for yourself?" I went to one of my "resident experts" for the answer. Here's Patrick Anderson with some very hard-hitting, realistic information:

> A lot of people think there must be an easy way to gain that top spot. Here's the challenge: there are over 4 million Web pages listed on Infoseek when you search for the word, *business.* You are shown ten of them at a time. What makes a person think their page has any more chance of getting listed on top than the other 3,999,999 pages? If it was really that easy to figure out, everyone would do it. Then, however, everyone would still not be on the first page. It's similar to the freeway at rush hour. You want to find a direct route home. So does everyone else.
>
> So, what do you do? If you want all the traffic you are either going to pay for the education or you are going to pay for the service. There is no other way to do it. It is not easy. It is not magic. It takes time, effort, and knowledge. Then it takes continual monitoring to keep the position you worked so hard to get in the first place. The competition is fierce and severe for those top spots, which is why the search engines can charge so much money to sell keyword banners.
>
> If you don't have the time or money, then concentrate your efforts on getting listed on Yahoo. Since Yahoo does not rely on automated routines that can be tricked by clever programmers, it is the most reasonable search engine to acquire good placement on. Some studies suggest that it is also the most popular search engine for people who are purchasing online. Here's our strategy for finding the perfect spot for your home page on Yahoo: First, do some research. Look through Yahoo to find useful information, bargain deals, or great entertainment sites related to your business. Think and act like your customers. Skip the pages that have a thousand listings. Get a little more specific and settle on a category that has 40 to 100 pages. This is where your customers will also be looking. Write a snappier headline and more interesting description than anybody else. Change the title of your Web site to match this new headline. Be sure to start your headline with the letter "A" or "B" (you can see why, right?). It sounds simple, but it works. One more note—erase all the meta tags and keyword stuffing tricks from your homepage before submitting.
>
> If you want to have any chance of getting close to the top on the other search engines, buy these two books and give them to your Web designer: *The Step by Step Guide to Successfully Promoting a Web*

Site by John DeUlloa (order online at http://www.promoteone
.com/var2) and *The Unfair Advantage Internet Book on Winning the
Search Engines War* by Stephen Mahaney (order online at
http://www.searchenginehelp.com/promote). They are the best.
And stay tuned to the *Hits to Sales* e-zine which always has an
updated section on search engine secrets, and it's free. You can find
that at http://www.hitstosales.com.

Name Capture—Another Advantage of Your Web Site

Once you draw someone to your Web site, the next goal, other than
hopefully to sell your product or service (or begin the process of
acquiring another networking partner), is to add that name to your
database. Even if the person didn't buy right now or express any interest in doing so, the fact is, if a person has taken time out of their daily
"surfing" to visit your Web site, there's a good chance they are a qualified prospect for your product or service. It's your job, while they are
there, to be sure they register their names and e-mail addresses in
order to receive future information from you.

What I'm saying is, "This is your chance to get them on your list!" In
Online Marketing Handbook, Dan Janal says, "Capturing names and
addresses of readers is of paramount importance to create relationships—think in terms of the long-term value of your customers." He
suggests that several ways of accomplishing this include providing a
registration form, creating an interactive game of sorts, giving away
some free information to those who register, and asking the visitor to
add comments about your home page.

One particularly important point made by Janal throughout his
book is to make it easy for your prospects and customers to do business with you. Not only should the process of name registration be
simple for them, the *buying* process should be easy as well. I can recall
one instance in particular where I wanted to buy something over the
Internet but could simply not figure out what they needed me to do. If
I hadn't really wanted that product, I wouldn't have bothered doing
what was necessary to obtain it. As it is, I picked up my telephone and
called to have one of their service people walk me through the process.
Do you really want to take a chance that your prospects want to do
business with you that badly? Probably not. I know I don't. Make it
easy for them to do business with you.

Overall View of Marketing through the Internet (Inter-Net-working)

As mentioned several times during this chapter, utilizing the Internet as a marketing tool needs to be viewed as—well, just that—another great business building tool, not a replacement for the full spectrum of your effective marketing strategy, most importantly, relationship building! Internet marketing can be a welcome and valuable addition to what you are already doing correctly, so long as it's not seen as the panacea or cure for an otherwise ineffective marketing game plan.

Most experts agree that as we head into the twenty-first century, effective utilization of the Internet will become more and more important. Certainly, it levels the playing field and allows us "little guys" to fight the good fight with the major corporations on a more even keel. To take advantage of the Internet, however, we must learn from the proper sources, get the right information, and look at Internet marketing as a continuing, long-term situation as opposed to a quick fix.

Internet marketing authority Terry Williams, author of the free weekly e-zine, *Internet Marketing Issues* (http://www.intersuccess. com/imi/), says:

> There are many very good resources on the Internet today that are available to home-based and small business entrepreneurs. The problem lies in where to *find* relative information that these people can use and profit from. Many of these resources are just not cost effective, or the entrepreneur doesn't have the resources available to them to take advantage of the global marketplace.
>
> In order to compete well into the next century, a business must have a well-defined Internet business presence and online marketing strategy to remain successful. The key is in finding the right balance between the costs involved and finding the best tools available to maximize their online marketing and advertising efforts.

My suggestion is to read books by the authorities in this field, check out and study the teachings that people such as Terry and others put forth in their e-zines, take classes that are offered, and discuss the ideas with others in situations similar to yours. Share information. Discover what is and isn't working, and test, test, test, until you have your own process systemized.

Also, keep in mind that with the Internet just beginning to boom, many self-proclaimed "experts" are selling information on how to succeed/get rich/profit, etc., on the Internet. This, in and of itself, is certainly okay, so long as they are legitimately knowledgeable with actual experience. It's up to you to make sure you're getting your advice from the correct sources.

Acknowledgment

Many people took time to provide me with information regarding online marketing and Inter-Net-working. Among them were several who invested time away from their own businesses in order to help me provide the knowledge in this area for you the reader. Patrick Anderson and Mike Henderson devoted hours of time via the telephone, fax, and Internet, sending me reams of information making my research much easier and of higher quality. And Daniel S. Janal also provided his time to answer my numerous questions and to point me in the right direction.

Key Points

- *Online marketing* has been defined by the author and online marketing authority Daniel S. Janal as "a system for selling products and services to target audiences who use the Internet and commercial online services, by utilizing online tools and services in a strategic manner consistent with the company's overall marketing program."

- According to online marketing authorities Patrick Anderson and Mike Henderson, "When the principles of this book are applied to the online world, it becomes *Inter-Net-working*."

- The principles of networking remain the same. In fact, know you, like you, and trust you becomes more critical than ever while establishing yourself in this new medium.

- E-mail, or electronic mail, is the most basic tool of online marketing, yet it is also among the most important. It is the primary way the online marketer can stay in touch with his or her prospect, customer, or client. And e-mail has been called the "common denominator" for reaching people.

- Be sure to include your e-mail address—as well as your Web site domain, if you have one—on all your business stationery and marketing tools.

- Trading links is the fundamental spirit of networking on the Internet. It is the golden hook that pulls people into your Web site, while you send people to theirs. This will provide an immediate increase in traffic to your Web site, bringing new, prequalified prospects to your doorstep.

- When prospecting on the Internet, investigate Web sites, newsgroups, listservs (mailing lists), and chat rooms.

- The bottom line: generating traffic should be your first priority in establishing a business presence on the Internet.

- Dan Janal says, "Capturing names and addresses of visitors is of paramount importance to creating relationships—think in terms of the long-term value of your customers." He suggests that name capture can be accomplished by:
  1. Providing a registration form
  2. Creating an interactive game of sorts
  3. Giving away free information to those who register
  4. Asking for visitor comments about your home page

Resource Guide

The following is merely a partial list to get you started. I suggest continually seeking out additional resources as well.

Books

Bayne, Kim: *The Internet Marketing Plan.* New York, John Wiley & Sons, 1997.

Chase, Larry: *Essential Business Tactics for the Net.* New York, John Wiley & Sons, 1998.

Daniels, Jim: *Email Marketing.* Smithfield, RI, JDD Publishing, 1997.

Daniels, Jim: *Insider Internet Marketing.* Smithfield, RI, JDD Publishing, 1997.

DeUlloa, John: *The Step by Step Guide to Successfully Promoting a Web Site.* Order online at http://www.promoteone.com/var2.

Edwards, Paul, Sarah Edwards, and Linda Rohrbough: *Making Money in Cyberspace.* Tarcher/Putnam, New York, 1998.

Janal, Daniel S.: *101 Successful Businesses You Can Start On The Internet.* New York, John Wiley & Sons, 1997.

Janal, Daniel S.: *Online Marketing Handbook.* New York, John Wiley & Sons, 1998.

Mahaney, Stephan: *The Unfair Advantage Internet Book on Winning the Search Engines War.* Order online at http://www.searchenginehelp.com/promote.

McCarthy, Ken: Internet-for-Business (kit). Order online at http://www.e-media.com.

O'Keefe, Steve: *Publicity on The Internet.* New York, John Wiley & Sons, 1996.

Stern, Jim: *Customer Service on the Internet: Building Relationships, Increasing Loyalty, and Staying Competitive.* New York, John Wiley & Sons, 1996.

Stern, Jim: *What Makes People Click.* New York, John Wiley & Sons, 1997.

A Few Interesting E-Zines/Newsletters

Bizweb E-Gazette, http://www.bizweb2000.com.

Business to Business Magazine, http://www.business2business.on.ca/welcome.html.

Chase Online Marketing Strategies, http://chaseonline.com.

Computer Profits Electronic Newsletter, http://www.uran.net/pearson/whichnws.html.

Cyberphoenix Weekly, subscribe@freedom-mall.com.

Dan Janal's Online Marketing Newsletter, http:\\www.janal.com.

DEMC's E-Magazine, subscribe@demc2.com.

Electronic Money Tree (Netrepreneur's Digest), http://www.soos.com/$tree.

Entrepreneur Weekly, http://www.eweekly.com.

Hits to Sales, http://www.hitstosales.com.

Home Money Free Email Newsletter, www.homeincome.com/homebiz/.

Internet Marketing Issues, http://www.intersuccess.com/imi/.

Larry Chase's Web Digest for Markets, http://wdfm.com.

Mizel, Jonathan, several Internet marketing articles, http://www.cyberwave.com.

NETResults News Service, http://www.copywriter.com.

Netrepreneur, http://www.talkbiz.com/digest.

Network Ink, http://www.profnet.com.

Small Business Advisor Newsletter, http://www.isquare.com.

SOHO BizAlert!, http://www.iwatch.com/SOHO/sohoba.html.

VirtualBusiness News, http://www.virtualbusiness.net.

Web Marketing Today, http://www.wilsonweb.com.

Weekly Success Tip, http://www.choicemall.com/successstyles.

Worldprofit Worldgram Electronic Newsletter, http://www.worldprofit.com.

Your-Biz Newsletter, http://pages.prodigy.com/business.

Your Business Newsletter, http://www.interlog.com/~gcn.

16

The Foundation
of Effective
Communication

I'd like to begin this chapter by sharing with you a recent incident. I believe it is the quintessential example of how easy it is to either get along, or not get along, with others. It shows just how much power each of us truly has to add positively or negatively to our network and to our world. Here's what happened.

My neighbor Carol, a staff supervisor for a local midsized business, called to invite me to a local dinner theater. As a holiday bonus her company had decided to send the entire staff to the theater for a night of fine food and entertainment, and Carol invited me to come as her guest.

Because the person with the tickets had not yet arrived, the manager would not let us into the main dining area to sit down and begin eating. Instead, he politely asked us to wait at the bar. Nursing a soft drink, I waited with the rest, when I sensed the first sign of trouble.

Carol announced she was not happy with the situation. She wanted us to begin eating right away so that we'd have plenty of time to enjoy our food. As far as Carol was concerned, the manager knew we were simply waiting for the person with the tickets to arrive, so "Why couldn't we just go in there now?" (I happened to have been in total agreement with Carol, but as a guest, I felt it wasn't my place to say so.)

Then Carol said the magic words—the words that told me I was absolutely right to sense trouble. "I'm going to raise a fuss about this!" Oh no, I thought. This was supposed to be a fun, relaxing evening.

Carol summoned the manager over and began to verbally assault him. Well, he got stubborn and simply repeated, "Ma'am, it's against the rules. As far as I know, the person with the tickets may want to assign the seats." And every time Carol countered with an insult to his intelligence (or lack thereof), he countered with the same excuse.

I came to an executive decision: enough was enough. When Carol finally took a breath between words, I simply, and with a smile, politely asked the manager, "Sir, aside from the seating arrangements, would there be any other reason why seating us now would be uncomfortable for you?" He replied, "Not at all."

Praying to myself that Carol would not interrupt, which I could sense she was genuinely contemplating, I continued, "Well, I understand exactly how you feel, and in a similar situation I might feel the same way. Let me ask, if we were to assume total responsibility for the seating assignments—in fact, if I could get the staff supervisor herself to agree that you would be totally off the hook—would you consider letting us go in now?"

He responded with a smile and said, "That wouldn't be a problem." I replied, "Great, because being able to eat our meal without having to hurry would certainly add to our enjoyment of the show. And by the way, I appreciate your help and understanding." How did he respond? "My pleasure." As a matter of fact, at that point he personally escorted us to our seats and then checked on our comfort several times throughout the evening.

Carol was delighted and amazed. "How did you do that? What's your secret?"

"There is no secret," I answered. "It's simply a philosophy. An attitude and a decision to genuinely care about someone else's needs so that they, in turn, *want* to care about yours."

Incidents such as the above occur in my life quite often. I'm known as a person who can get people to do things for me that they ordinarily wouldn't do for others. The objective is a win-win outcome. As mentioned earlier in this book, isn't that really what networking is all about?

And my techniques for pulling off the seemingly impossible, ranging from extinguishing possible verbal and emotional fires to getting civil servants to cut through red tape and get things done for me quickly, is also a learned skill. Because I had the very best teacher! You see, there are probably only a few people in the history of the universe who have ever had *natural* people skills to the extent of a Dale Carnegie. One was Dale Carnegie himself; the other is my dad, Mike Burg.

He is one of the world's greatest natural networkers, one of those rare human beings who, despite his more-than-humble beginnings, has helped change the lives of many and positively affected the lives of many others. With everything I've learned and experienced regarding networking in the business sense, what I've learned about networking in the *human* sense has proven many times as valuable.

As we discuss certain philosophies and techniques in this chapter, I'll combine some of the thoughts and lessons I've learned from my dad, as well as from other "people experts," both modern and ancient.

Make People Feel Good About Themselves

Probably my dad's greatest strength is his ability to make those with whom he comes into contact feel important as human beings. And he does this not through manipulation or false compliments, but by genuine caring. We touched on that in Chapter 2 when we discussed asking feel-good questions that get people talking about themselves. But this philosophy goes much deeper than that. It's realizing that when we look at a person, what we and the rest of the world see is not necessarily the whole truth.

The business Dad founded and ran was a gymnasium school called the Academy of Physical and Social Development. This was a unique, psychodynamically oriented gymnasium school that helped countless individuals and families learn to communicate more effectively with each other. It was based on Dad's philosophy that if you could make a person feel good about himself, he would lead a healthy and productive life. Word got around about the success of the Academy and this resulted in a *Time* magazine feature story.

While I was growing up, I watched all sorts of people come into the Academy. I'd see a family walk in: the man, big and handsome; the woman, pretty and trim, with an air of confidence; the child, attractive and well-dressed, looking like a million bucks. They looked like the all-American family.

But when you got to know them, you realized that this guy with muscles didn't *feel* so strong, this pretty woman didn't *feel* attractive, and the youngster was not happy being their child. You realized that there was more to this than met the eye, and that only when people feel good about themselves do they feel strong and pretty. And when they are successful and make their parents happy with them, they feel very welcome in the family.

The Academy had a motto that I feel is timeless: "To have a body does not make one a man. To have a child does not make one a parent." What we see is not always what we get, and we need to approach people as individuals whose lives we can somehow make better by making them feel better about themselves.

This philosophy is easy to relate to networking, isn't it? After all, what comes to mind when we approach center-of-influence types? They might *appear* to have it all together. We know they might be successful in business, have lots of friends around them, and appear to be always happy. Yet, below the surface, things may not be so wonderful.

Think about it. We don't know what is going on with their family. We don't know what their pressures of business are at that time. We don't really know what's in their heads, and as a result, they can use a lot of good, positive strokes. And, if done in a sincere, genuine manner, they are going to be very grateful because it's going to make them feel good. That is where confidence comes in. The more confident this person feels, the more he is going to appreciate your coming into his life.

Five Questions of Life

Dad's mentor, so to speak, was a post-Biblical sage by the name of ben Zoma, whose philosophy dealt with different states of being and appreciation, as expressed through four basic questions. Dad later added a fifth question, which followed along the same lines.

Question 1: Who Is a Wise Person?

ben Zoma's answer to this first question was, "One who learns from others."

How many famous quotes and sayings run along those same lines? For example, "We have two ears and only one mouth for a reason." Isn't that true? When we talk, we must be saying something that we already know (or think we know). Only by listening can we become wiser in whatever situation we happen to be involved.

Let's take, for example, a doctor. A patient comes into his or her office looking sick. Regardless of the numerous years of education and vast amount of knowledge this doctor has concerning medicine and the human body, the easiest way to get to the root of the patient's problem is for the doctor to first ask about and *listen* to what the patient describes as symptoms. Only then can the doctor intelligently suggest a particular treatment.

In networking we can relate this question to that person who actively listens to other people. What do they feel? How do they feel? Why do they feel? What's working in their life or business, and what isn't? As we find their needs, we know what direction to take with them. If a doctor provides a diagnosis and prescription without first knowing the symptoms, that's malpractice. If we, as salespeople, try and sell a product or service to someone without first knowing his true needs, isn't that malpractice as well?

Question 2: Who Is a Mighty Person?

"One who can control his or her emotions and make of an enemy a friend," says ben Zoma.

This means nothing more than having enough self-control and discipline to take a bad situation and make it work for you. Imagine approaching someone who isn't particularly friendly or open, but having enough strength or being mighty enough to turn that person to your side. And usually, when we can win people over and turn them in our direction, they turn out to be our biggest supporters.

Abraham Lincoln once said, "I don't like that person—I'm going to have to get to know him better." How many friendships do you currently have with others that began in a sort of less-than-amiable fashion? If you have one, several, or many, you know that those are some of your most rewarding relationships. If you have none, then set a goal to try to turn one "enemy" into a friend. Just one at first. Watch what happens. I assure you, the results will be habit-forming.

Question 3: Who Is a Rich Person?

A truly rich person is one who appreciates his or her lot. In other words, somebody who is happy with himself, somebody who really feels good enough about his life and lifestyle that he can be a pretty complete or contented person.

Of course, the standard response to that question from most people is, "Someone who has money." And certainly there's nothing wrong with having money. It's just that money, in and of itself, can only make a person wealthy. It can't make one rich.

In relation to networking, this would translate into a person who appreciates and enjoys the individuals in his or her network, even if not yet receiving immediate referrals from those people.

Question 4: Who Is an Honored Person?

One who honors others, one who makes others feel good about themselves, is herself an honored person. In networking, this means liking and caring about your networking prospects enough so that they feel it. In turn, they will honor you. Here's a good practice exercise: next time you are at a social or business function, begin introducing people to each other. Have a one-sentence, complimentary statement about everyone you introduce. As you *honor* everyone you introduce (even by just taking the time to make the introduction) watch how you become the hit of the function. It works every time.

Question 5: Who Is a Brave Person?

This question is my father's. A brave person is one who is smart enough to be afraid and still do their job. According to Dad, "I've met a lot of people, both during the war and outside of the service, who were willing to physically fight it out. Although they were willing to go into battle, so to speak, to do things others might not do, they really did not have the sense of appreciation of themselves. They weren't scared because they didn't have a reason to be scared. They didn't know enough to be scared. They didn't have anything to be scared about.

"While you have to give those people credit for what they do, it's the person who has real feelings about being scared and goes ahead anyway, trying to accomplish what he or she set out to do, who deserves a real pat on the back."

How does that relate to networking? Simply this: It is the true networker who, though smart enough to recognize potential rejection, still reaches out to give of himself or herself.

Truth, Justice, Peace, and Love

Four ingredients that add to a successful networking recipe are truth, justice, peace, and love. Although my feelings about these four can be argued semantically, you'll see where the philosophies fit into the style of the successful networker throughout this book.

> *Truth:* What is vital to realize is that truth (or the correct way of doing things) in your own mind doesn't necessarily mean that the person you're dealing with sees the truth in the same way. And, unless you are transacting with someone who can communicate in a positive way, a lack of communication or negative communication will be the result: hostile feelings or misunderstandings that will not work for the benefit of any of the parties concerned.
> My friend and fellow speaker Jim Cathcart, author of *Relationship*

Selling, explains what he calls the Platinum Rule. The Golden Rule, of course, is "Do unto others as you would have them do unto you." According to Jim, the Platinum Rule is "Do unto others as *they* want to be done unto."

In other words, just because we, in our mind, see the perfect business relationship being a certain way and following certain rules or procedures, that doesn't mean the other person feels the same way. What is the truth? As far as I'm concerned, if we want a positive business relationship with that person, we must try to see the truth from *that person's* point of view.

Justice: This is maturity. It's the ability to say, "Hey, I'm wrong. I can do something about it, and I *will* do something about it. I will change." In networking we must be able to admit when we are wrong. So many confrontations occur and continue because of the inability to admit shortcomings, when admitting those shortcomings will only make you more of a hero in the other person's eyes.

Peace: Peace comes about when there is comfort and a lack of stress when dealing with people. You're not afraid to say things to them; you're not under pressure, because if there is any kind of misunderstanding about the truth, you will be able to work it out. People are willing to deal with the justice that accompanies understanding. In networking, peace results from two or more people having a mutual respect.

Love: This means putting the other person ahead of yourself. The other person becomes more important to you than yourself. In networking, realistically, we don't love our networking prospects as we love our own families, but we care about them, their families, and their needs, which in return will influence them to have good feelings about us.

From what I've experienced, putting another person's needs ahead of one's own seems to be a struggle few are able to overcome. Too many people ask themselves, "How does doing that benefit me?" I can only say that the successful networkers I know, the ones receiving tons of referrals and feeling truly happy about themselves, continually put the other person's needs ahead of their own. Let me say this one more time because it is so important:

> The successful networkers I know, the ones receiving tons of referrals and feeling truly happy about themselves, continually put the other person's needs ahead of their own.

Do You Network as a Parent, Adult, or Child?

In the best-selling book *Games People Play,* author Eric Berne, often credited with being the father of transactional analysis, points out three distinct personality states: Parent, Adult, and Child. These are states taken on and displayed by each of us, depending upon what we are feeling at that particular point in time. The following is my paraphrased explanation of these three states and how they relate to networking.

The Child in all of us is the victim. He or she feels like a baby, put down, blamed, punished, controlled. As a result, the person is angry and looking to get even. And usually the Child wants to get even with the person who assumes the Parent role.

The Parent in all of us is usually a victim of our own upbringing, biases, and environment. People in the Parent role mean well; they just don't recognize negative communication. They don't realize that they're putting somebody down. They don't realize that they're making somebody feel bad.

The Adult in all of us, which is the ideal, is the negotiator, the communicator—the respectful, honest, active listener who's trustworthy and just. And somebody you would just love doing business with.

Isn't it a fact that we have all three of those situations in the networking process? There are people who talk down to us. They are the Parent and we are the Child. In that situation we have to know that it's not something to be taken personally, but that we have to bring ourselves up to the Adult level. At the same time, we have to make sure we don't come across like the Parent talking down to them as the Child, but as Adult to Adult.

It's also important to keep in mind that you can't expect prospects to act like adults just because *you* know how to. So don't feel put down if they can't respond that way. I realize that is easier said than done. The way to overcome that is to make a game out of it. Be aware the next time you are in a negative transaction, and see if you can *win.* Of course, you don't win by emotionally *beating* that person, but by *building* that person to an Adult level, in order to match the level to which you have risen.

Networking Disciplines

Networking discipline says that if you don't abide by networking techniques, you won't get all the referrals you are capable of getting. If you do, you will get referrals—lots and lots of them. Let's number the seven networking disciplines right down the line:

First, get the necessary knowledge needed to effectively network. Review the techniques you've learned throughout this book until you really know them, because the more you practice, the better you are going to feel and the more effective you're going to be. The same goes for other books you read and tapes you listen to.

Second, place yourself in front of potential networking prospects. Understand that you can have fear and anxiety and still be brave enough to do it and be effective. We all have trepidations when going into a room full of people we don't know. And we've all experienced rejection and don't enjoy the feeling. Despite this, we can succeed. Realize that the more you practice, the easier it is to face any new situation. Also know that the more new situations you face, the less intimidating they become.

Third, be wise by learning from others, especially your networking prospects, and learn how you can help *them.*

Fourth, give unrequited referrals. Help the others in your network without expecting an immediate payback. Don't look for a "shake" just because you're being effective and good about your actions.

Fifth is tact. This is so important! Tact is the language of strength. If we could listen on tape to what we say in everyday conversations, we'd be amazed at the lack of tact and sensitivity in the way we relate to others. There's a great deal of truth in the old saying, "You can catch more flies with honey than you can with vinegar." Make an agreement with yourself to analyze the way you talk to others for just 21 days. Watch your improvement every day and be proud of yourself.

Sixth, allow yourself to be rewarded with endless referrals after showing persistence. Follow through in gratitude.

And seventh, realize that discipline and networking are nothing more than learning how to benefit from being the "boss of yourself" so you may constructively help and influence others to network. Only *you* can determine how you are going to handle an individual person or situation. By being the boss of yourself, you control the situation, and your own success, while adding positively to those whose lives you touch. As my dad says, "We are ideally put on earth to help others." And as we help others, we eventually and invariably help ourselves.

As a postscript to this chapter, let me point out that, regardless of what you are used to doing, regardless of the way you presently handle conflict with others, effective communication is a *learned skill.* Fellow speaker and author Anthony Robbins says, "Your past does not equal your future." No matter what your shortcomings in communicating and networking with others have been, you can use the techniques presented in this book to begin developing a powerful network of contacts.

Even the story I began with about my neighbor, Carol, who was looking for a fight with the theater manager, contains a lesson. How can you use that as a guide for turning potential lemons into lemonade—or potential enemies into friends?

Living your life from a perspective of strength is a lot more fun and rewarding. Do we need to continually work at this in order to make it effective? Yes! And it's worth it.

Key Points

- Whenever possible, make others feel good about themselves.
- People are not always what they seem to be.
- To have a body does not make one a man. To have a child does not make one a parent.
- These are the five questions of life:
  1. *Who is a wise person?* One who learns from others.
  2. *Who is a mighty person?* One who can control his or her emotions and make of an enemy a friend.
  3. *Who is a rich person?* One who appreciates his or her lot.
  4. *Who is an honored person?* One who honors others.
  5. *Who is a brave person?* One who is smart enough to be afraid and still do their job.
- The four key ingredients in a successful networking recipe are truth, justice, peace, and love.
- The successful networkers I know, the ones receiving tons of referrals and feeling truly happy about themselves, continually put the other person's needs ahead of their own.
- We each display three personality states:
  1. *The Child:* The Child feels like the victim, like a baby—put down, blamed, punished, controlled.
  2. *The Parent:* The Parent means well but is domineering and controlling.
  3. *The Adult:* The Adult is the ideal—the negotiator, the communicator, win-win–oriented.
- There are seven networking disciplines:
  1. Acquire knowledge.
  2. Place yourself in front of potential networking prospects.

3. Be wise by learning from others—especially your networking prospects. Learn how you can help them.
4. Give unrequited referrals. Help others in your network without expecting an immediate payback.
5. Be tactful. Tact is the language of strength.
6. Allow yourself to be rewarded with endless referrals after showing persistence. Follow through in gratitude.
7. Realize that discipline and networking are nothing more than learning how to benefit from being the "boss of yourself" so that you can constructively help and influence others to network. We are ideally put on earth to help others. And, of course, as we help others we invariably help ourselves.

17
Networking: Begin Now

It is one of the most beautiful compensations
of life that no one can sincerely try to help
another without helping him or herself.
RALPH WALDO EMERSON

Isn't the above statement a great summation of what we've been discussing throughout this entire book? Regardless of whether it's working a crowd or networking in a one-on-one situation, positioning yourself through the media, asking questions, having better follow-up than anybody else, providing excellent customer service, running your own organized networking group, or just helping others succeed in their businesses, the more you do for the benefit of others, the more successful you will be.

What never stops fascinating me is the fact that the people who give the most of themselves to others, without expecting anything in return, seem to get back many times over what they give out. And truly successful networkers do the little things right consistently, knowing that they will eventually reap the harvest from the seeds they have planted. But there's one more thing to keep in mind, as well.

This brings us to the final point. Throughout this book you've been exposed to techniques that can and will account for a dramatic increase in both your personal happiness and financial earnings, but only if you take the information and apply it!

How often has it been noted that knowledge without action is the same as having no knowledge at all? To succeed in your quest for endless referrals, you must take the information you have learned and absolutely begin applying it to your life right now!

Unfortunately, many people read a book such as this as though it were a novel, skimming through, finding some ideas interesting, maybe even saying to themselves, "One of these days I'm going to use that technique," but they never actually get around to it. I call these people "as soon as" people.

You know the type: really nice, well-intentioned people. Unfortunately, they are always in the process of "getting ready." They're "going to" do something based on future, unrelated events that one day may take place. For example, "I'm going to learn the 10 open-ended, feel-good questions `as soon as' the kids start the school year." Or "I'll develop a benefit statement `as soon as' the next sales contest starts." (That would be a great time, wouldn't it? After all, it wouldn't make sense to start now, so that the benefit statement is internalized *before* the contest begins!) Unfortunately, all too often, that attitude is directly reflected in the size of their paycheck.

I can't stress enough how important it is to jump-start your new-found knowledge into action *now*. Go back to the beginning and read this book through again and again. See, feel, and hear yourself picking up new ideas each time through, while strengthening and internalizing others at the same time.

Skip around to different chapters, seeking information for particular projects and needs. Study and internalize the various questions, methods, techniques, and skills. Do you want to focus on cross-promotion? Then sink yourself into Chapter 11. Looking to position yourself as an expert through the various media? Turn to Chapter 9. Need a review of how to work a crowd? There's Chapter 3.

I'm so excited for you. Based on the amount of calls and letters I receive from my seminar attendees all over North America, as well as those who own my cassette tapes, I know that people are applying this system with incredible success. You can do it too! Will the payoff be immediate? Maybe, maybe not. Will you do everything perfectly the first time out? Probably not. I'm still learning how to do it perfectly. (When that day actually arrives, I'll *really* begin to worry.)

The point is this: Begin! Begin right away! Also, the ability to stick with it is a key point. If you get knocked down, get back up. If you get knocked down again, get back up again. And you will get knocked down again. The fact is, we all get knocked on our rear ends from time to time. But we don't lose as a result of getting knocked down—only by staying down. The following saying was shared with me by my Dad, and I'd like to share it with you.

You are beaten to Earth
Well, well, what's that?
Come up with a smiling face.
It's nothing against you to fall down flat
But to lie there, that's disgrace.

The harder you're thrown
Why, the higher you'll bounce.
Be proud of your blackened eye.
It isn't the fact that you're licked that counts
It's how did you fight . . . and why.

As long as we keep our why, our dream, our reason for doing in mind, we'll overcome anything in our way and proceed until we eventually overcome and conquer. As Dexter Yager, one of the most successful businessmen in the world, is often quoted as saying, "If the dream is big enough, the facts don't count."

Do whatever it takes to stay in the race. Among my favorite self-motivators is a poem authored by a very successful man. I'm sure you've heard it before. It's entitled, "Persistence," and it reads as follows:

Persistence

Nothing in the world can take the place of persistence.

Talent will not.

Nothing is more common than unsuccessful people with talent.

Genius will not.

Unrewarded genius is almost a proverb.

Education will not.

The world is full of educated derelicts.

The slogan "Press on" has solved and always will solve the problems
of the human race.

CALVIN COOLIDGE, 30TH PRESIDENT

My suggestion is to be persistent. Do the little things right, do them consistently, and realize that selling, networking, and life itself is simply a numbers game. Of course, when following proven techniques, the numbers seem to get a lot better.

Learn the techniques, implement them beginning now, and be persistent, and you will network your everyday contacts into sales.

Resource Guide

Allard, Lloyd: *Selling*, Gretna, LA, Pelican Publishing, 1991.

Alessandra, Tony, Phil Wexler, and Rick Barrera: *Nonmanipulative Selling*. Englewood Cliffs, NJ, Prentice-Hall, 1987.

Alessandra, Tony, and Michael O'Connor: *The Platinum Rule*. New York, Warner Books, 1997.

Alexander, Scott: *Advanced Rhinocerology*. Laguna Hills, CA, Rhino's Press, 1981.

Alexander, Scott: *Rhinoceros Success*. Laguna Hills, CA, Rhino's Press, 1980.

Alexander, Scott: *Rhinocerotic Relativity*. Laguna Hills, CA, Rhino's Press, 1983.

Amos, Wally "Famous," and Gregory Amos: *The Power in You*. New York, Donald I. Fine, 1988.

Andrews, Andy: *Storms of Perfection*. Nashville, TN, Lightning Crown, 1992.

Andrews, Andy: *Storms of Perfection 2*. Nashville, TN, Lightning Crown, 1994.

Andrews, Andy: *Storms of Perfection 3*. Nashville, TN, Lightning Crown, 1996.

Andrews, Andy: *Storms of Perfection 4*. Nashville, TN, Lightning Crown, 1997.

Anderson, Peggy, compiler: *Great Quotes from Great Leaders*. Lombard, IL, Celebrating Excellence Publishing, 1990.

Anthony, Robert: *The Ultimate Secrets of Total Self-Confidence*. New York, Berkeley Books, 1979.

Ash, Mary Kay: *Mary Kay: The Success Story of America's Most Dynamic Businesswoman*. New York, Harper & Row. 1987.

Axelrod, Alan, and Jim Holtje: *201 Ways to Deal with Difficult People*. New York, McGraw-Hill, 1997.

Bach, Richard: *Jonathan Livingston Seagull*. New York, Simon & Schuster, 1970.

Bach, Richard: *Illusions*. New York, Dell, 1977.

Bander, Richard, and John Grinder: *Frogs into Princes*. Moab, UT, Real People Press, 1979.

Beavis, Wes: *Become the Person You Dream of Being*. Los Angeles, Powerborn, 1995.

Beckwith, Harry: *Selling the Invisible*. New York, Time Warner Books, 1997.

Berne, Eric: *Transactional Analysis in Psychotherapy: A Systematic Individual and Social Psychiatry*. New York, Ballantine, 1986.

Berne, Eric: *Games People Play*. New York, Ballantine, 1985.

Bernstein, Daryl: *Venture Adventure*. Tulsa, OK, Global Support Network, 1996.

Bethel, Sheila Murray: *Making a Difference.* New York, Berkeley Books, 1990.

Bettger, Frank: *How I Raised Myself from Failure to Success in Selling.* New York, Simon & Schuster, 1947.

Biggs, Dick: *If Life Is a Balancing Act, Why Am I So Darn Clumsy?* Roswell, GA, Chattahoochee Publishers, 1993.

Biro, Brian D.: *Beyond Success.* Pagmillion, MT, 1997.

Blackman, Jeff: *Peak Your Profits.* Franklin Lakes, NJ, Career Press, 1996.

Blanchard, Kenneth, and Spencer Johnson: *The One-Minute Manager.* New York, Berkeley Books, 1987.

Bland, Glenn: *Success! The Glenn Bland Method.* Wheaton, IL, Living Books, 1972.

Boe, Anne, and Bettie B. Youngs: *Is Your "Net" Working?* New York, John Wiley, 1989.

Boone, Louis E.: *Quotable Business.* New York, Random House, 1992.

Borg, Tom: *The Service Factor.* Detroit, MI, Wilcockson & Antoinette, 1991.

Brooks, Michael: *Instant Rapport.* New York, Warner Books, 1990.

Brooks, Michael: *The Power of Business Rapport.* New York, Harper Collins, 1991.

Brown, H. Jackson, and Robyn Spizman: *A Hero in Every Heart.* Nashville, TN, Thomas Nelson Publishers, 1996.

Brown, H. Jackson, and Robyn Spizman: *Life's Little Instruction Book.* Nashville, TN, Rutledge Hill Press, 1997.

Burg, Bob: *Winning Without Intimidation.* Jupiter, FL, Samark Publishing, 1998.

Burg, Bob: *The Memory System.* Overland Park, KS, National Press, 1992.

Burros, Daniel A.: *Technotrends: How to Use Technology to Go Beyond Your Competition.* New York, HarperBusiness, 1993.

Canine, Craig: *Dream Reaper.* New York, Alfred A. Knopf, 1995.

Capozzi, John M.: *Why Climb the Corporate Ladder When You Can Take the Elevator?* New York, Penguin Books, 1994.

Canfield, Jack, and Mark Victor Hansen: *The Aladdin Factor.* New York, Berkeley Books, 1995.

Canfield, Jack, and Mark Victor Hansen: *Chicken Soup for the Soul.* Deerfield Beach, FL, Health Communication, 1993.

Canfield, Jack, and Mark Victor Hansen: *A 2nd Helping of Chicken Soup for the Soul.* Deerfield Beach, FL, Health Communication, 1995.

Canfield, Jack, and Mark Victor Hansen: *A 3rd Serving of Chicken Soup for the Soul.* Deerfield Beach, FL, Health Communication, 1996.

Canfield, Jack, and Mark Victor Hansen: *A 4th Course of Chicken Soup for the Soul.* Deerfield Beach, FL, Health Communication, 1997.

Carlson, Richard: *Don't Sweat the Small Stuff...and It's All Small Stuff.* New York, Hyperion, 1997.

Carnegie, Dale: *How to Win Friends and Influence People.* New York, Simon & Schuster, 1982.

Carnegie, Dale: *Lincoln the Unknown.* Garden City, NY, Dale Carnegie & Associates, 1959.

Carson, Gayle: *Winning Ways: How to Get to the Top and Stay There.* Miami Beach, FL, 1988.

Cates, Bill: *Unlimited Referrals*. Wheaton, MD, Thunder Hill, 1996.

Cathcart, Jim: *The Acorn Principle*. New York, St. Martin's Press, 1998.

Cathcart, Jim: *Relationship Selling: The Key to Getting and Keeping Customers*. New York, Perigree-Putnam, 1990.

Chopra, Deepak: *The Seven Spiritual Laws of Success*. Novato, CA, Amber-Allen Publishing, 1994.

Clason, George S.: *The Richest Man in Babylon*. New York, Signet, 1955.

Cohen, Herb: *You Can Negotiate Anything*. New York, Bantam, 1983.

Conner, Tim: *The Soft Sell*. Ann Arbor, MI, Training Associates International, 1981.

Conwell, Russell H.: *Acres of Diamonds*. Harrington Park, NJ, R. H. Sommer, 1987.

Covey, Stephen R.: *The 7 Habits of Highly Effective People*. New York, Simon & Schuster, 1989.

Cox, Danny, and John Hoover: *Leadership When the Heat's On*. New York, McGraw-Hill, 1992.

Crandall, Rick, ed.: *Marketing for People Not in Marketing*. Corte Madera, CA, Select Press, 1998.

Davidson, Jeff: *Breathing Space*. New York, Master Media LTD, 1991.

Davis, Kevin: *Getting into Your Customer's Head*. New York, Random House, 1996.

Decker, Bert: *You've Got to Be Believed to Be Heard*. New York, St. Martin's Press, 1992.

DeVos, Rich: *Compassionate Capitalism*. New York, Penguin Group, 1994.

Dornan, James M.: *Strategies for Success*. San Diego, CA, Network TwentyOne, 1977.

Dyer, Wayne W.: *Everyday Wisdom*. Carson, CA, Hay House, 1993.

Erdman, Ken, and Tom Sullivan: *Network Your Way to Success*. Philadelphia, Marketers Book Shelf, 1992.

Faris, Jack: *Small Business under Siege*. Washington, DC, National Federation of Independent Business, 1994.

Fisher, Donna: *People Power*. Austin, TX, Bard Press, 1995.

Fisher, Mark: *The Instant Millionaire*. San Rafael, CA, New World Library, 1990.

Floyd, Elaine: *Marketing with Newsletters*. St. Louis, MO, Newsletter Resources, 1997.

Fogg, John Milton: *The Greatest Networker in the World*. Charlottesville, VA, MLM Publishing, 1992.

Frank, Milo O.: *How to Get Your Point across in 30 Seconds or Less*. New York, Pocket Books, 1986.

Frankl, Viktor E.: *Man's Search for Meaning*. New York, Washington Square Press, 1984.

Franklin, Benjamin: *The Autobiography and Other Writings*. New York, Signet Classic, 1961.

Gates, Bill: *The Road Ahead*. New York, Penguin Books, 1996.

Gee, Bobbie: *Winning the Image Game: A Ten-Step Master Plan for Achieving Power, Prestige and Profit*. Berkeley, CA, PageMill Press, 1991.

Gerber, Michael E.: *The E Myth*. New York, Harper Business, 1986.

Giblin, Les: *How to Have Confidence and Power in Dealing with People.* Englewood Cliffs, NJ, Prentice-Hall, 1971.

Girard, Joe, and Stanley H. Brown: *How to Sell Anything to Anybody.* New York, Warner Books, 1986.

Gitomer, Jeffrey H.: *The Sales Bible.* New York, William Morrow, 1994.

Griessman, Gene: *The Words Lincoln Lived By.* New York, Simon & Schuster, 1997.

Gross, T. Scott: *Positively Outrageous Service: New and Easy Ways to Win Customers for Life.* New York, MasterMedia, 1991.

Gschwandtner, Gerhard: *Thoughts to Sell By.* Fredricksburg, VA, Personal Selling Power, 1995.

Guiducci, Joan: *Power Calling: A Fresh Approach to Cold Calls and Prospecting.* Mill Valley, CA, Tonino, 1992.

Guiducci, Joan: *Power Calling II.* Mill Valley, CA, Tonino, 1995.

Harrell, Wilson: *For Entrepreneurs Only.* Hawthorne, NJ, Career Press, 1994.

Harris, Amy Bjork, and Thomas A. Harris: *Staying OK.* New York, Avon, 1986.

Harris, Thomas A.: *I'm OK—You're OK.* New York, Avon, 1976.

Hartley, Joan: *The Business Owners Basic Tool Kit for Success.* Wilsonville, OR, BookPartners, 1998.

Hedges, Burke: *You, Inc.* Tampa, FL, INTI Publishing, 1996.

Helmsetter, Shad: *What to Say When You Talk to Your Self.* New York, Pocket Books, 1982.

Henderson, Robyn: *Networking for $uccess.* New South Wales, Australia, Murray, Child & Co. Pty, Ltd., 1992.

Hennig, James F.: *The Familiar Stranger.* Milwaukee, WI, International Management Publication, 1990.

Hill, Napoleon: *Law of Success.* Evanston, IL, Success Unlimited, 1979.

Hill, Napoleon: *Think and Grow Rich,* New York, Fawcett Publications, 1987.

Hill, Rick: *The Fishing Trip.* Tucson, AZ, Pinnacle Publishing, 1993.

Hoffman, Gloria, and Pauline Graivier: *Speak the Language of Success.* New York, Berkeley Books, 1983.

Hopkins, Tom: *How to Master the Art of Selling.* New York, Warner Books, 1988.

Hyken, Shep: *Moments of Magic.* St. Louis, MO, Alan Press, 1993.

James, Larry: *The First Book of Life $kill: Ten Ways to Maximize Your Personal and Professional Potential!* Tulsa, OK, Career Assurance Press, 1992.

Jeary, Tony: *Inspire Any Audience.* Dallas, TX, Trophy Publishing, 1996.

Jeffers, Susan: *Feel the Fear and Do It Anyway.* New York, Fawcett Columbine, 1987.

Johnson, Spencer, and Larry Wilson: *The One Minute Sales Person.* West Caldwell, NJ, William Morrow, 1984.

Johnson, Spencer: *The Precious Present.* New York, Doubleday, 1984.

Jones, Charlie "Tremendous": *Life Is Tremendous.* Wheaton, IL, Living Books, 1968.

Jones, Charlie "T": *Quotes Are Tremendous.* Mechanicsburg, PA, Executive Books, 1995.

Joyner, Rick: *Leadership, Management.* Charlotte, NC, Morning Star, 1990.

Kennedy, Dan S.: *How to Succeed in Business by Breaking All the Rules.* New York, Dutton, 1997.

Kennedy, Dan S.: *The Ultimate Information Entrepreneur.* Phoenix, AZ, Empire Communications, 1990.

Kennedy, Danielle: *Selling the Danielle Kennedy Way.* Englewood Cliffs, NJ, Prentice-Hall, 1991.

Keyes, Ralph: *The Wit & Wisdom of Harry Truman.* New York, Harper Collins Publishing, 1995.

Kinder, Jack, and Gary Kinder: *21st Century Positioning.* Dallas, TX, Taylor Publishing, 1996.

Kiam, Victor: *Going for It!* New York, William Morrow, 1986.

King, Larry, with Bill Gilbert: *How to Talk to Anyone, Anytime, Anywhere.* New York, Crown Publishers, 1994.

Koller, John: *Encyclopedia of Sales and Selling.* Scottsdale, AZ, Performance Consulting, 1995

Koltnow, Emily, and Lynne S. Dumas: *Congratulations! You've Been Fired: Sound Advice for Women Who've Been Terminated, Pink-Slipped, Downsized or Otherwise Unemployed.* New York, Fawcett, 1990.

Kordis, Paul, and Dudley Lynch: *Strategy of the Dolphin.* New York, Morrow, 1989.

Kroc, Ray, with Robert Anderson: *Grinding It Out.* New York, St. Martin's Press, 1977.

Kushner, Harold S.: *When Bad Things Happen to Good People.* New York, Schocken Books, 1981.

Kyne, Peter B.: *The Go-Getter.* Markham, Ontario, Fizhenry and Whiteside LTD, 1921.

Lant, Jeffrey: *How to Make a Whole Lot More than $1,000,000 Writing, Commissioning, Publishing and Selling `How-To' Information.* Cambridge, MA, JLA Publications, 1990.

LeBoeuf, Michael: *GMP: The Greatest Management Principle in the World.* New York, Berkeley Books, 1989.

LeBoeuf, Michael: *How to Win Customers and Keep Them for Life.* New York, Berkeley Books, 1989.

Leduc, Bob: *How to Build Your Small Business Fast with Simple Postcards.* Las Vegas, NV, 1996.

Levinson, Jay Conrad: *Guerrilla Advertising: Cost-Effective Tactics for Small-Business Success.* Boston, Houghton Mifflin, 1994.

Levinson, Jay Conrad, and Seth Godin: *Guerrilla Marketing Handbook.* Boston, Houghton Mifflin, 1994.

Levinson, Jay Conrad, and Seth Godin: *Get What You Deserve! How to Guerrilla Market Yourself.* New York, Avon Books, 1997.

Levinson, Jay Conrad, Mark S. A. Smith, and Orval Ray Wilson: *Guerrilla Trade Show Selling.* New York, John Wiley & Sons, 1997.

Levinson, Jay Conrad: *The Way of the Guerrilla: Achieving Success and Balance as an Entrepreneur in the 21st Century.* Boston, Houghton Mifflin, 1997.

Lewis, Herschell Gordon: *Direct Mail Copy that Sells!* Englewood Cliffs, NJ, Prentice-Hall, 1986.

Lipnack, Jessica, and Jeffrey Stamps: *The Networking Book.* New York, Viking Penguin, 1988.

Littauer, Florence: *Personality Plus.* Grand Rapids, MI, Fleming H. Revell, 1993.

Lontos, Pam: *Don't Tell Me It's Impossible Until After I've Already Done It.* New York, William Morrow, 1986.

Lorayne, Harry, and Jerry Lucas: *The Memory Book.* New York, Dorset Press, 1989.

Lord, Alan: *Everyone Lives by Selling Something.* Icon Publications, 1989.

Lowndes, Leil: *How to Talk to Anybody about Anything.* Secaucus, NJ, Citadel Press, 1993.

Lundy, Jim: *Lead, Follow or Get out of the Way.* New York, Berkeley, 1991.

Mackay, Harvey B.: *Swim with the Sharks without Being Eaten Alive.* New York, Ivy Books, 1988.

Mackay, Harvey B. *Beware the Naked Man Who Offers You His Shirt.* New York, Ivy Books, 1991.

Mackay, Harvey B.: *The Harvey Mackay Rolodex Network Builder.* Secaucus, NJ, Taylor Publishing, 1991.

Mackay, Harvey B. *Sharkproof.* New York, HarperCollins, 1993.

Maltz, Maxwell: *PsychoCybernetics.* North Hollywood, CA, Wilshire Books, 1973.

Mandino, Og: *The Choice.* New York, Bantam Books, 1984.

Mandino, Og: *The Greatest Miracle in the World.* New York, Bantam Books, 1981.

Mandino, Og: *The Greatest Salesman in the World.* Nashville, TN, Thomas Nelson Publishers, 1988.

Mandino, Og: *The Greatest Secret in the World.* Nashville, TN, Thomas Nelson Publishers, 1972.

Mandino, Og: *University of Success.* New York, Bantam Books, 1982.

Mandino, Og: *The Spellbinder's Gift.* New York, Fawcett, 1995.

Mansfield, Stephen: *Never Give In.* Elkton, MD, Highland Books, 1995.

Marcinko, Richard: *Leadership Secrets of the Rogue Warrior.* New York, Pocket Books, 1996.

Marden, Orison Swett: *Peace-Power and Plenty.* New York, Thomas & Crowell, 1909.

Mason, John L.: *Let Go of Whatever Makes You Stop.* Tulsa, OK, Insight International, 1994.

Maxwell, John C.: *Be All You Can Be!* Wheaton, IL, SP Publications, 1977.

Maxwell, John C.: *Developing the Leader within You.* Nashville, TN, Thomas Nelson Publishers, 1993.

Maxwell, John C.: *Developing the Leaders Around You.* Nashville, TN, Thomas Nelson Publishers, 1995.

Maxwell, John C., and Jim Dornan: *Becoming a Person of Influence.* Nashville, TN, Thomas Nelson Publishers, 1997.

Mays, Carl: *A Strategy for Winning: Winning in Business, in Sports, in Family, in Life.* Gatlinburg, TN, Lincoln-Bradley, 1991.

McCarthy, Kevin W.: *The On-Purpose Person.* Colorado Springs, CO, Pinon Press, 1992.

McCormack, John, with David R. Legge: *Self Made in America.* New York, Addison-Wesley Publishing, 1990.

McNally, David. *Even Eagles Need a Push.* New York, Dell Trade, 1971.

Mesiti, Pat: *Wake Up and Dream.* Fyshwick Canberra, ACT, Australia, Pirie Printers, 1994.

Misner, Ivan R., and Robert Davis: *Business by Referral.* Austin, TX, Bard Press, 1998.

Misner, Ivan R.: *Seven Second Marketing.* Austin, TX, Bard Press, 1996.

Misner, Ivan R: *The World's Best Known Marketing Secret.* Austin, TX, Bard & Stephen, 1994.

Naisbitt, John: *Megatrends.* New York, Warner Books, 1988.

Newman, Bill: *Soaring with Eagles.* Toowond, Qld, Australia, Bill Newman International, 1994.

Paluch, Jim: *5 Important Things.* Mechanicsburg, PA, Executive Books, 1996.

Peale, Norman Vincent: *The Power of Positive Thinking.* New York, Ballantine, 1991.

Peck, Scott M.: *The Road Less Traveled.* New York, Touchstone Book, 1978.

Pennington, Randy, and Marc Bockman: *On My Honor, I Will: How One Simple Oath Can Lead You to Success in Business.* New York, Warner Books, 1992.

Perez, Rosita: *The Music Is You.* Granville, OH, Trudy Knox, 1985.

Phillips, Donald T.: *Lincoln on Leadership—Executive Strategies for Tough Times.* New York, Warner Books, 1992.

Pinskey, Raleigh: *101 Ways to Promote Yourself.* New York, Avon, 1997.

Piper, Watty: *The Little Engine That Could.* New York, Platt & Munk, 1976.

Pitino, Rick, with Bill Reynolds: *Success Is A Choice.* New York, Broadway Books, 1997.

Popcorn, Faith: *The Popcorn Report: Faith Popcorn on the Future of Your Company, Your World, Your Life.* New York, Doubleday, 1991.

Proctor, Bob: *You Were Born Rich.* Cartersville, GA, Life Success Productions, 1997.

Quain, Bill: *10 Rules to Break & 10 Rules to Make.* Tampa, FL, INTI Publishing, 1997.

Qubein, Nido: *The Time Is Now, the Person Is You.* High Point, NC, Executive Press, 1997.

Qubein, Nido R.: *Stairway to Success.* High Point, NC, Creative Services, 1996.

Qubein, Nido R.: *Achieving Peak Performance.* High Point, NC, Creative Services, 1996.

Qubein, Nido R.: *How to Be a Great Communicator.* High Point, NC, Creative Services, 1997.

Reck, Ross R., and Brian G. Long: *The Win-Win Negotiator.* New York, Pocket Books, 1985.

Redfield, James: *The Celestine Prophecy.* New York, Warner Books, 1993.

Ries, Al, and Jack Trout: *Bottom Up Marketing.* New York, Penguin Books, 1990.

Ries, Al, and Jack Trout: *Positioning: The Battle for Your Mind.* New York, Warner Books, 1987.

RoAne, Susan: *How to Work a Room: A Guide to Successfully Managing the Mingling,* New York, Warner Books, 1989.

RoAne, Susan: *The Secrets of Savvy Networking.* New York, Warner Books, 1993.

RoAne, Susan: *What Do I Say Next?* New York, Warner Books, 1998.

Robbins, Anthony: *Awaken the Giant Within.* New York, Simon & Schuster, 1992.

Robbins, Anthony: *Personal Power.* New York, Fawcett, 1987.

Robbins, Anthony: *Notes from a Friend.* New York, Simon & Schuster, 1995.

Robbins, Anthony: *Giant Steps.* New York, Simon & Schuster, 1994.

Roberts, Wess: *Leadership Secrets of Attila the Hun.* New York, Warner Books, 1985.

Rohn, Jim: *7 Strategies for Wealth and Happiness.* Prima Publishing, 1996.

Ruettiger, Rudy, and Mike Celizic: *Rudy's Rules.* Waco, TX, WRS Publishing, 1995.

Sanborn, Mark: *Sanborn on Success.* Glendale, CA, Griffin Publishing, 1996.

Sanborn, Mark: *TeamBuilt: Making Teamwork Work.* New York, Master Media, 1992.

Scevola, John: *Sales Dragon.* Hollywood, FL, Lifetime Books, 1997.

Schuller, Robert H.: *Tough Times Never Last But Tough People Do!* New York, Bantam, 1983.

Schulte, Gary: *Successful Life Insurance Selling.* Dearborn Financial Publishing, 1995.

Schwartz, David: *The Magic of Thinking Big.* New York, Simon & Schuster, 1987.

Schwartz, David J.: *The Magic of Thinking Success.* Hollywood, CA, Wilshire Books, 1987.

Sewell, Carl, and Paul B. Brown: *Customers for Life.* New York, Pocket Books, 1991.

Shafer, Ross: *How to Get Famous.* Woodland Hills, CA, Shafer Productions, 1992.

Slutsky, Jeff: *Streetfighter Marketing.* New York, Lexington Books, 1995.

Slutsky, Jeff, and Mark Slutsky: *How to Get Clients.* New York, Warner Books, 1992.

Spence, Gerry: *How to Argue and Win Everytime.* New York, St. Martin's Press, 1995.

Stanley, Thomas J.: *Marketing to the Affluent.* New York, McGraw-Hill, 1988.

Stanley, Thomas J., and William D. Danko: *The Millionaire Next Door.* New York, McGraw-Hill, 1998.

Stettner, Morey: *The Art of Winning Conversation.* Englewood Cliffs, NJ, Prentice-Hall, 1995.

Stone, Conway D.: *Follow Your Dreams.* Louisville, KY, 1995.

Swets, Paul W.: *The Art of Talking So That People Will Listen.* New York, Fireside, 1983.

Tannen, Deborah: *You Just Don't Understand.* New York, William Morrow, 1990.

Taylor, Stu: *How to Turn Trends into Fortunes.* Secaucus, NJ, Birch Lane Press, 1993.

Tarkenton, Fran: *What Losing Taught Me about Winning.* New York, Simon & Schuster, 1998.

Templeton, John Marks: *Worldwide Laws of Life.* Philadelphia, PA, Templeton Foundation Press, 1997.

Templeton, John: *Golden Nuggets*. Radnor, PA, Templeton Foundation Press, 1997.

Thomas, David R.: *Dave's Way*. New York, Berkeley Books, 1992.

Truax, Bill, and Sue Truax: *The Blitz Call*. Chagrin Falls, OH, Trufield Publishing, 1993.

Van Fleet, James K.: *Lifetime Conversation Guide*. Englewood Cliffs, NJ, Prentice-Hall, 1984.

Vance, Mike, and Diane Deacon: *Think out of the Box*. Franklin Lakes, NJ, Career Press, 1995.

Vilas, Sandy, and Donna Fisher: *Power Networking*. Bard Press, 1991.

Tzu, Sun, trans. by Thomas Cleary: *The Art of War*. Boston, MA, Shambhala, 1986.

Waitley, Denis: *The Double Win*. New York, Berkeley Books, 1984.

Waitley, Denis: *The Psychology of Winning*. New York, Berkeley Books, 1984.

Waitley, Denis: *The Winner's Edge*. New York, Berkeley Books, 1980.

Waitley, Denis: *Seeds of Greatness: The Ten Best Kept Secrets of Total Success*. Tarrytown, NY, Fleming H. Revell, 1988.

Walters, Dottie, and Lilly Walters: *Speak and Grow Rich*. Englewood Cliffs, NJ, Prentice-Hall, 1989.

Walters, Dottie, and Lilly Walters: *101 Simple Things to Grow Your Business*, Menlo Park, CA, Crisp Publications, 1997.

Walters, Lilly: *Secrets of Successful Speakers*. New York, McGraw-Hill, 1993.

Walther, George: *Phone Power*. New York, Berkeley Books, 1987.

Walther, George: *Power Talking: 50 Ways to Say What You Mean and Get What You Want*. New York, Berkeley Books, 1991.

Walton, Sam: *Made in America*. New York, Doubleday, 1992.

Warren, Arnie: *The Great Connection*. Ft. Lauderdale, FL, Pallium Books, 1997.

Watson, Lillian Eichler: *Light from Many Lamps*. New York, Simon & Schuster, 1951.

Wexler, Phillip S., W. A. Adams, and Emil Bohn: *The Quest for Service Quality: RX's for Achieving Excellence*. Sandy, UT, Maxcomm Associates, 1992.

Weylman, Richard C.: *Opening Closed Doors*. New York, McGraw-Hill, 1994.

Williams, Bill: *Get Sales Prospects Galore by Networking for Referrals*. Houston, TX, Gamala Publishing, 1998.

Williamson, Porter B.: *Gen. Patton's Principles, for Life and Leadership*. Tucson, AZ, MCS, Inc., 1988.

Yager, Dexter, and Ron Ball: *Everything I Know at the Top I Learned at the Bottom*. Wheaton, IL, Tyndale House Publishers, 1991.

Yager, Dexter: *Dynamic People Skills*. Charlotte, NC, InterNET Services, 1997.

Yager, Dexter: *Millionaire Mentality*. Charlotte, NC, InterNET Services, 1993.

Yoho, David Alan: *The Art and Science of Personal Influence*. Bethesda, MD, Professional Educators Group, 1993.

Ziglar, Zig: *Over the Top*. Nashville, TN, Thomas Nelson, 1994.

Ziglar, Zig: *See You at the Top*. Gretna, LA, Pelican, 1984.

Ziglar, Zig: *Secrets of Closing the Sale*, New York, Berkeley Books, 1987.

Index

Index

About the Author

Bob Burg, president of Burg Communications, Inc., is a professional speaker and consultant on the topics of communication skills and business networking. A former television news anchor, salesman, and sales manager, he is a much-sought-after keynote speaker for major corporations, associations, and sales organizations throughout North America. He lives and works in Jupiter, Florida.

BOB BURG LIVE

As a speaker at major sales and corporate conventions, Bob Burg shares information on two topics vital to both business and personal success:

**How to Cultivate a Network of
Endless Referrals**
and
**Winning *Without* Intimidation
(How to Master the Art of Positive Persuasion)**

He has earned acclaim for his presentation style, combining humor and entertainment with hard-hitting, immediately applicable, profit-generating information.

Bob has shared the platform with some of the world's best-known speakers and celebrities, including Zig Ziglar, CNN's Larry King, Coach Lou Holtz, Mary Lou Retton, Tom Hopkins, radio legend Paul Harvey, Dr. Joyce Brothers, Les Brown, Dr. Denis Waitley, Harvey Mackay, former U.S. President Gerald Ford, and many others.

He also has a full line of audio and video programs based on his books, which can be used for individual growth, and/or company in-house training.

If you'd like information on having Bob speak at your company convention, or if you would like to order his audio and video resources and motivational items, please call or write:

Burg Communications, Inc.
P.O. Box 7002
Jupiter, FL 33468-7002
(561) 575-2114 or (800) 726-3667
Fax (561) 575-2304
http://www.Burg.com